AMERICAN FICTION, 1900-1950

AMERICAN LITERATURE, ENGLISH LITERATURE, AND WORLD LITERATURES IN ENGLISH: AN INFORMATION GUIDE SERIES

Series Editor: Theodore Grieder, Curator, Division of Special Collections, Fales Library, New York University, New York, New York

Associate Editor: Duane DeVries, Adjunct Assistant Professor, York College of the City University of New York, New York

Other books on American Literature in this Series:

AMERICAN FICTION TO 1900—*Edited by David K. Kirby**

CONTEMPORARY FICTION IN AMERICA AND ENGLAND, 1950-1970—*Edited by Alfred F. Rosa and Paul A. Eschholz**

AFRO-AMERICAN FICTION, 1853-1973—*Edited by Robert A. Corrigan**

AMERICAN DRAMA, 1900-1970—*Edited by Paul Hurley**

AMERICAN POETRY TO 1900—*Edited by Bernice Slote**

AMERICAN POETRY, 1900-1950—*Edited by William White and Artem Lozynsky**

CONTEMPORARY POETRY IN AMERICA AND ENGLAND, 1950-1970—*Edited by Calvin Skaggs**

THE LITERARY JOURNAL IN AMERICA TO 1900—*Edited by Edward E. Chielens**

THE LITERARY JOURNAL IN AMERICA, 1900-1970—*Edited by Edward E. Chielens**

THE LITTLE MAGAZINE IN AMERICA AND ENGLAND, 1950-1970—*Edited by Jackson R. Bryer**

AMERICAN PROSE AND CRITICISM, 1900-1950—*Edited by John Clendenning**

*in preparation

The above series is part of the
GALE INFORMATION GUIDE LIBRARY

The Library consists of a number of separate Series of guides covering major areas in the social sciences, humanities, and current affairs.

General Editor: Paul Wasserman, Professor and former Dean, School of Library and Information Services, University of Maryland

AMERICAN FICTION, 1900-1950

A Guide to Information Sources

James Woodress
*Professor of English and Chairman of the Department,
University of California at Davis*

Volume 1
*American Literature, English Literature,
and World Literatures In English:
An Information Guide Series*

Gale Research Company
Book Tower, Detroit, Michigan 48226

Library of Congress
Cataloging in Publication Data

Woodress, James Leslie.
   American fiction, 1900-1950.

   (American literature, English literature, and world literatures in English,
v.1) (Gale information guide library)
   1. American fiction--20th century--History and criticism--Bibliography.
I. Title.
Z1231.F4W64   016.813'03   73-17501
ISBN 0-8103-1201-8

Copyright © 1974 by
Gale Research Company

CONTENTS

BD
18.00
8|75

CONTENTS

TABLE OF ACRONYMS AND ABBREVIATIONS

The following acronyms and abbreviations have been used in PART TWO to refer to periodicals in which articles appeared that have been cited in the various bibliographical essays. Also a number of books or series of books referred to frequently have been assigned acronyms or have been cited by the author's name.

SPECIAL NOTE: The asterisk (*) has been used to designate novels or collections of stories of special importance.

AAL   Lewis Leary, ARTICLES ON AMERICAN LITERATURE, 1900-1950.
           (Durham, N.C., 1954); ARTICLES ON AMERICAN LITERATURE,
           1950-1967. (Durham, N.C., 1970)

ABC   AMERICAN BOOK COLLECTOR (formerly AMATEUR BOOK COLLEC-
           TOR)

AH   AMERICAN HERITAGE

AL   AMERICAN LITERATURE

ALM   AMERICAN LITERARY MANUSCRIPTS (Austin, Tex., 1960)

ALR   AMERICAN LITERARY REALISM

ALS   AMERICAN LITERARY SCHOLARSHIP: AN ANNUAL. (Durham,
           N.C., 1965-   ).

AM   AMERICAN MERCURY

AQ   AMERICAN QUARTERLY

AR   ANTIOCH REVIEW

ArQ   ARIZONA QUARTERLY

AS   AMERICAN SPEECH

ASch   AMERICAN SCHOLAR

ASt   ASIAN STUDIES

AtlM   ATLANTIC MONTHLY

BAASB BRITISH ASSOCIATION FOR AMERICAN STUDIES BULLETIN

BB   BULLETIN OF BIBLIOGRAPHY

BlackW BLACK WORLD (formerly NegroD)

BNYPL BULLETIN OF THE NEW YORK PUBLIC LIBRARY

BuR   BUCKNELL REVIEW

CE   COLLEGE ENGLISH

CF   CANADIAN FORUM

CHSQ   CALIFORNIA HISTORICAL SOCIETY QUARTERLY

CJ   CLASSICAL JOURNAL

CLAJ   COLLEGE LANGUAGE ASSOCIATION JOURNAL

ClarQ CLAREMONT QUARTERLY

CLQ   COLBY LIBRARY QUARTERLY

ColQ   COLORADO QUARTERLY

CR   CENTENNIAL REVIEW

Crit   CRITIQUE: STUDIES IN MODERN FICTION

DA, DAI DISSERTATION ABSTRACTS (now DISSERTATION ABSTRACTS INTER-
         NATIONAL)

DAL   James Woodress, DISSERTATIONS IN AMERICAN LITERATURE, 1891-
         1966 (Durham, N.C., 1968)

DR   DALHOUSIE REVIEW

EA   ETUDES ANGLAISES

EJ   ENGLISH JOURNAL

ES   ENGLISH STUDIES

Expl   EXPLICATOR

GaR   GEORGIA REVIEW

Gersten- Donna Gerstenberger and George Hendrick, THE AMERICAN NOVEL,
berger   1789-1959: A CHECKLIST OF TWENTIETH-CENTURY CRITICISM.
         (Denver, 1961, 1970)

GSE   GOTHENBURG STUDIES IN ENGLISH

HarM   HARVARD MONTHLY

HLB   HARVARD LIBRARY BULLETIN

HM   HARPER'S MONTHLY

IQ   ITALIAN QUARTERLY

JA   JAHRBUCH FUR AMERIKASTUDIEN

JCMVASA JOURNAL OF THE CENTRAL MISSISSIPPI VALLEY AMERICAN
         STUDIES ASSOCIATION (later MASJ)

JEGP   JOURNAL OF ENGLISH AND GERMANIC PHILOLOGY

JISHS   JOURNAL OF THE ILLINOIS STATE HISTORICAL SOCIETY

JLN   JACK LONDON NEWSLETTER

Johnson   Jacob Blanck, ed., MERLE JOHNSON'S AMERICAN FIRST EDI-
TIONS, 4th ed. (Waltham, Mass., 1965)

JPC   JOURNAL OF POPULAR CULTURE

JSH   JOURNAL OF SOUTHERN HISTORY

KanQ   KANSAS QUARTERLY

KFR   KENTUCKY FOLKLORE RECORD

KHSR   KENTUCKY HISTORICAL SOCIETY REGISTER

KR   KENYON REVIEW

LCUP   LIBRARY CHRONICLE OF THE UNIVERSITY OF PENNSYLVANIA

LCUT   LIBRARY CHRONICLE OF THE UNIVERSITY OF TEXAS

LE&W   LITERATURE EAST AND WEST

LHUS   R.E. Spiller, et al., eds., LITERARY HISTORY OF THE UNITED
STATES (New York, 1948, 1963)

LonM   LONDON MAGAZINE

LUB   LINCOLN UNIVERSITY BULLETIN

MASJ   MID-CONTINENT AMERICAN STUDIES JOURNAL (formerly
JCMVASA)

MFS   MODERN FICTION STUDIES

MH   MINNESOTA HISTORY

MissQ   MISSISSIPPI QUARTERLY

MLA   MODERN LANGUAGE ASSOCIATION

MLR   MODERN LANGUAGE REVIEW

ModQ   MODERN QUARTERLY

MQ   MIDWEST QUARTERLY

MQR   MICHIGAN QUARTERLY REVIEW

MR   MASSACHUSETTS REVIEW

MTJ   MARK TWAIN JOURNAL (formerly MTQ-MARK TWAIN QUARTERLY)

NAR   NORTH AMERICAN REVIEW

NCF   NINETEENTH-CENTURY FICTION

NCol   NEW COLOPHON

NegroD   NEGRO DIGEST (now BlackW)

NeL   NEW LEADER

NEQ   NEW ENGLAND QUARTERLY

NL   NOUVELLES LITTERAIRES

NLB   NEWBERRY LIBRARY BULLETIN

NMQ   NEW MEXICO QUARTERLY

N&Q   NOTES AND QUERIES

NR   NEW REPUBLIC

NY   NEW YORKER

NYHTB   NEW YORK HERALD TRIBUNE BOOK REVIEW

NYTBR   NEW YORK TIMES BOOK REVIEW

NYTM   NEW YORK TIMES MAGAZINE

PBSA   PAPERS OF THE BIBLIOGRAPHICAL SOCIETY OF AMERICA

PELL   PAPERS ON ENGLISH LANGUAGE AND LITERATURE (now PLL-PAPERS ON LITERATURE)

PMHB   PENNSYLVANIA MAGAZINE OF HISTORY AND BIOGRAPHY

PMLA   PUBLICATIONS OF THE MODERN LANGUAGE ASSOCIATION

PS   PACIFIC SPECTATOR

PULC   PRINCETON UNIVERSITY LIBRARY CHRONICLE

QJLC   QUARTERLY JOURNAL OF THE LIBRARY OF CONGRESS

QQ   QUEEN'S QUARTERLY

RALS   RESOURCES FOR AMERICAN LITERARY STUDY

RLM   REVUE DES LETTRES MODERNES

SA   STUDI AMERICANI

SAQ   SOUTH ATLANTIC QUARTERLY

SatR   SATURDAY REVIEW (formerly SRL)

SB   STUDIES IN BIBLIOGRAPHY

SBL   STUDIES IN BLACK LITERATURE

SDR   SOUTH DAKOTA REVIEW

SELit   STUDIES IN ENGLISH LITERATURE (University of Tokyo)

SEP   SATURDAY EVENING POST

SFQ   SOUTHERN FOLKLORE QUARTERLY

SHR   SOUTHERN HUMANITIES REVIEW

SMAA   Jackson Bryer, ed., SIXTEEN MODERN AMERICAN AUTHORS
        (Durham, N.C., 1974)

SNL   SATIRE NEWSLETTER

SoR   SOUTHERN REVIEW

SovR   SOVIET REVIEW

SR   SEWANEE REVIEW

SRL   SATURDAY REVIEW OF LITERATURE (later SatR)

SSF   STUDIES IN SHORT FICTION

SWR   SOUTHWEST REVIEW

TArts   THEATER ARTS MONTHLY

TC   TWENTIETH CENTURY

TCL   TWENTIETH CENTURY LITERATURE

TLS   TIMES LITERARY SUPPLEMENT

TQ   TEXAS QUARTERLY

TR   TEXAS REVIEW

TriQ   TRI-QUARTERLY

TSE   TULANE STUDIES IN ENGLISH

TSL   TENNESSEE STUDIES IN LITERATURE

TSLL   TEXAS STUDIES IN LITERATURE AND LANGUAGE

TUSAS   TWAYNE UNITED STATES AUTHORS SERIES

UKCR   UNIVERSITY OF KANSAS CITY REVIEW (later UNIVERSITY REVIEW)

UMPAW   UNIVERSITY OF MINNESOTA PAMPHLETS ON AMERICAN WRITERS

UPLL   UNIVERSITY OF UTAH PAPERS IN LANGUAGE AND LITERATURE

UTQ   UNIVERSITY OF TORONTO QUARTERLY

VQR   VIRGINIA QUARTERLY REVIEW

WAL   WESTERN AMERICAN LITERATURE

WF   WESTERN FOLKLORE

WHR   WESTERN HUMANITIES REVIEW

WR   WESTERN REVIEW

WSCL   WISCONSIN STUDIES IN CONTEMPORARY LITERATURE

YULG   YALE UNIVERSITY LIBRARY GAZETTE

YR   YALE REVIEW

ACKNOWLEDGMENTS

In the course of preparing these bibliographical essays I have incurred numerous obligations. I should like to thank Laurel Weeks and Charles Kollerer, who acted as my bibliographical assistants; my students in English 200, who worked on bibliographical projects that aided me materially in collecting my data; the Research Committee of the University of California at Davis, which made grants two years running to help bring this project to fruition; and Elaine Bukhari, who typed the manuscript and rendered invaluable editorial assistance.

Davis, California

August, 1973

VITA

James Woodress is currently professor of English and formerly chairman at the University of California at Davis. He received his A.B. from Amherst College, his M.A. from New York University, and his Ph.D. from Duke University. Woodress has taught at Grinnell College, Butler University, and California State University, Northridge, where he also chaired the English Department and served as Dean of Letters and Science. Academic honors awarded to Woodress include Ford and Guggenheim fellowships; in addition he was a Fulbright lecturer in France and Italy and during 1974-75 will be a visiting professor at the Sorbonne.

Woodress was editor of AMERICAN LITERARY SCHOLARSHIP: AN ANNUAL from 1965-1969 and recently has resumed its editorship. He edited, with Richard B. Morris, VOICES FROM AMERICA'S PAST, edited the revision of EIGHT AMERICAN AUTHORS, compiled DISSERTATIONS IN AMERICAN LITERATURE, and has written HOWELLS AND ITALY, BOOTH TARKINGTON: GENTLEMAN FROM INDIANA, A YANKEE'S ODYSSEY: THE LIFE OF JOEL BARLOW, and WILLA CATHER: HER LIFE AND ART.

AMERICAN FICTION, 1900–1950
INTRODUCTION

The 44 writers chosen for this volume are those who seem in 1973 to be the
most significant producers of fiction during the first half of the twentieth century. They have been selected on the basis of the critical esteem accorded
them during the 23 years that have passed since 1950, the cutoff date for this
collection of bibliographic essays. It would be safe to assume that some writers
discussed here will not survive to the end of the century. One might hazard a
guess that Faulkner and Hemingway will continue to be read in the year 2000,
but the literary position of Henry Miller or Richard Wright at the end of the
century is less of a certainty. It is likely that some lesser authors included
here, like Robert Herrick, Floyd Dell, Owen Wister, and Joseph Hergesheimer,
who still attract minor critical attention, appear in this volume only because of
an earlier momentum that already is dying. Other minor authors such as Winston
Churchill, Zona Gale, George Ade, O.E. Rolvaag, and Kenneth Roberts, who
certainly would have been included twenty years ago, seem now to have dimmed
to third or fourth magnitude importance and thus have been omitted.

While it is hazardous to make judgements about the permanence of contemporary
writers, one now can generalize with some confidence about the state of fiction
in 1900. American fiction then was dominated by William Dean Howells, Henry
James, and Mark Twain, the writers whose work has been the most influential
and lasting. These three are still widely read, and in the case of James certainly, better known now than during their lifetimes. In 1900 no critic, except
perhaps Howells himself, knew the importance of James and Twain, although
most perceptive readers and critics would have ranked Howells high.

The average critic or even serious reader in 1900 was, as today, lost in the
forest of his own contemporary fiction. The most esteemed writers at the turn
of the century were certainly not always the authors who have managed to escape oblivion. As Jay B. Hubbell demonstrates in a fascinating study of shift-
ing literary reputations, WHO ARE THE MAJOR AMERICAN WRITERS? (Durham,
N.C., 1972), even the most astute readers cannot separate successfully the
sheep from the goats. Hubbell reprints the results of a poll taken among readers of the magazine LITERATURE in 1899, in which subscribers were asked to
name the writers most worthy to become members of the newly proposed American Academy of Arts and Letters. Heading the list was William Dean Howells,
who seemed to almost everyone the dean of the literary establishment, though,
as everyone knew, his books were not best-sellers. Most people then were buying Charles Major's WHEN KNIGHTHOOD WAS IN FLOWER, just as most
people in recent years have been buying PEYTON PLACE or THE VALLEY OF
THE DOLLS and not the works of Edward Dahlberg or Nathanael West.

Mark Twain was number three in LITERATURE's poll, a choice no one would
quarrel with today, but the number two selection was the completely forgotten
historian John Fiske. In the fourth and fifth positions, ironically, were Thomas
Bailey Aldrich and Frank R. Stockton, both forgotten writers, and not ever likely to be rediscovered. Henry James ranked sixth, which seems in retrospect a
rather good showing because his novels were then almost totally neglected.
Equally astonishing as the positions of Aldrich and Stockton above James are the
rankings of S. Weir Mitchell and Bret Harte in seventh and eighth places. Stephen Crane, of course, does not appear at all. He was well known in 1900,
but THE RED BADGE OF COURAGE, which had sold briskly, apparently was
regarded as just another historical novel by those who responded to the magazine's poll. When the American Academy actually was set up in 1904 Howells
was elected president and Twain was one of the first seven members chosen.
The original group of seven included, besides Howells and Twain, two artists,
a composer, and a poet, plus one other writer—John Hay. Not many people
today remember Hay as a writer, though they might just possibly recall that he
was then Secretary of State.

A great deal happened to American fiction between 1900 and 1950. Writers like Nathanael West, not even born in 1900, had lived and died by the middle of the century. Important authors who had come to maturity early in the century, like Sherwood Anderson, Willa Cather, and Theodore Dreiser, had died in the 1940's. Thomas Wolfe, F. Scott Fitzgerald, and Ring Lardner, who belonged to the post-World War I generation, also had ended their careers by dying young. Ernest Hemingway and William Faulkner were still productive, and the best of today's living writers were just beginning their careers. Saul Bellow's first novel appeared in 1944, Norman Mailer's THE NAKED AND THE DEAD was published in 1948, and John Barth and J.D. Salinger still were waiting in the wings.

The changes between 1900 and 1950 were wide ranging. Howells and Twain and most of the minor novelists in 1900 were writing novels that were in no great way different in structure and technique from the novels of Jane Austen. James was beginning to move beyond the nineteenth century realistic novel in technique, and the subjects that interested writers had expanded in variety as the nation had grown in diversity and population. It was essentially the Victorian novel that readers were consuming at the turn of the century.

In one sense the change was a shift from Victorian reticence to the wide permissiveness of American sexual mores today. Stephen Crane's inability to find a publisher for MAGGIE: A GIRL OF THE STREETS until after THE RED BADGE OF COURAGE became a best-seller and Thomas Hardy's disgust over the censorship of JUDE THE OBSURE demonstrated the artist's conflict with the repressive society of the 1890's. Dreiser's struggles with censorship down to World War I showed the issue at a later stage. Still another decade and a half passed before ULYSSES could legally be imported into the United States; but by 1950, after two world wars, the Society for the Suppression of Vice was in full retreat. It was still to be nearly a dozen years, however, before the courts would admit LADY CHATTERLEY'S LOVER and Henry Miller's TROPIC OF CANCER, but by 1950 it was clear that an author soon would be hemmed in only by his artistic limitations.

The changes in style, structure, and narrative technique were just as startling as the changes in candor and the widening of subject matter. When Henry James wrote THE AMBASSADORS in 1903 at the age of 60, he was taking the novel into new territory. His remarkable use of the controlled point of view exerted a great influence on the twentieth-century novel, but he could not have foreseen how far the innovations would go. He was followed by Proust and Joyce, whose influence on American writers was deep and lasting. When Faulkner began writing in the 1920's, the break with the past was assured, and the novel was never to be quite the same again. THE SOUND AND THE FURY (1929) baffled readers expecting traditional fiction and broke ground for whatever experiments writers of the future wanted to try.

If American literature has undergone great changes, it also has maintained a measure of continuity; for American writers always have been attuned to the life about them. Bryant and Whitman were active in politics; Whittier wrote propaganda for the anti-slavery movement; Hawthorne was an officeholder and writer of a campaign biography. Howells put his neck on the block in defending the Chicago Anarchists; Mark Twain's work is full of contemporary material. And, as noted above, John Hay served Presidents McKinley and Theodore Roosevelt as Secretary of State. In our century the number of writers who have written social protest or sought by overt means to bring about social change is legion. One thinks of Upton Sinclair writing THE JUNGLE, his expose of the meatpacking industry, and later running for governor of California. Or of Dos Passos joining other writers in protesting the conviction of Sacco and Vanzetti. Of Jack London writing socialist tracts and John Steinbeck dramatizing his sympathy for migrant farm workers in California.

One could say that the majority of the significant writers of this century have been social gadflies or satirists in their attempts to improve the quality of American life. Dreiser's massive novels exposed the corruption of the robber barons in his Frank Cowperwood trilogy and posed the dilemmas in our culture faced by Clyde Griffiths in AN AMERICAN TRAGEDY. Sinclair Lewis wielded a satiric scalpel on the mindlessness of "Babbittry" and the smugness of "Main Street." Ring Lardner's tremendously popular humor was only a thin veneer to cover angry satire, while the impassioned criticism of Nathanael West and Edward Dahlberg

went almost unread. Although the Supreme Court had not yet issued its deseg-
regation decision in 1950, Richard Wright already was exposing angrily American
racial attitudes, and Faulkner was probing the same problem more soberly.

Some of the writers mentioned in the last two paragraphs might be classed as
"angry young men," but the predilection of American writers for dealing with
social issues extended even to our well-mannered authors. One would never ac-
cuse Willa Cather, Ellen Glasgow, Edith Wharton, J.P. Marquand, or Booth
Tarkington of being angry young men, but their work also reflected American
problems. Bigness, materialism, money, business all take their lumps from these
writers, albeit the attack usually is administered with a velvet glove. These
writers, one might say, inherit the genteel traditions of the nineteenth-century
realists like Howells and James. They share the earlier generation's belief that
fiction should be civilized. Whitman might have understood and applauded
Henry Miller's barbaric yawp, but certainly Howells would not have.

Another aspect of American fiction which exhibits continuity between the nineteenth and twentieth centuries is the exploitation of the provinces. The use of
regional peculiarities in the decades after the Civil War was called local color,
and it continued on as regionalism after 1900. The best of this fiction is deeply
rooted in its time and place but universal in its depiction of character and in
its treatment of theme. The work of our greatest contemporary novelist, William
Faulkner, illustrates best this facet of twentieth-century fiction, but he is only
the first among a good many regionalists. Willa Cather's use of Nebraska,
Thomas Wolfe's evocation of North Carolina, Steinbeck's settings in California
all illustrate the point. And there is Tarkington's Indiana, Caldwell's Georgia,
Wister's Wyoming, O. Henry's New York, James T. Farrell's Chicago, Langston
Hughes' Harlem, and the Kentucky of Elizabeth Madox Roberts and Jesse Stuart.
The list could go on and on.

While the international novel seems in retrospect an invention of Henry James,
twentieth-century writers have carried on the fictional depiction of Americans
abroad. Tarkington and Edith Wharton were writing international novels before
World War I, but this use of foreign settings became a natural vehicle for the

rather sizeable group of expatriates who grew to maturity after the war. Hemingway's THE SUN ALSO RISES (1926) is almost the archetypal sample of this genre, but one thinks almost simultaneously of other fine novels like F. Scott Fitzgerald's TENDER IS THE NIGHT (1934), or Katherine Anne Porter's SHIP OF FOOLS (1962). And then too there is much of the work of our most famous expatriate, Gertrude Stein, and also that completely uninhibited exile, Henry Miller. The subject that began practically with DAISY MILLER (1878), the fictional examination of the American in Europe, has continued, though the contrast in style and technique between James' novel and, for example, THE TROPIC OF CANCER illustrates how much the American novel has changed since the last century.

Although this brief view of trends in twentieth-century fiction began by emphasizing change, it should conclude with a restatement of the continuity of the American literary tradition. The changes in style and technique have been profound, but some good writers like James Gould Cozzens and J.P. Marquand have gone on writing old-fashioned novels, and the stories of William Saroyan are not much different in narrative method from those of O. Henry, who was writing during the first decade of the century. But even where the changes in style and technique have been great and influential, as with Hemingway and Faulkner, our writers for the most part have felt themselves to be a part of American life. Fitzgerald's marvelous creation of THE GREAT GATSBY (1925) probed the perversion of the American dream and was as true a scrutiny of our national experience as Mark Twain's nineteenth-century report in THE ADVENTURES OF HUCKLEBERRY FINN. And the ordeal of Thomas Wolfe in his several autobiographical novels is as serious a study of American life as Melville's treatment of Ishmael's wandering in MOBY DICK. American writers have examined their society from new perspectives, but the act of examination links them with their nineteenth-century predecessors.

PART 1

Section 1

BACKGROUND SOURCE MATERIAL

REFERENCE WORKS

A-1 ABSTRACTS OF ENGLISH STUDIES (1958–   ); AMERICAN LITERATURE
ABSTRACTS (1967–72); MLA ABSTRACTS (1972–   ).

All contain abstracts of articles from current periodicals.

A-2 Hart, James D. THE OXFORD COMPANION TO AMERICAN LITERA-
TURE. 4th ed. New York: Oxford University Press, 1965.

Indispensable dictionary of authors, works, topics.

A-3 Herzberg, Max, Jr. THE READER'S ENCYCLOPEDIA OF AMERICAN
LITERATURE. New York: Crowell, 1962.

Similar to the above work.

A-4 Holman, C. Hugh. A HANDBOOK TO LITERATURE. 3rd ed. New
York: Odyssey, 1972.

Definitions of literary terms, very thorough.

A-5 Kunitz, Stanley J., and Haycraft, Howard. TWENTIETH CENTURY
AUTHORS. New York: H.W. Wilson, 1944.

Mainly biographical.

A-6 Kunitz, Stanley J. TWENTIETH CENTURY AUTHORS: FIRST SUPPLE-
MENT. New York: H.W. Wilson, 1955.

A-7 Magill, Frank N. MASTERPLOTS: AMERICAN FICTION SERIES. New
York: Salem Press, 1964.

A-8 Malone, Dumas, and Johnson, Allen, eds. DICTIONARY OF NATIONAL
BIOGRAPHY. 20 vols. New York: Scribners, 1928–37.

Authoritative sketches; supplements published, 1946, 1958, 1973; includes only persons deceased before 1946.

A-9 Warfel, Harry R. AMERICAN NOVELISTS OF TODAY. New York: American Book, 1951.

Sketches of 575 writers.

A-10 WHO'S WHO IN AMERICA. Chicago: A.N. Marquis, 1899- .

Biennial pub. of living persons, who supply their own sketches. For deceased persons see WHO WAS WHO.

BIBLIOGRAPHIES OF AMERICAN LITERATURE AND FICTION

B-1 AMERICAN LITERATURE (1929-).

Quarterly journal of literary history, criticism, and bibliography, the leader in the field. Each issue contains "Articles on American Literature Appearing in Current Periodicals."

B-2 Blanck, Jacob. BIBLIOGRAPHY OF AMERICAN LITERATURE. 10 vols. New Haven: Yale University Press, 1955- .

Vol. 6 (Longstreet through Parsons) expected in 1974. No writer included who was alive in 1931.

B-3 Bryer, Jackson R., ed. SIXTEEN MODERN AMERICAN AUTHORS: A SURVEY OF RESEARCH AND CRITICISM. Durham, N.C.: Duke University Press, 1973.

Includes Anderson, Cather, Dreiser, Faulkner, Fitzgerald, Hemingway, Steinbeck, Wolfe. Each essay is by an authority.

B-4 Chapman, Abraham. THE NEGRO IN AMERICAN LITERATURE AND A BIBLIOGRAPHY OF LITERATURE BY AND ABOUT NEGRO AMERICANS. Oshkosh, Wisc.: Wisconsin Council of Teachers of English, 1960.

B-5 Coan, Otis, and Lillard, Richard G. AMERICA IN FICTION: AN ANNOTATED LIST OF NOVELS THAT INTERPRET ASPECTS OF LIFE IN THE UNITED STATES, CANADA, AND MEXICO. 5th ed. Palo Alto, Calif.: Pacific Books, 1967.

B-6 Dickinson, A.T. AMERICAN HISTORICAL FICTION. 3rd ed. Metuchen, N.J.: Scarecrow, 1971.

B-7 Gerstenberger, Donna, and Hendrick, George. THE AMERICAN NOVEL, 1789-1959: A CHECKLIST OF TWENTIETH-CENTURY CRITICISM. Vol.

1. Denver: Swallow, 1961.

    Vol. 2 covering 1960–68 appeared in 1970. Contains about
    16,000 items.

B-8 Gohdes, Clarence. BIBLIOGRAPHICAL GUIDE TO THE STUDY OF THE
LITERATURE OF THE U.S.A. 3rd ed. Durham, N.C.: Duke University
Press, 1970.

An indispensable guide which ranges far beyond literature narrowly defined and begins with "Aids to Information on All
Subjects."

B-9 Havlice, Patricia P. INDEX TO AMERICAN AUTHOR BIBLIOGRAPHIES.
Metuchen, N.J.: Scarecrow, 1971.

Restricted to bibliographies in periodicals but includes many
minor writers.

B-10 Holman, C. Hugh. THE AMERICAN NOVEL THROUGH HENRY JAMES.
New York: Appleton-Century-Crofts, 1966.

Besides background material includes brief bibliographies of
Dreiser, Glasgow, London, Wharton, and Sinclair.

B-11 Johnson, Merle D. AMERICAN FIRST EDITIONS. 4th ed. Rev. and
enlarged by Jacob Blanck. Waltham, Mass.: Mark Press, 1965.

B-12 Jones, Howard M., and Ludwig, Richard M. GUIDE TO AMERICAN
LITERATURE AND ITS BACKGROUNDS SINCE 1890. 4th ed. Cambridge,
Mass.: Harvard University Press, 1973.

Especially good for background; part two contains reading lists
topically and chronologically arranged.

B-13 Leary, Lewis G. ARTICLES ON AMERICAN LITERATURE, 1900–1950.
Durham, N.C.: Duke University Press, 1954.

A second volume covering 1950–67 appeared in 1970. Both
together contain about 35,000 items, though neither is exhaustive.

B-14 McNamee, Lawrence F. DISSERTATIONS IN ENGLISH AND AMERICAN
LITERATURE. New York: Bowker, 1968.

Coverage is from 1865 to 1964 of British, American, and German theses. A supplement covering 1964–68 appeared in 1969.

B-15 Marshall, Thomas F. AN ANALYTICAL INDEX TO "AMERICAN LITERA-
TURE": VOLUMES I–XXX, MARCH 1929–JANUARY 1959. Durham,
N.C.: Duke University Press, 1963.

This index may be used as a general bibliography of articles
and book reviews on American literature.

B-16 Millett, Fred B. CONTEMPORARY AMERICAN AUTHORS. New York: Harcourt Brace, 1940.

Critical survey and over 200 bio-bibliographies; superseded but still valuable.

B-17 MLA INTERNATIONAL BIBLIOGRAPHY OF BOOKS AND ARTICLES ON THE MODERN LANGUAGES AND LITERATURES. Vol. 1. New York: Modern Language Association, 1972- .

This important compilation began as "American Bibliography for 1921" in PMLA 37 (1922), though American literature was first treated for 1922. Since 1972 it has been published separately as a multi-volume work. Vol. 1 contains a section on American literature. The 1971 bibliography appeared in 1973 and contained 2842 items on American literature.

B-18 Nevius, Blake. THE AMERICAN NOVEL: SINCLAIR LEWIS TO THE PRESENT. New York: Appleton-Century-Crofts, 1970.

Includes brief bibliographies of 23 of the writers in this vol.

B-19 Nilon, Charles H. BIBLIOGRAPHY OF BIBLIOGRAPHIES IN AMERICAN LITERATURE. New York: Bowker, 1970.

Arranged by individual author and by subject.

B-20 Rubin, Louis D., Jr., ed. A BIBLIOGRAPHICAL GUIDE TO THE STUDY OF SOUTHERN LITERATURE. Baton Rouge, La.: Louisianna State University Press, 1969.

The most extensive bibliography of its kind, divided into general topics and checklists of 134 writers from all periods.

B-21 Spiller, Robert E. et al. LITERARY HISTORY OF THE UNITED STATES: BIBLIOGRAPHY. New York: Macmillan, 1948.

3rd ed. rev., 1963, contains an updated bibliography covering 1948-58 prepared by Richard M. Ludwig. To this should be added BIBLIOGRAPHY SUPPLEMENT II (1972), also by Ludwig.

B-22 Walker, Warren S. TWENTIETH-CENTURY SHORT STORY EXPLICATION: INTERPRETATIONS, 1900-1966, OF SHORT FICTION SINCE 1800. 2nd ed. Hamden, Conn.: Shoestring Press, 1967.

Supplement I to 2nd ed. covering 1967-69 appeared in 1970; Supplement II in press, December 1973.

B-23 Whiteman, Maxwell. A CENTURY OF FICTION BY AMERICAN NE-GROES, 1853-1952: A DESCRIPTIVE BIBLIOGRAPHY. Philadelphia [privately printed], 1955.

B-24 Woodress, James, ed. AMERICAN LITERARY SCHOLARSHIP: AN AN-
NUAL. Durham, N.C.: Duke University Press, 1965-   .

> From 1969-74 ed. by J.A. Robbins. Separate chaps. on Faulk-
> ner, Hemingway-Fitzgerald, fiction: 1900 to the 1930's, fic-
> tion: 1930's to the present, each by a specialist. Reviews
> the year's scholarship.

B-25 _____. DISSERTATIONS IN AMERICAN LITERATURE, 1891-1966. Durham, N.C.: Duke University Press, 1968.

> Broader coverage for dissertations in American literature than
> B-14, as it includes all foreign countries and theses done in
> departments other than English.

LITERARY HISTORY (AND CRITICISM):
NINETEENTH AND TWENTIETH CENTURIES

C-1 Berthoff, Warner. THE FERMENT OF REALISM: AMERICAN LITERATURE,
1884-1919. New York: Free Press, 1965.

C-2 Brashers, Howard C. AN INTRODUCTION TO AMERICAN LITERATURE
FOR EUROPEAN STUDENTS. Stockholm: Bonniers, 1965.

C-3 Brooks, Van Wyck. THE CONFIDENT YEARS: 1885-1915. New York:
Dutton, 1952.

> Vol. 5 of MAKERS AND FINDERS: A HISTORY OF THE
> WRITER IN AMERICA, 1800-1915.

C-4 Cunliffe, Marcus. THE LITERATURE OF THE UNITED STATES. 3rd ed.
Baltimore: Penguin, 1967.

> A survey by an English scholar.

C-5 Foerster, Norman. IMAGE OF AMERICA: OUR LITERATURE FROM PU-
RITANISM TO THE SPACE AGE. Notre Dame, Ind.: University of
Notre Dame Press, 1962.

> The collected intros. to the several sections of Foerster's an-
> thology, AMERICAN POETRY AND PROSE.

C-6 Hicks, Granville. THE GREAT TRADITION: AN INTERPRETATION OF
AMERICAN LITERATURE SINCE THE CIVIL WAR. Rev. ed. New York:
Macmillan, 1935, 1968.

> A Marxist interpretation.

C-7 Horton, Rod W., and Edwards, Herbert W. BACKGROUNDS OF AMERI-

CAN LITERARY THOUGHT. 2nd ed. New York: Appleton-Century-Crofts, 1967.

Elementary textbook treatment.

C-8 Howard, Leon. LITERATURE AND THE AMERICAN TRADITION. Garden City, N.Y.: Doubleday, 1960.

C-9 Kazin, Alfred. ON NATIVE GROUNDS. New York: Reynal and Hitchcock, 1942.

American prose literature from 1890.

C-10 Martin, Jay. HARVESTS OF CHANGE: AMERICAN LITERATURE, 1865-1914. Englewood Cliffs, N.J.: Prentice Hall, 1967.

C-11 Pattee, Fred Lewis. A HISTORY OF AMERICAN LITERATURE SINCE 1870. New York: The Century Co., 1917.

By the pioneer scholar in American literature.

C-12 _____. THE NEW AMERICAN LITERATURE, 1890-1930. New York: The Century Co., 1930.

C-13 Quinn, Arthur H. et al. THE LITERATURE OF THE AMERICAN PEOPLE. New York: Appleton-Century-Crofts, 1951.

Twentieth-century section written by George F. Whicher.

C-14 Spiller, Robert E. et al. LITERARY HISTORY OF THE UNITED STATES. 3rd ed. New York: Macmillan, 1963.

See B-21.

C-15 Spiller, Robert E. THE CYCLE OF AMERICAN LITERATURE. New York: Macmillan, 1955.

The best brief over-all survey.

C-16 Taylor, Walter F. THE STORY OF AMERICAN LETTERS. Chicago: Regnery, 1956.

A rev. of the earlier A HISTORY OF AMERICAN LETTERS. (1936).

LITERARY HISTORY (AND CRITICISM): TWENTIETH CENTURY ONLY

D-1 Aaron, Daniel, WRITERS ON THE LEFT: EPISODES IN AMERICAN LITERARY COMMUNISM. New York: Harcourt Brace and World, 1961.

D-2   Aldridge, John W. AFTER THE LOST GENERATION: A CRITICAL STUDY OF THE WRITERS OF TWO WARS. New York: McGraw-Hill, 1951.

D-3   Brooks, Van Wyck. THE OPINIONS OF OLIVER ALLSTON. New York: Dutton, 1941.

    Attacks literature of previous quarter century.

D-4   Cargill, Oscar. INTELLECTUAL AMERICA: IDEAS ON THE MARCH. New York: Macmillan, 1941.

    Impact of foreign ideas; writers grouped as naturalists, deca- dents, primitivists, the intelligentsia, the Freudians.

D-5   Cowley, Malcolm, ed. AFTER THE GENTEEL TRADITION: AMERICAN WRITERS, 1910-1930. Rev. ed. Carbondale, Ill.: Southern Illinois University Press, 1964.

    Reissue of essays by various critics covering 1910-30, orig. pub. in 1937. Essays on Dreiser, Sinclair, Cather, Anderson, Lewis, Dos Passos, Hemingway, Wolfe.

D-6   _____. EXILE'S RETURN: A LITERARY ODYSSEY OF THE 1920s. New ed. New York: Viking, 1951.

    Literary history by a participant; orig. pub. in 1934 with sub- title: "A Narrative of Ideas."

D-7   _____. THE LITERARY SITUATION. New York: Viking, 1954.

D-8   _____. THINK BACK ON US: A CONTEMPORARY CHRONOLOGY OF THE 1930'S. Ed. with intro. by Henry Dan Piper. Carbondale, Ill.: Southern Illinois University Press, 1967.

    Essays and reviews from NR, 1929-41.

D-9   Duffey, Bernard. THE CHICAGO RENAISSANCE IN AMERICAN LETTERS. Lansing, Mich.: Michigan State University Press, 1954.

    Covers period 1890-1930.

D-10 Fishman, Solomon. THE DISINHERITED OF ART: WRITER AND BACK- GROUND. Berkeley: University of California Press, 1953.

    Discusses alienation, nationalism, naturalism, Marxism, agrarian- ism.

D-11 French, Warren, ed. THE THIRTIES: FICTION, POETRY, DRAMA. De- land, Fla.: Everett Edwards, 1967.

Essays by various hands with intro by ed.

D-12 _____. THE FORTIES: FICTION, POETRY, DRAMA. Deland, Fla.: Everett Edwards, 1969.

D-13 _____. THE FIFTIES: FICTION, POETRY, DRAMA. Deland, Fla.: Everett Edwards, 1971.

D-14 Hoffman, Frederick J. THE TWENTIES: AMERICAN WRITING IN THE POSTWAR DECADE. 3rd ed. New York: Viking, 1965.

D-15 Knight, Grant C. THE STRENUOUS AGE IN AMERICAN LITERATURE. Chapel Hill, N.C.: University of North Carolina Press, 1954.

Treats the decade 1900-10.

D-16 Langford, Richard E., and Taylor, William E., eds. THE TWENTIES: POETRY AND PROSE. Deland, Fla.: Everett Edwards, 1966.

Similar to D-11-13.

D-17 Loggins, Vernon. I HEAR AMERICA: LITERATURE IN THE UNITED STATES SINCE 1900. New York: Crowell, 1937.

D-18 Madden, David, ed. PROLETARIAN WRITERS OF THE THIRTIES. Carbondale, Ill.: Southern Illinois University Press, 1968.

Essays by various hands on Wright, Dos Passos, Dahlberg, B. Traven, and general topics.

D-19 _____, ed. TOUGH GUY WRITERS OF THE THIRTIES. Carbondale, Ill.: Southern Illinois University Press, 1968.

Companion vol. to the above with essays on Hemingway, Chandler, and general topics.

D-20 Major, Mabel, and Pearce, T.M. SOUTHWEST HERITAGE: A LITERARY HISTORY WITH BIBLIOGRAPHIES. 3rd ed., rev. and enlarged. Albuquerque: University of New Mexico Press, 1972.

D-21 Straumann, Heinrich. AMERICAN LITERATURE IN THE TWENTIETH CENTURY. 3rd ed. New York: Harper and Row, 1965.

A good survey by a Swiss professor.

D-22 Thorp, Willard. AMERICAN WRITING IN THE TWENTIETH CENTURY. Cambridge, Mass.: Harvard University Press, 1960.

Very good.

D-23 Wilson, Edmund. CLASSICS AND COMMERCIALS: A LITERARY CHRO-
NOLOGY OF THE FORTIES. New York: Farrar, Straus, 1950.

D-24 _____. THE SHORES OF LIGHT: A LITERARY CHRONICLE OF THE
TWENTIES AND THIRTIES. New York: Farrar, Straus, and Young,
1952.

LITERARY HISTORY (AND CRITICISM): SPECIAL TOPICS

E-1 Carpenter, Frederic I. AMERICAN LITERATURE AND THE DREAM. New
York: Philosophical Library, 1955.

E-2 Commager, Henry Steele. THE AMERICAN MIND: AN INTERPRETA-
TION OF AMERICAN THOUGHT AND CHARACTER SINCE THE 1800'S.
New Haven: Yale University Press, 1954.

Deals somewhat with literature, by an historian.

E-3 Hoffman, Frederick J. FREUDIANISM AND THE LITERARY MIND. Baton
Rouge, La.: Louisiana State University Press, 1957.

E-4 Jones, Howard Mumford. IDEAS IN AMERICA. Cambridge, Mass.: Harvard University Press, 1945.

Deals with the need for literary history and the responsibilities
of contemporary American literature.

E-5 _____. THE THEORY OF AMERICAN LITERATURE. Rev. ed. Ithaca,
N.Y.: Cornell University Press, 1965.

Orig. pub. in 1948.

E-6 Krause, Sydney J., ed. ESSAYS ON DETERMINISM IN AMERICAN
LITERATURE. Kent, Ohio: Kent State University Press, 1964.

Includes essays on Farrell and Dos Passos.

E-7 Levin, Harry. SYMBOLISM AND FICTION. Charlottesville, Va.: University of Virginia Press, 1956.

Slim little vol. but provocative.

E-8 Luccock, Halford E. CONTEMPORARY AMERICAN LITERATURE AND
RELIGION. Chicago: Willet, Clark, 1934.

E-9 Lukacs, Gyorgy. REALISM IN OUR TIME: LITERATURE AND THE CLASS
STRUGGLE. Trans. by John and Necke Mander. New York: Harper
and Row, 1964.

11

By the leading Eastern European critic.

E-10 Walcutt, Charles C. AMERICAN LITERARY NATURALISM: A DIVIDED
STREAM. Minneapolis: University of Minnesota Press, 1956.

Traces naturalism through London, Dreiser, Anderson, Farrell,
Steinbeck, Hemingway, Dos Passos.

Section 2

SPECIALIZED SOURCE MATERIAL - THE NOVEL

GENERAL HISTORY (AND CRITICISM): NINETEENTH AND TWENTIETH CENTURIES

F-1　Allen, Walter. THE MODERN NOVEL IN BRITAIN AND THE UNITED STATES. New York: Dutton, 1964.

F-2　Chase, Richard. THE AMERICAN NOVEL AND ITS TRADITION. Garden City, N.Y.: Doubleday, 1957.

F-3　Quinn, Arthur Hobson. AMERICAN FICTION: AN HISTORICAL AND CRITICAL SURVEY. New York: Appleton-Century, 1936.

F-4　Snell, George D. THE SHAPERS OF AMERICAN FICTION, 1798-1947. New York: Dutton, 1947; Cooper Square, 1961.

F-5　Stegner, Wallace, ed. THE AMERICAN NOVEL FROM JAMES FENIMORE COOPER TO WILLIAM FAULKNER. New York: Basic Books, 1965.

　　　Anderson, Dreiser, Wharton, London, Cather, Lewis, Fitzgerald, Hemingway, Wolfe, Faulkner. Essays prepared as talks on Voice of America by prominent scholars.

F-6　Van Doren, Carl. THE AMERICAN NOVEL, 1789-1939. New York: Macmillan, 1940.

F-7　Wagenknecht, Edward. CAVALCADE OF THE AMERICAN NOVEL. New York: Henry Holt, 1952.

THE NOVEL: TWENTIETH CENTURY HISTORY (AND CRITICISM)

G-1　Aldridge, John W. IN SEARCH OF HERESY. New York: McGraw-Hill, 1956.

G-2 Baldwin, Charles C. THE MEN WHO MAKE OUR NOVELS. Rev. ed. New York: Dodd, Mead, 1924.

G-3 Beach, Joseph Warren. AMERICAN FICTION: 1920-1940. New York: Macmillan, 1941.

G-4 Boynton, Percy H. AMERICA IN CONTEMPORARY FICTION. Chicago: University of Chicago Press, 1940; New York: Russell and Russell, 1963.

G-5 Bradbury, Malcolm, and Palmer, David, eds. THE AMERICAN NOVEL AND THE 1920'S. Stratford-on-Avon Studies, no. 13. London: Edward Arnold, 1971.

G-6 Burgum, Edwin Berry. THE NOVEL AND THE WORLD'S DILEMMA. New York: Oxford University Press, 1947; Russell and Russell, 1963.

> Essays on Stein, Hemingway, Faulkner, Wright, Saroyan, Steinbeck, Dreiser, Wolfe.

G-7 Eisinger, Chester E. FICTION OF THE FORTIES. Chicago: University of Chicago Press, 1963.

G-8 French, Warren. THE SOCIAL NOVEL AT THE END OF AN ERA. Carbondale, III.: Southern Illinois University Press, 1966.

> Treats Faulkner, Hemingway, Steinbeck, Wright, fiction of the decade before World War II.

G-9 Geismar, Maxwell. AMERICAN MODERNS: FROM REBELLION TO CONFORMITY. New York: Hill and Wang, 1958.

> Deals with Dreiser, Hemingway, Dos Passos, Faulkner, Lewis, Wolfe, Cozzens, Steinbeck, Marquand.

G-10 _____. THE LAST OF THE PROVINCIALS: THE AMERICAN NOVEL, 1915-1925. Boston: Houghton Mifflin, 1947.

> Discusses Lewis, Cather, Anderson, Fitzgerald.

G-11 _____. REBELS AND ANCESTORS: THE AMERICAN NOVEL, 1890-1915. Boston: Houghton Mifflin, 1953.

> Treats London, Glasgow, Dreiser.

G-12 _____. WRITERS IN CRISIS: THE AMERICAN NOVEL, 1925-1940. Boston: Houghton Mifflin, 1942; New York: Hill and Wang, 1961.

> Covers Lardner, Hemingway, Dos Passos, Faulkner, Wolfe, Steinbeck.

G-13 Hartwick, Harry. THE FOREGROUND OF AMERICAN FICTION. New York: American Book Co., 1934; Gordian Press, 1967.

Covers years 1890-1930.

G-14 Hatcher, Harlan. CREATING THE MODERN AMERICAN NOVEL. New York: Farrar and Rinehart, 1935; Russell and Russell, 1965.

G-15 Hoffman, Frederick J. THE MODERN NOVEL IN AMERICA: 1900-1950. Chicago: Regnery, 1951.

G-16 McCole, C. John. LUCIFER AT LARGE. New York: Longmans, Green, 1937.

An idiosyncratic survey of American literature from Dreiser to the 1930's.

G-17 Millgate, Michael. AMERICAN SOCIAL FICTION: JAMES TO COZ-ZENS. New York: Barnes and Noble, 1964.

Treats Wharton, Dreiser, Anderson, Lewis, Fitzgerald, Dos Passos, and Cozzens.

G-18 O'Faolain, Sean. THE VANISHING HERO: STUDIES OF NOVELISTS OF THE TWENTIES. Boston: Little, Brown, 1957.

Essays on Hemingway and Faulkner.

G-19 Simon, Jean. LE ROMAN AMERICAIN AU XXe SIECLE. Paris: Boivin, 1950.

G-20 Van Doren, Carl. CONTEMPORARY AMERICAN NOVELISTS, 1900-1920. New York: Macmillan, 1922.

THE NOVEL: SPECIAL ASPECTS TECHNIQUE AND STRUCTURE

H-1 Beach, Joseph Warren. THE OUTLOOK FOR AMERICAN PROSE. Chicago: University of Chicago Press, 1926.

Essays on style.

H-2 _____. THE TWENTIETH-CENTURY NOVEL: STUDIES IN TECHNIQUE. New York: Century, 1932.

H-3 Booth, Wayne C. THE RHETORIC OF FICTION. Chicago: University of Chicago Press, 1961.

H-4 Brace, Gerald Warner. THE STUFF OF FICTION. New York: Norton,

1969.

> By a distinguished novelist-teacher.

H-5 DeVoto, Bernard. THE WORLD OF FICTION. Boston: Houghton Mifflin, 1950.

> An analysis of the relationship between reader and writer.

H-6 Edel, Leon. THE MODERN PSYCHOLOGICAL NOVEL. New York: Grove Press, 1955.

> Concerns itself with the manner in which emotional and sensory experience has been rendered into fiction.

H-7 Forster, E.M. ASPECTS OF THE NOVEL. New York: Harcourt, Brace, 1927.

> Frequently repr.

H-8 Friedman, Melvin J. STREAM OF CONSCIOUSNESS: A STUDY IN LITERARY METHOD. New Haven: Yale University Press, 1955.

> See also H-12.

H-9 Frye, Northrop. ANATOMY OF CRITICISM. Princeton, N.J.: Princeton University Press, 1957.

> Pp. 243-337 deal with the theory of genres.

H-10 Handy, William J. MODERN FICTION: A FORMALIST APPROACH. Carbondale, Ill.: Southern Illinois University Press, 1971.

> Chaps. on Dreiser, Faulkner, Hemingway.

H-11 Hicks, Granville. THE LIVING NOVEL: A SYMPOSIUM. New York: Macmillan, 1957.

H-12 Humphrey, Robert. STREAM OF CONSCIOUSNESS IN THE MODERN NOVEL. Berkeley: University of California Press, 1954.

> See also H-8.

H-13 Lever, Katherine. THE NOVEL AND THE READER. New York: Appleton-Century-Crofts, 1961.

H-14 Lubbock, Percy. THE CRAFT OF FICTION. New York: Scribners, 1921.

> Reissued by Viking, 1957. A pioneering work in treating fiction as art.

H-15 Magny, Claude-Edmonde. THE AGE OF THE AMERICAN NOVEL: THE FILM AESTHETIC OF FICTION BETWEEN THE TWO WARS. New York: Ungar, 1972.

> Orig. pub. in France in 1948; treats film technique's influence on American novel. Chaps. on Dos Passos, Steinbeck, Faulkner.

H-16 Muir, Edwin. THE STRUCTURE OF THE NOVEL. London: Hogarth, 1928, 1946.

H-17 O'Connor, William Van, ed. FORMS OF MODERN FICTION. Minneapolis: University of Minnesota Press, 1948.

> Includes essays by Allen Tate, Lionel Trilling, Mark Schorer, Edmund Wilson, et al.

H-18 Perkins, George, ed. THE THEORY OF THE AMERICAN NOVEL. New York: Holt, Rinehart, Winston, 1970.

> Statements by novelists about writing from H.H. Brackenridge to Nabokov.

H-19 Perosa, Sergio. LE VIE DELLA NARRATIVA AMERICANA. Milan: Mursia, 1965.

H-20 Sale, Roger, ed. DISCUSSIONS OF THE NOVEL. Boston: Heath, 1960.

H-21 Scholes, Robert, ed. APPROACHES TO THE NOVEL: MATERIALS FOR A POETICS. Rev. ed. San Francisco: Chandler, 1966.

> Includes many writers listed in this section plus Ian Watt, Harry Levin, R.S. Crane, Virginia Woolf, Nathalie Sarraute, et al.

H-22 Scholes, Robert, and Kellogg, Robert. THE NATURE OF NARRATIVE. New York: Oxford University Press, 1966.

H-23 Stevick, Philip, ed. THE THEORY OF THE NOVEL. New York: Free Press, 1967.

> A rich anthology.

H-24 Warren, Austin, and Wellek, René. THE THEORY OF LITERATURE. New York: Harcourt, Brace, 1949.

> Chaps. 16 and 17 deal with literary genres. Frequently repr.

THE NOVEL: SPECIAL ASPECTS - TYPES

DETECTIVE

I-1   Harper, Ralph. THE WORLD OF THE THRILLER. Cleveland: Press of
       Case Western Reserve, 1969.

       An anatomy of the suspense novel.

1-2   Haycraft, Howard. MURDER FOR PLEASURE: THE LIFE AND TIMES OF
       THE DETECTIVE STORY. New York: Appleton-Century, 1941.

I-3   Murch, A.E. THE DEVELOPMENT OF THE DETECTIVE NOVEL. London:
       Peter Owen, 1958; New York: Greenwood, 1968.

I-4   Symons, Julian. BLOODY MURDER: FROM THE DETECTIVE STORY TO
       THE CRIME NOVEL--A HISTORY. London: Faber and Faber, 1972.

HISTORICAL

I-5   Blake, Nelson M. NOVELISTS' AMERICA: FICTION AS HISTORY,
       1910-1940. Syracuse: Syracuse University Press, 1963.

       A social and cultural historian discusses Wolfe, Lewis, Fitz-
       gerald, Faulkner, Steinbeck, Farrell, Dos Passos, Wright.

I-6   Dickinson, A.T. AMERICAN HISTORICAL FICTION. Metuchen, N.J.:
       Scarecrow, 1958.

       This ed. contains 92-page essay on historical fiction. Later eds.
       are pure bibliography. See B-6.

I-7   Leisy, Ernest E. THE AMERICAN HISTORICAL NOVEL. Norman, Okla.:
       University of Oklahoma Press, 1950.

       Appendix lists novels.

I-8   Phillips, William et al. AMERICAN HISTORY IN THE NOVEL, 1585-
       1900. Jefferson City, Mo.: Lincoln University, 1956.

       Repr. from MIDWEST JOURNAL 8 (1956) : 274-406. Essays
       by Phillips, James Woodress, Walter Harding, Charles Kaplan
       discussing many twentieth-century novels; includes bibliographies.

HOLLYWOOD [See also H-15]

I-9   Bluestone, George. NOVELS INTO FILM. Baltimore: Johns Hopkins
       Press, 1957.

Special chaps. on THE GRAPES OF WRATH and THE OX-BOW
INCIDENT.

I-10 Spatz, Jonas. HOLLYWOOD IN FICTION: SOME VERSIONS OF THE
AMERICAN MYTH. The Hague: Mouton, 1969.

I-11 Wells, Walter. TYCOONS AND LOCUSTS: A REGIONAL LOOK AT
HOLLYWOOD FICTION OF THE 1930'S. Carbondale, Ill.: Southern
Illinois University Press, 1973.

POLITICS

I-12 Blotner, Joseph. THE POLITICAL NOVEL. Doubleday Short Studies in
Political Science. Garden City, N.Y.: Doubleday, 1955.

Appendix contains a reading list.

I-13 _____. THE MODERN AMERICAN POLITICAL NOVEL, 1900-1960.
Austin: University of Texas Press, 1966.

I-14 Milne, Gordon. THE AMERICAN POLITICAL NOVEL. Norman, Okla.:
University of Oklahoma Press, 1966.

SCIENCE FICTION

I-15 Bailey, James O. PILGRIMS THROUGH SPACE AND TIME: TRENDS
AND PATTERNS IN SCIENTIFIC AND UTOPIAN FICTION. New York:
Argus Books, 1947.

I-16 Davenport, Basil, et al. THE SCIENCE FICTION NOVEL: IMAGINA-
TION AND SOCIAL CRITICISM. Chicago: Advent, 1959.

WAR AND MILITARY

I-17 Cooperman, Stanley. WORLD WAR I AND THE AMERICAN NOVEL.
Baltimore: Johns Hopkins Press, 1967.

Treats Cather, Dos Passos, Hemingway, Faulkner, Wharton.

I-18 Luchting, Wolfgang A. DAS ERLEBNIS DES KRIEGES IM AMERIKANIS-
CHEN ROMAN UBER DEN ZWEITEN WELTKRIEG. Munich: [privately
printed], 1956.

I-19 Miller, Wayne C. AN ARMED AMERICA: ITS FACE IN FICTION—A
HISTORY OF THE AMERICAN MILITARY NOVEL. New York: New
York University Press, 1970.

1-20 Waldemeir, Joseph J. AMERICAN NOVELS OF THE SECOND WORLD WAR. The Hague: Mouton, 1968.

MISCELLANEOUS

1-21 Barnett, James H. DIVORCE AND THE AMERICAN DIVORCE NOVEL, 1858-1937. Philadelphia: [privately printed], 1939; Russell and Russell, 1968.

1-22 Berry, Thomas E. THE AMERICAN NEWSPAPER IN THE AMERICAN NOVEL, 1900-1969. Metuchen, N.J.: Scarecrow, 1970.

1-23 Folsom, James K. THE AMERICAN WESTERN NOVEL. New Haven: College and University Press, 1966.

      From Cooper to the present.

1-24 Frohock, W.M. THE NOVEL OF VIOLENCE IN AMERICA. Rev. and enlarged ed. Dallas: Southern Methodist University Press, 1957; Boston: Beacon, 1964.

      See also L-3.

1-25 Gelfant, Blanche H. THE AMERICAN CITY NOVEL. Norman, Okla.: University of Oklahoma Press, 1954.

      Anderson, Wolfe, Dos Passos, Farrell.

1-26 Herron, Ima H. THE SMALL TOWN IN AMERICAN LITERATURE. Durham, N.C.: Duke University Press, 1939; New York: Pageant Books, 1959.

      Deals mostly with the nineteenth century.

1-27 Lyons, John O. THE COLLEGE NOVEL IN AMERICA. Carbondale, Ill.: Southern Illinois University Press, 1962.

1-28 Meyer, Roy W. THE MIDDLE WESTERN FARM NOVEL IN THE TWEN-TIETH CENTURY. Lincoln: University of Nebraska Press, 1965.

1-29 Rideout, Walter B. THE RADICAL NOVEL IN THE UNITED STATES, 1900-1954. Cambridge, Mass.: Harvard University Press, 1956.

1-30 Tuttleton, James W. THE NOVEL OF MANNERS IN AMERICA. Chapel Hill, N.C.: University of North Carolina Press, 1972.

      Chaps. on Wharton, Lewis, Fitzgerald, Marquand, Cozzens.

THE NOVEL: SPECIAL ASPECTS - CHARACTERS (See also NEGRO)

J-1 Deegan, Dorothy Yost. THE STEREOTYPE OF THE SINGLE WOMAN IN AMERICAN NOVELS: A SOCIAL STUDY WITH IMPLICATIONS FOR THE EDUCATION OF WOMEN. New York: King's Crown, 1951.

J-2 Feied, Frederick. NO PIE IN THE SKY: THE HOBO AS AMERICAN CULTURAL HERO IN THE WORKS OF JACK LONDON, JOHN DOS PASSOS, AND JACK KEROUAC. New York: Citadel, 1964.

J-3 Fiedler, Leslie A. THE JEW IN THE AMERICAN NOVEL. Herzl Institute Pamphlet, no. 10. New York: Herzl, 1959.

J-4 Karolides, Nicholas J. THE PIONEER IN THE AMERICAN NOVEL, 1900-1950. Norman, Okla.: University of Oklahoma Press, 1967.

J-5 Liptzin, Solomon. THE JEW IN AMERICAN LITERATURE. New York: Bloch, 1966.

J-6 Morsand, Joseph. TRADITIONS IN AMERICAN LITERATURE: A STUDY OF JEWISH CHARACTERS AND AUTHORS. New York: Modern Chapbooks, 1939.

J-7 Pinsker, Sanford. THE SCHLEMIEL AS METAPHOR: STUDIES IN THE YIDDISH AND AMERICAN JEWISH NOVEL. Carbondale, Ill.: Southern Illinois University Press, 1971.

Mostly deals with period after 1950.

J-8 Witham, W. Tasker. THE ADOLESCENT IN THE AMERICAN NOVEL, 1920-1960. New York: Ungar, 1964.

Extensive bibliographical appendix.

J-9 Wisse, Ruth. THE SCHLEMIEL AS MODERN HERO. Chicago: University of Chicago Press, 1971.

A more general study than J-7.

THE NOVEL: SPECIAL ASPECTS - THEMES AND MOTIFS

CHRISTIAN

K-1 Gardiner, Harold C., S.J., ed. FIFTY YEARS OF THE AMERICAN NOVEL: A CHRISTIAN APPRAISAL. New York: Scribners, 1952; Gordian, 1968.

Essays on 13 novelists treated in this work.

K-2   Stewart, Randall. AMERICAN LITERATURE AND CHRISTIAN DOCTRINE.
Baton Rouge, La.: Louisiana State University Press, 1958.

Deals mostly with nineteenth century.

PSYCHOLOGICAL

K-3   Beja, Morris. EPIPHANY IN THE MODERN NOVEL. Seattle: University of Washington Press, 1971.

General essays plus chaps. on Wolfe and Faulkner.

K-4   Bowden, Edwin T. THE DUNGEON OF THE HEART: HUMAN ISOLA-
TION AND THE AMERICAN NOVEL. New York: Macmillan, 1961.

K-5   Malin, Irvin, ed. PSYCHOANALYSIS AND AMERICAN FICTION. New
York: Dutton, 1965.

Includes essays on Cather, Caldwell, Faulkner.

K-6   Lesser, Simon O. FICTION AND THE UNCONSCIOUSNESS. Boston:
Beacon, 1957.

MISCELLANEOUS

K-7   Bluefarb, Sam. THE ESCAPE MOTIF IN THE AMERICAN NOVEL: MARK
TWAIN TO RICHARD WRIGHT. Columbus: Ohio State University Press,
1972.

K-8   Fiedler, Leslie A. LOVE AND DEATH IN THE AMERICAN NOVEL.
Rev. ed. New York: Stein and Day, 1966.

Highly personal thematic study "especially on the duplicity"
with which the themes of love and death are handled in the
United States.

K-9   Fuller, Edmund. MAN IN MODERN FICTION: SOME MINORITY
OPINIONS ON CONTEMPORARY AMERICAN WRITING. New York:
Random House, 1958.

Argues that a "debased image of man" has become current in
contemporary fiction.

K-10 Hilfer, Anthony C. THE REVOLT FROM THE VILLAGE, 1915-1930.
Chapel Hill, N.C.: University of North Carolina Press, 1969.

Chaps. on Cather, Lewis, Wolfe, et al.

K-11 Lehan, Richard. A DANGEROUS CROSSING: FRENCH LITERARY EXISTENTIALISM AND THE MODERN AMERICAN NOVEL. Carbondale, Ill.: Southern Illinois University Press, 1973.

Deals particularly with Dos Passos, Hemingway, Faulkner, Wright.

K-12 Lutwack, Leonard. HEROIC FICTION: THE EPIC TRADITION AND AMERICAN NOVELS OF THE TWENTIETH CENTURY. Carbondale, Ill.: Southern Illinois University Press, 1971.

Steinbeck and Hemingway.

K-13 Lynn, Kenneth S. THE DREAM OF SUCCESS: A STUDY OF THE MODERN AMERICAN IMAGINATION. Boston: Little, Brown, 1955.

Deals among others with Dreiser, London, Herrick.

K-14 Maxwell, D.E.S. AMERICAN FICTION: THE INTELLECTUAL BACKGROUND. New York: Columbia University Press, 1963.

K-15 Mizener, Arthur. THE SENSE OF LIFE IN THE MODERN NOVEL. Boston: Houghton Mifflin, 1964.

Essays on Cozzens, Faulkner, Fitzgerald, Hemingway.

K-16 Muller, Herbert J. MODERN FICTION: A STUDY OF VALUES. New York: Funk and Wagnalls, 1937.

Examples of quaint, passe criticism.

K-17 Wasserstrom, William. HEIRESS OF ALL THE AGES: SEX AND SENTIMENT IN THE GENTEEL TRADITION. Minneapolis: University of Minnesota Press, 1959.

Last chap. deals with twentieth century.

K-18 White, George L. SCANDINAVIAN THEMES IN AMERICAN FICTION. Philadelphia: [privately printed], 1937.

THE NOVEL: SPECIAL ASPECTS - REGIONALISM: SOUTH

L-1 Bradbury, John M. RENAISSANCE IN THE SOUTH: A CRITICAL HISTORY OF THE LITERATURE, 1920-1960. Chapel Hill, N.C.: University of North Carolina Press, 1963.

Includes many minor novelists.

L-2 Davenport, F. Garvin, Jr. THE MYTH OF SOUTHERN HISTORY: HISTORICAL CONSCIOUSNESS IN TWENTIETH-CENTURY SOUTHERN LIT-

ERATURE. Nashville: Vanderbilt University Press, 1970.

L-3　Gossett, Louise Y. VIOLENCE IN RECENT SOUTHERN FICTION. Durham, N.C.: Duke University Press, 1965.

　　Caldwell, Wolfe, Faulkner treated in part one.

L-4　Hoffman, Frederick J. THE ART OF SOUTHERN FICTION: A STUDY OF SOME MODERN NOVELISTS. Carbondale, Ill.: Southern Illinois University Press, 1967.

　　Treats only Katherine Anne Porter, and to a slight extent, Caroline Gordon, of writers included in this vol.

L-5　Holman, C. Hugh. THE ROOTS OF SOUTHERN WRITING: ESSAYS ON THE LITERATURE OF THE AMERICAN SOUTH. Athens, Ga.: University of Georgia Press, 1972.

　　Essays on Glasgow, Wolfe, Faulkner, lesser treatment of Cabell, Caldwell.

L-6　_____. THREE MODES OF MODERN SOUTHERN FICTION: ELLEN GLASGOW, WILLIAM FAULKNER, THOMAS WOLFE. Athens, Ga.: University of Georgia Press, 1966.

　　Regional differentiation emphasized.

L-7　Rubin, Louis D., Jr. THE FARAWAY COUNTRY: WRITERS OF THE MODERN SOUTH. Seattle: University of Washington Press, 1963.

　　Treats Faulkner, Wolfe as well as later writers.

L-8　Rubin, Louis D., Jr., and Jacobs, Robert D. SOUTH: MODERN SOUTHERN LITERATURE IN ITS CULTURAL SETTING. Garden City, N.Y.: Doubleday, 1961.

　　Essays by various hands, some repr.

L-9　_____ and _____. SOUTHERN RENASCENCE: THE LITERATURE OF THE MODERN SOUTH. Baltimore: Johns Hopkins Press, 1953.

L-10 Stewart, John L. THE BURDEN OF TIME: THE FUGITIVES AND AGRARIANS. Princeton, N.J.: Princeton University Press, 1965.

　　Probably the best of several books on the Nashville Fugitives. For others see B-8 under "Fugitives."

THE NOVEL: SPECIAL ASPECTS - NEGRO

M-1　Bigsby, C.W.E., ed. THE BLACK AMERICAN WRITER: VOLUME 1--

FICTION. Deland, Fla.: Everett Edwards, 1969.

Essays by various hands, black and white.

M-2 Bone, Robert A. THE NEGRO NOVEL IN AMERICA. Rev. ed. New Haven: Yale University Press, 1965.

From 1853 to date.

M-3 Brawley, Benjamin G. THE NEGRO IN LITERATURE AND ART IN THE UNITED STATES. New York: Duffield, 1930; AMS, 1971.

M-4 Brown, Sterling. THE NEGRO IN AMERICAN FICTION. Port Washington, N.Y.: Kennikat, 1968.

Orig. pub. in 1937.

M-5 Ford, Nick Aaron. THE CONTEMPORARY NEGRO NOVEL: A STUDY IN RACE RELATIONS. Boston: Meador, 1936.

M-6 Gloster, Hugh M. NEGRO VOICES IN AMERICAN FICTION. Chapel Hill, N.C.: University of North Carolina Press, 1948.

M-7 Gross, Seymour L., and Hardy, John E., eds. IMAGES OF THE NEGRO IN AMERICAN LITERATURE. Chicago: University of Chicago Press, 1966.

Repr. crit.

M-8 Hemenway, Robert, ed. THE BLACK NOVELIST. Columbus: Merrill, 1970.

Essays about black novelists and essays by black writers.

M-9 Hill, Herbert, ed. ANGER AND BEYOND: THE NEGRO WRITER IN THE UNITED STATES. New York: Harper and Row, 1966.

Symposium on Wright, essays on general topics and younger writers.

M-10 Huggins, Nathan. HARLEM RENAISSANCE. New York: Oxford University Press, 1971.

M-11 Hughes, Carl M. [pseud. of John Milton Charles Hughes] THE NEGRO NOVELIST: A DISCUSSION OF THE WRITINGS OF AMERICAN NEGRO NOVELISTS, 1940-1950. New York: Citadel, 1953.

M-12 Littlejohn, David. BLACK ON WHITE: A CRITICAL SURVEY OF WRITING BY AMERICAN NEGROES. New York: Grossman, 1966.

M-13 Margolies, Edward. NATIVE SONS: A CRITICAL STUDY OF TWEN-
TIETH-CENTURY NEGRO AMERICAN AUTHORS. Philadelphia: Lippin-
cott, 1968.

> From W.E.B. DuBois to LeRoi Jones.

M-14 Starke, Catherine J. BLACK PORTRAITURE IN AMERICAN FICTION:
STOCK CHARACTERS, ARCHETYPES, AND INDIVIDUALS. New York:
Basic Books, 1971.

THE NOVEL: SPECIAL ASPECTS - BEST SELLERS

N-1 Hackett, Alice P. SEVENTY YEARS OF BEST SELLERS, 1895-1965. New
York: Bowker, 1967.

N-2 Hart, James D. THE POPULAR BOOK: A HISTORY OF AMERICA'S
LITERARY TASTE. New York: Oxford University Press, 1950.

N-3 Hubbell, Jay B. WHO ARE THE MAJOR AMERICAN WRITERS? Durham, N.C.: Duke University Press, 1972.

> Interesting study based on various opinion polls.

N-4 Stuckey, W.J. THE PULITZER PRIZE NOVELS: A CRITICAL LOOK
BACKWARD. Norman, Okla.: University of Oklahoma Press, 1966.

THE NOVEL: SPECIAL ASPECTS - FOREIGN RECEPTION

O-1 Anderson, Carl L. THE SWEDISH ACCEPTANCE OF AMERICAN LITERA-
TURE. Philadelphia: University of Pennsylvania Press, 1957.

> Treats London, Sinclair, and particularly Lewis.

O-2 Brown, Deming B. SOVIET ATTITUDES TOWARD AMERICAN WRITING.
Princeton, N.J.: Princeton University Press, 1962.

> Dos Passos, London, Sinclair, W.S. Porter, Lewis, Dreiser,
> and Hemingway treated at length.

O-3 Chapman, Arnold. THE SPANISH AMERICAN RECEPTION OF UNITED
STATES FICTION, 1920-1940. University of California Publications in
Modern Philology, no. 77. Berkeley: University of California Press,
1966.

> Anderson, Dreiser, Lewis, Faulkner, Caldwell, Buck.

O-4 Durham, Philip, and Mustanoja, Tauno F. AMERICAN FICTION IN

FINLAND: AN ESSAY AND BIBLIOGRAPHY. Memoires de la Societe Neophilologique de Helsinki, vol. 24. Helsinki: Societe Neophilologique, 1960.

O-5 Kunzova, Hela, and Hava Rybakova. AMERICAN LITERATURE IN CZECHOSLOVAKIA, 1945-1965. Prague: n.p., 1966.

O-6 Price, Lawrence M. THE RECEPTION OF UNITED STATES LITERATURE IN GERMANY. Chapel Hill: University of North Carolina Press, 1966.

Includes fiction writers in a survey extending from colonial times to the present.

O-7 Smith, Thelma M., and Miner, Ward L. TRANSATLANTIC MIGRATION: THE CONTEMPORARY AMERICAN NOVEL IN FRANCE. Durham, N.C.: Duke University Press, 1955; New York: Greenwood, 1968.

O-8 Springer, Anne M. THE AMERICAN NOVEL IN GERMANY: A STUDY OF THE CRITICAL RECEPTION OF EIGHT AMERICAN NOVELISTS BETWEEN THE TWO WORLD WARS. Hamburg: Cram, De Gruyter, 1960.

Treats London, Sinclair, Lewis, Dreiser, Dos Passos, Hemingway, Faulkner, Wolfe.

THE NOVEL: CRITICISM -- ESSAY COLLECTIONS

P-1 Aldridge, John W., ed. CRITIQUES AND ESSAYS ON MODERN FICTION, 1920-1951. New York: Ronald, 1952.

A large anthology covering many writers and general topics.

P-2 _____. TIME TO MURDER AND CREATE: THE CONTEMPORARY NOVEL IN CRISIS. New York: McKay, 1966.

Some discussion of K.A. Porter, Fitzgerald, Hemingway, Lewis.

P-3 Auchincloss, Louis. PIONEERS AND CARETAKERS: A STUDY OF NINE AMERICAN WOMEN NOVELISTS. Minneapolis: University of Minnesota Press, 1965.

Treats E.M. Roberts, K.A. Porter, Wharton, Glasgow, Cather.

P-4 Bode, Carl, ed. THE YOUNG REBEL IN AMERICAN LITERATURE: SEVEN LECTURES. London: Heineman, 1959; Folcroft, Pa.: Folcroft Library Editions, 1972.

On Lewis, Fitzgerald, Steinbeck, Faulkner.

P-5 French, Warren, and Kidd, Walter E., eds. AMERICAN WINNERS OF

THE NOBEL LITERARY PRIZE. Norman, Okla.: University of Oklahoma Press, 1968.

Essays on Lewis, Buck, Faulkner, Hemingway, Steinbeck.

P-6 Gohdes, Clarence, ed. ESSAYS ON AMERICAN LITERATURE IN HONOR OF JAY B. HUBBELL. Durham, N.C.: Duke University Press, 1967.

Essays on W.S. Porter, London, Dashiell Hammett, Wilder.

P-7 Litz, A. Walton, ed. MODERN AMERICAN FICTION: ESSAYS IN CRITICISM. New York: Oxford University Press, 1963.

Essays on Dreiser, Stein, Anderson, Lewis, Fitzgerald (3), Dos Passos, Faulkner (4), Hemingway (4), Wolfe, Steinbeck.

P-8 Mizener, Arthur. TWELVE GREAT AMERICAN NOVELS. New York: New American Library, 1967.

Treats Wharton, Dos Passos, Fitzgerald, Hemingway, Faulkner, Cozzens.

P-9 Moore, Harry T. AGE OF THE MODERN AND OTHER LITERARY ESSAYS. Carbondale, Ill.: Southern Illinois University Press, 1971.

Chaps. on Wolfe, Fitzgerald, Sinclair, Hemingway, Dos Passos, Miller, Dreiser, Steinbeck.

P-10 Morgan, H. Wayne. WRITERS IN TRANSITION: SEVEN AMERICANS. New York: Hill and Wang, 1963.

Cather, Anderson, Wolfe.

P-11 Morris, Wright. THE TERRITORY AHEAD. New York: Harcourt, Brace, 1958.

Includes essays on Hemingway, Fitzgerald, Faulkner, Wolfe.

P-12 O'Connor, William Van. SEVEN MODERN AMERICAN NOVELISTS. Minneapolis: University of Minnesota Press, 1964.

Wharton, Lewis, Fitzgerald, Faulkner, Hemingway, Wolfe, West. Orig. pub. as separate pamphlets in UMPAW.

P-13 Rubin, Louis D., Jr., and Moore, John R., eds. THE IDEA OF AN AMERICAN NOVEL. New York: Crowell, 1961.

Chaps. on Dreiser, Lewis, Hemingway, Fitzgerald, Dos Passos, Farrell, Wolfe, Faulkner.

P-14 Shapiro, Charles, ed. TWELVE ORIGINAL ESSAYS ON GREAT AMERI-

CAN NOVELS. Detroit: Wayne State University Press, 1958.

>Treats Anderson, Dreiser, Fitzgerald, Hemingway, Faulkner, Wharton.

P-15 Squires, J.C. et al. CONTEMPORARY AMERICAN AUTHORS. New York: Holt, 1928.

>Intro. by H.S. Canby; essays by critics of London MERCURY, who discuss Cather, Lewis, Dreiser, Wharton, Hergesheimer.

P-16 Stallman, Robert W. THE HOUSES THAT JAMES BUILT AND OTHER LITERARY STUDIES. East Lansing: Michigan State University Press, 1961.

>Essays on Fitzgerald, Hemingway, Faulkner.

P-17 Sutherland, William O.S., Jr., ed. SIX CONTEMPORARY NOVELS: SIX INTRODUCTORY ESSAYS IN MODERN FICTION. Austin: University of Texas Department of English, 1962.

>Faulkner, Hemingway.

P-18 Whipple, T.K. SPOKESMEN: MODERN WRITERS AND AMERICAN LIFE. New York: Appleton, 1928.

>Treats Anderson, Cather, Dreiser, Lewis.

P-19 _____. STUDY OUT THE LAND. Berkeley: University of California Press, 1943.

>Includes essays on London, Steinbeck, and Dos Passos.

P-20 Whitbread, Thomas B., ed. SEVEN CONTEMPORARY AUTHORS: ESSAYS ON COZZENS, MILLER, WEST, GOLDING, HELLER, ALBEE AND POWERS. Austin: University of Texas Press, 1966.

P-21 Wilson, Edmund. THE WOUND AND THE BOW: SEVEN STUDIES IN LITERATURE. Boston: Houghton Mifflin, 1941.

>Wharton and Hemingway.

Section 3

SPECIALIZED SOURCE MATERIAL - THE SHORT STORY

Q-1 Lieberman, Elias. THE AMERICAN SHORT STORY: A STUDY OF THE INFLUENCE OF LOCALITY IN ITS DEVELOPMENT. Ridgewood, N.J.: The Editor Co., 1912.

Q-2 O'Brien, Edward J. THE ADVANCE OF THE AMERICAN SHORT STORY. New York: Dodd, Mead, 1931.

By the ed. of the annual BEST SHORT STORIES (1914-40).

Q-3 Pattee, Fred Lewis. THE DEVELOPMENT OF THE AMERICAN SHORT STORY: AN HISTORICAL SURVEY. New York: Harper, 1923, 1966.

Q-4 Peden, William. THE AMERICAN SHORT STORY: FRONT LINE IN THE NATIONAL DEFENSE OF LITERATURE. Boston: Houghton Mifflin, 1964.

Appendix contains checklist of 100 "notable" American short story writers, 1940-63.

Q-5 West, Ray B., Jr. THE SHORT STORY IN AMERICA, 1900-1950. Chicago: Regnery, 1952; Freeport, N.Y.: Books for Libraries, 1968.

More criticism than history.

Q-6 Williams, Blanche. OUR SHORT STORY WRITERS. New York: Moffat, 1920.

Q-7 Wright, Austin M. THE AMERICAN SHORT STORY IN THE TWENTIES. Chicago: University of Chicago Press, 1961.

Section 4

SPECIALIZED SOURCE MATERIAL
INTERVIEWS WITH AUTHORS

R-1 Cowley, Malcolm, ed. WRITERS AT WORK: THE "PARIS REVIEW" IN-
TERVIEWS. New York: Viking, 1958.

Faulkner, Wilder.

R-2 Paris Review. WRITERS AT WORK: THE "PARIS REVIEW" INTERVIEWS.
2nd Ser. New York: Viking, 1963.

Prepared for pub. by George Plimpton; interviews include K.A.
Porter, Hemingway, and Henry Miller.

R-3 Van Gelder, Robert. WRITERS AND WRITING. New York. Scribners,
1946.

Brief interviews first pub. in NYTBR.

PART 2

Section 5

SHERWOOD ANDERSON   (1876-1941)

Sherwood Anderson (hereafter SA or A) was born in Camden, Ohio, the third child of an itinerant harness-maker. Although the family moved frequently, most of A's childhood was spent in the town of Clyde (the Winesburg of his fiction). A spent a year in the army during the Spanish-American War and afterwards went into business. In 1912 while operating his own paint manufacturing firm in Elyria, Ohio, he suffered a breakdown from trying to be a businessman by day and a writer by night. He left his wife and children and went to Chicago and for the rest of his life was a writer. Although his work is uneven in quality, he is one of the more influential figures in contemporary American letters. In Chicago before World War I he was part of the group that included Sandburg, Dell, and others; he knew both Hemingway and Faulkner in their formative years; he met and developed a friendship with Gertrude Stein in Paris in the Twenties.

BIBLIOGRAPHY AND MANUSCRIPTS

There is need for a complete and up-to-date bibliography, which would include both primary and secondary materials. The best available at this writing is Eugene Sheehy and Kenneth Lohf, SA: A BIBLIOGRAPHY (Los Gatos, Calif., 1960), which is a checklist only, but it does contain both lists of A's works and works about him. Supplemental to this compilation is G.T. Tanselle's "Additional Reviews of SA's Work," PBSA 56 (1962): 358-65. The Sheehy-Lohf bibliography builds on an earlier compilation by Raymond Gozzi, published in part as "A Bibliography of SA's Contributions to Periodicals," NLB 2 (1948): 71-82. Another checklist of secondary material is Roger Asselineau, "Selection bibliographique des etudes consacrees a SA," RLM 10 (1963): 137-57. Finally, there is an excellent bibliographical essay by Walter Rideout in SMAA.

There is a vast collection of MSS, letters, documents, clippings, correspondence with others, and various miscellaneous materials at the Newberry Library. This huge collection documents A's entire life as a writer. There are in addition supplemental collections at Columbia, Princeton, Yale, and Notre Dame, the Universities of North Carolina and Virginia, Smith College, and the Enoch Pratt Library in Baltimore.

SHERWOOD ANDERSON

WORKS OF FICTION

Novels: WINDY MCPHERSON'S SON (1916), MARCHING MEN (1917), POOR WHITE (1920), MANY MARRIAGES (1923), *DARK LAUGHTER (1925), BEYOND DESIRE (1932), KIT BRANDON (1936).

Stories: *WINESBURG, OHIO (1919), *THE TRIUMPH OF THE EGG (1921), *HORSES AND MEN (1923), DEATH IN THE WOODS (1933).

EDITIONS AND REPRINTS

There has been published at the University Press of Case Western Reserve a partial edition of A's works, edited by R.L. White. These are critical editions with notes on the texts, explanation of editorial principles, lists of variant readings, but they are not published under the auspices of the Modern Language Association's Center for Editions of American Authors. So far the following have appeared: A STORY TELLER'S STORY (1968), TAR: A MIDWEST CHILDHOOD (1969), MARCHING MEN (1972). White also has edited SA'S MEMOIRS (Chapel Hill, N.C., 1969). In this edition he has restored A's original version from the MSS and typescripts at the Newberry Library. The original edition published after A's death was rearranged, rewritten in part, and heavily edited by Paul Rosenfeld.

WINESBURG, OHIO has been carefully edited by Malcolm Cowley (1960), and there are in all four editions in print. Three of A's novels, BEYOND DESIRE, DARK LAUGHTER, and POOR WHITE are available in paperback editions. Other editions of note are Paul Rosenfeld, ed., THE SA READER (Boston, 1947), which contains some previously unpublished material; R.L. White's edition of MARCHING MEN, which contains an appendix with previously uncollected "Selected Essays: 1902-1914"; Horace Gregory, ed., THE PORTABLE SA (New York, 1949, 1956, 1972); Maxwell Geismar, ed., SA: SHORT STORIES (New York, 1962); White, ed., RETURN TO WINESBURG: SELECTIONS FROM FOUR YEARS OF WRITING FOR A COUNTRY NEWSPAPER (Chapel Hill, N.C., 1967); W.D. Taylor, ed., THE BUCK FEVER PAPERS (Charlottesville, Va., 1971), a collection of A's columns from the SMYTH COUNTY NEWS and the MARION DEMOCRAT, 1927-1931. Separate reprints of novels with introductions include: WINDY MCPHERSON'S SON (Chicago, 1965) by Wright Morris; DARK LAUGHTER (New York, 1960) by H.M. Jones; BEYOND DESIRE and POOR WHITE (New York, 1961, 1966) by Walter Rideout.

BIOGRAPHY

William Sutton's Ohio State dissertation (1943), "SA's Formative Years, 1876-1913," has long furnished scholars with the most authoritative source of biographical information on SA down to the time he left his paint business and family

* Of Special Importance

to write. Parts of this work have been published here and there over the years,
but now it is in print in one place with recent material incorporated as THE
ROAD TO WINESBURG: A MOSAIC OF THE IMAGINATIVE LIFE OF SA (Metuchen, N.J., 1972). There have been two good book-length critical biographies: SA by Irving Howe (New York, 1951; repr. Stanford, Calif., 1966) and
SA: HIS LIFE AND WORK by James Schevill (Denver, 1951). Both make use
of Sutton's work and the Newberry Library collection. These works may be sup-
plemented by H.M. Jones and Walter Rideout, eds., LETTERS OF SA, 2 vols.
(Boston, 1953); R.L. White, ed., SA/GERTRUDE STEIN: CORRESPONDENCE
AND PERSONAL ESSAYS (Chapel Hill, N.C., 1972); letters to Rosenfeld in
Jerome Mellquist and Lucie Wiese, eds., PAUL ROSENFELD: VOYAGER IN
THE ARTS (New York, 1948); to Van Wyck Brooks in STORY 19 (September-
October, 1941): 42-62; to R.M. Lovett and Ferdinand Schevill, BERKELEY 1
(October 1947): 1-4; to August Derleth, N&Q 12 (1965): 266-73; to Floyd
Dell, MLR (1963): 532-37.

A was an indefatigable writer about himself, although his autobiographical volumes were never intended to be literal fact. They are important, however.
See A STORY TELLER'S STORY (1924, 1968), SA'S NOTEBOOK (1926), TAR:
A MIDWEST CHILDHOOD (1926), SA'S MEMOIRS (1942, 1969). Other biographical material Is to be found in Karl Anderson's "My Brother SA," SatR 31
(4 September 1948): 6-7, 26-28, the special A number of the NLB 2 (December 1948); and various memoirs and reminiscences of A's friends, including among
others, Margaret Anderson, Harry Hansen, Ben Hecht, Floyd Dell, and Edward
Dahlberg. Stein speaks of A in THE AUTOBIOGRAPHY OF ALICE B. TOKLAS
and Faulkner writes "An Appreciation" in AtlM 191 (June 1953): 27-29.

CRITICISM

Walter Rideout in his excellent essay (see above) summarizes A's critical fortunes as follows: In the 1910's he was attacked by the "Establishment" but
praised by the rebels; in the 1920's he was seen as an important innovator in
the short story; in the 1930's he "was dismissed as a confused man of failing
talent"; in the 1940's his rejection continued as a writer technically and intel-
lectually deficient; in the 1950's the reexamination began of a neglected writer;
in the 1960's the reexamination became the reevaluation of an important writer.
He was one of 16 twentieth-century authors (nine fiction writers) included in
SMAA .

The best brief introduction to SA is Brom Weber's pamphlet (UMPAW, 1964),
which skillfully sums up his career and calls for a reassessment. Weber finds
A a pioneer in the literary field later tilled by Carson McCullers, Bernard Mal-
amud, Flannery O'Connor, Saul Bellow, and others. A longer study, but still
a slim volume, is Rex Burbank's SA (TUSAS, 1964), a reliable overview of A's
entire corpus. Burbank gives most of his attention to A's major works and
doesn't attempt to dwell on "such palpably bad efforts" as MANY MARRIAGES
or BEYOND DESIRE. He devotes the last two chapters before his conclusion
to A STORY TELLER'S STORY and the MEMOIRS, both of which he treats as
confessions rather than autobiographies, and considers superior creations. Irving

Howe's SA (cited under "Biography") is more criticism than biography, but it is not entirely sympathetic to A's work. Yet its analysis of WINESBURG, OHIO and the short stories is penetrating and acute. Howe is not, however, as negative as Lionel Trilling in THE LIBERAL IMAGINATION (New York, 1950), who argues that A is a writer of minor importance.

More recent than any of the books cited above is David (no relation) Anderson's SA: AN INTRODUCTION AND INTERPRETATION (New York, 1967). The treatment is sympathetic, but the argument of the book is "essentially on amplification in detail of Maxwell Geismar's thesis [that A's work was an effort to discover the meaning of existence in the United States] ... as stated in THE LAST OF THE PROVINCIALS [Boston, 1947]" (Rideout, SMAA). The first two books on A, however, appeared in the 1920's: Cleveland Chase, SA (New York, 1927, 1972), and N.B. Fagin, THE PHENOMENON OF SA (Baltimore, 1927). Chase was hostile and accused A of writing to escape from life and thought his work was full of softness and sentimentality. Fagin's book illustrates the anti-establishment defense of A in the early decades of his career.

There have been many discussions of A in books of criticism or literary history through the years. Some of the early ones still have historic interest: "D.H. Lawrence and SA" in THE COLLECTED ESSAYS OF JOHN PEALE BISHOP (New York, 1948; orig. pub., 1921); Percy Boynton in MORE CONTEMPORARY AMERICANS (Chicago, 1926); J.W. Beach in THE OUTLOOK FOR AMERICAN PROSE (Chicago, 1927); T.K. Whipple in SPOKESMEN (New York, 1928); Stuart Sherman in CRITICAL WOODCUTS (New York, 1926). More recent discussions of value include: Alfred Kazin in ON NATIVE GROUNDS (New York, 1942); H.S. Canby in LHUS; Bernard Duffey in THE CHICAGO RENAISSANCE IN AMERICAN LETTERS (East Lansing, Mich., 1954); C.C. Walcutt in AMERICAN LITERARY NATURALISM (Minneapolis, 1956); R.B. West in THE SHORT STORY IN AMERICA, 1900-1950 (Chicago, 1952).

As Weber points out, "SA thought of himself at the end as merely a minor artist who had contributed only a minor classic--WINESBURG, OHIO--to American culture." That this work is generally regarded as a classic is apparent from the steady success the book has had, continuing sales, new editions, and critical exegesis. John H. Ferres, ed., WINESBURG, OHIO: TEXT AND CRITICISM (New York, 1966), brings together six contemporary reviews and 20 critical essays besides reprinting Malcolm Cowley's text of the work. Many of the selections already have been cited here such as Kazin, Cowley, Geismar, Howe, Anderson, Walcutt, Trilling, and Faulkner, but additional essays are these: William Phillips, "How SA Wrote WINESBURG, OHIO"; Walter Rideout, "The Simplicity of WINESBURG, OHIO"; Horace Gregory's introduction to THE PORTABLE SA; E. San Juan, Jr., "Vision and Reality: A Reconsideration of SA's WINESBURG, OHIO"; and J.T. Flanagan, "Hemingway's Debt to SA."

There is still another collection of reprinted criticism, edited by R.L. White: THE ACHIEVEMENT OF SA (Chapel Hill, N.C., 1966). Nine of the 20 pieces here are duplicated in the previously cited collection--not a surprising fact inasmuch as both books appeared in the same year. Some of the duplicated items not mentioned earlier: Edwin Fussell's "Winesburg, Ohio: Art and Isolation"; Waldo Frank's "WINESBURG, OHIO After Twenty Years"; a selection from F.J. Hoffman's FREUDIANISM AND THE LITERARY MIND. Both books together provide the student with a sizeable body of the best A criticism written over a period of 50 years. To these collections also should be added "Homage to SA," the special issue of STORY 19 (September-October 1941), and a special issue of SHENANDOAH 13 (Spring 1962). The latter contains, among other things, J.K. Feibleman's "A Memoir of SA"; articles by J.S. Lawry on "I Want to Know Why" and C.D. Williams on KIT BRANDON.

A never has attracted as much attention from dissertation writers or from foreign scholars as other major twentieth-century authors. Only 15 dissertations had been written on A through 1970, about one-sixth as many as on Faulkner but about the same number as on Steinbeck. The foreign interest in Steinbeck, however, always has been considerably greater than in A. In the twenty years between 1950 and 1970 only 18 articles on A appeared in foreign journals (as recorded in AAL and MLA listings), of which the Italians accounted for eight. The most significant work done on A outside the United States, however, is that of Roger Asselineau in France, who has written several important articles, one of which, "Langue et style de SA dans WINESBURG, OHIO," is reprinted in Ferres' collection (see above).

Section 6

PEARL (SYDENSTRICKER) BUCK (1892-1973)

Although she was the third of seven Americans (after Sinclair Lewis and Eugene O'Neill) to win the Nobel Prize for Literature, Pearl Buck (hereafter PSB, PB, or B) enjoys a very modest place in the esteem of scholars and critics of American literature. She rocketed to international fame with her second novel, THE GOOD EARTH (1931), but after that her literary output, which was prolific, was anticlimatic. Novels came from her typewriter annually as inevitably as the changing seasons. Born the daughter of missionaries, she grew up in China, married a missionary, whom she later divorced, and lived in China as a university teacher of English literature until the 1930's. She devoted most of her literary effort to oriental subjects, chiefly China.

BIBLIOGRAPHY AND MANUSCRIPTS

There is no up-to-date separately published bibliography, but one may consult Vito Brenni, "PB: A Selected Bibliography," BB 22 (1957): 65-69, 94-96; the appendix (annotated) to Paul Doyle, PSB (TUSAS, 1965); and Johnson. Also see a list of B's early writings in Richard Walsh (D's second husband), A BIO-GRAPHICAL SKETCH OF PSB (New York, 1936).

The principal MS collections are at Harvard and the New York Public Library. The Wisconsin Historical Society also has letters to and from B. In addition, one should check the NATIONAL UNION CATALOGUE OF MANUSCRIPT COLLECTIONS, where B is listed as a correspondent in over a dozen scattered MS holdings.

WORKS OF FICTION

Novels (not including those published under pseudonym "John Sedges"): EAST WIND: WEST WIND (1930), *THE GOOD EARTH (1931), *SONS (1932), THE YOUNG REVOLUTIONIST (1932), *THE MOTHER (1933), *A HOUSE DIVIDED (1935), THIS PROUD HEART (1938), THE PATRIOT (1939), OTHER GODS; AN

* Of Special Importance

AMERICAN LEGEND (1940), CHINA SKY (1942), DRAGON SEED (1942), THE
PROMISE (1943), CHINA FLIGHT (1945), PORTRAIT OF A MARRIAGE (1945),
PAVILION OF WOMEN (1946), PEONY (1948), THE BONDMAID (1949), KIN-
FOLK (1949), GOD'S MEN (1951), THE HIDDEN FLOWER (1952), COME, MY
BELOVED (1953), IMPERIAL WOMAN (1955), LETTER FROM PEKING (1957),
SATAN NEVER SLEEPS (1962), THE LIVING REED (1963), DEATH IN THE CAS-
TLE (1965), THE TIME IS NOON (1966), THE NEW YEAR (1968), THE THREE
DAUGHTERS OF MADAME LIANG (1969), MANDALA (1970), ALL UNDER
HEAVEN (1973).

Stories: THE FIRST WIFE AND OTHER STORIES (1933), FAR AND NEAR:
STORIES OF JAPAN, CHINA, AND AMERICA (1934), TODAY AND FOREVER:
STORIES OF CHINA (1941), TWENTY-SEVEN STORIES (1943), FOURTEEN
STORIES (1961), HEARTS COME HOME, AND OTHER STORIES (1962), ESCAPE
AT MIDNIGHT, AND OTHER STORIES (1964), THE GOOD DEED, AND OTHER
STORIES OF ASIA, PAST AND PRESENT (1969), ONCE UPON A CHRISTMAS
(1972).

Translation: ALL MEN ARE BROTHERS (1933), trans. of important medieval
Chinese novel, SHUI HU CH'UAN. For critical essay on this version, see Mark
Van Doren, PRIVATE READER (New York, 1942).

EDITIONS AND REPRINTS

THE GOOD EARTH, which has become a modern classic, won the Pulitzer Prize
in 1932 and was a best seller for two years. It has been translated into some
20 languages, filmed, and dramatized, and it has sold over a million copies.
Four editions now are in print. Most of B's books, some two dozen novels, several volumes of stories, and a baker's dozen of children's books are in print,
many both in paper and hardback editions. There, is no collected edition, but
HOUSE OF EARTH was issued as a trilogy containing THE GOOD EARTH,
SONS, A HOUSE DIVIDED; AMERICAN TRIPTYCH collected three "John Sedges"
novels; recently appeared PSB: THE COMPLETE WOMAN--SELECTIONS FROM
THE WRITINGS OF (1971).

BIOGRAPHY

Richard Walsh's sketch (noted above), which is the earliest biographical account,
was printed separately, then used in a shorter version as the introduction to THE
FIRST WIFE AND OTHER STORIES. The first full-length life was written by
Grace Yaukey (B's sister) under the pseudonym of Cornelia Spencer: THE EXILE'S
DAUGHTER: A BIOGRAPHY OF PSB (New York, 1944); but it is narrative
biography only. A semi-official life (title page notes "in consultation with
PSB") was prepared by Theodore Harris: PSB: A BIOGRAPHY (New York, 1969)
and expanded with a second volume (New York, 1971), the latter containing
substantial amounts of B's letters and speeches. Harris also recorded and published B's FOR SPACIOUS SKIES: JOURNEY IN DIALOGUE (New York, 1966).

To these studies should be added two autobiographical volumes: MY SEVERAL WORLDS (New York, 1954) and A BRIDGE FOR PASSING (New York, 1962); two books about B's parents, THE EXILE [her mother] and FIGHTING ANGEL: PORTRAIT OF A SOUL [her father] (both New York, 1936; repr. in one vol. as THE SPIRIT AND THE FLESH, 1944). See in addition "PB Talks of Her Life in China," CHINA WEEKLY REV. 62 (1932): 145-46; FRIEND TO FRIEND: A CANDID EXCHANGE BETWEEN PSB AND CARLOS P. ROMULO (New York, 1958).

CRITICISM

In view of B's low critical reputation in America it may come as a surprise to discover that she is rather widely read abroad. Besides the large number of translations of THE GOOD EARTH, many of her other books have been turned into versions as diverse as Slovenian, Danish, Latvian, and Hungarian. Two of the three dissertations written on her were done in Europe: Elfriede Kreuchel, "Die Stellung der Frau in PBs China-Romanen" (Vienna, 1950); Ilse Magnus, "Die Frau in China in den Werken PBs" (Kiel, 1954). The only American dissertation is Doan Ly, "The Image of the Chinese Family in PB's Novels" (St. John's, Brooklyn, 1965). The only recent book-length study of B is Doyle's competent but brief volume in the Twayne Series (see above).

Among American critics B has usually been treated in composite studies, almost all written more than 20 years ago. Typical are Carl Van Doren, THE AMERICAN NOVEL, 1789-1939, rev. ed. (New York, 1940) and Oscar Cargill, INTELLECTUAL AMERICA (New York, 1941). The latter work examines B at some length as an exponent of literary naturalism. Later she was treated by A.C. Cooper and C.A. Palmer in TWENTY MODERN AMERICANS (New York, 1942) and R.M. Bartlett in THEY WORK FOR TOMORROW (New York, 1943). Robert Van Gelder in WRITERS AND WRITING (New York, 1946) is informative about B's writing habits, and John and H.S. Cournos give her six pages in FAMOUS MODERN AMERICAN NOVELISTS (New York, 1952). The only recent American book discussing B, and a rather specialized study at that, is Warren French and Walter Kidd, eds., AMERICAN WINNERS OF THE NOBEL PRIZE (Norman, Okla., 1968), in which Dody Thompson contributes the chapter on B.

There have been only a few significant articles on B in the last 35 years. One of these is a pioneer and perceptive study, Phyllis Bentley, "The Art of PSB," EJ 24 (1935): 791-800; but most of the articles in the 1930's fall in the category of literary journalism with a cluster of articles appearing around the time of B's Nobel Prize. Other essays worth noting, however, are Ami Henchoz, "A Permanent Element in PB's Novels," ES 25 (1943): 97-103, a thoughtful, analytic article; Mamoru Shimizu, "On Some Stylistic Features, Chiefly Biblical, of THE GOOD EARTH," SELit 41 (1964): 117-34; Paul Doyle, "PB's Short Stories: A Survey," EJ 55 (1966): 62-68; Walter Langlois, "THE DREAM OF THE RED CHAMBER, THE GOOD EARTH, and MAN'S FATE: Chronicles of Social Change in China," LE&W 11 (1967): 1-10; George Cevasco, "PB and the Chinese Novel," ASt (1967): 437-50.

Section 7

JAMES BRANCH CABELL (1879-1958)

James Branch Cabell (hereafter JBC or C) was born in Richmond into an old Virginia family and lived most of his life in his native state. He graduated with high honors from William and Mary College and then went into journalism. He began writing novels in 1904, but it was not until the Society for the Suppression of Vice succeeded in having JURGEN suppressed in 1920 that C became a conspicuous literary figure. He is best known for a series of sophisticated, ironic pseudo-Medieval romances laid in a mythical land of Poictesme. Although he was pretty much neglected and unread during the last years of his life, his reputation has undergone a rejuvenation in the last decade.

BIBLIOGRAPHY AND MANUSCRIPTS

Two important bibliographical volumes appeared the year before C died and since he wrote no more in the last months, these compilations are complete for primary sources: Frances Brewer, JBC: A BIBLIOGRAPHY OF HIS WRITINGS, BIO-GRAPHY AND CRITICISM (Charlottesville, Va., 1957; repr. Freeport, N.Y., 1971); M.J. Bruccoli, JBC: A BIBLIOGRAPHY, PART II: NOTES ON THE C COLLECTIONS AT THE UNIVERSITY OF VIRGINIA (Charlottesville, 1957). Brewer lists both primary and secondary sources (257 entries) and records reviews. Primary sources are arranged in C's order of the Life of Manuel, the criticism chronologically. Bruccoli's work is a detailed descriptive bibliography of C's works and an account of MS and letter collections at Virginia. Both volumes together supersede earlier bibliographies. There are more recent compilations for secondary sources: Dorothy Schlegel's entry on C in Louis Rubin, ed., A BIBLIOGRAPHICAL GUIDE TO THE STUDY OF SOUTHERN LITERATURE (Baton Rouge, La., 1969); J.L. Davis's appendix to JBC (TUSAS, 1962), which is annotated. There also is bibliographical data in the issues of two new periodicals, KALKI, which began in 1967, and THE CABELLIAN, which began in 1968 and expired after two volumes.

More information on C's letters than is contained in Bruccoli's book may be found in Maurice Duke's "JBC's Personal Library," SB 23 (1970): 207-16. Also it should be noted that Yale has C's correspondence with Van Vechten, Princeton the correspondence with Fitzgerald. Other significant holdings of letters are at the University of California at Berkeley, the University of Chicago, Harvard, the New York Public Library, and the Virginia Historical Society at Richmond.

WORKS OF FICTION

Novels: THE EAGLE'S SHADOW (1904), THE CORDS OF VANITY (1909), THE SOUL OF MELICENT (1913; revised as DOMNEI, 1920), THE RIVET IN GRAND-FATHER'S NECK (1915), *THE CREAM OF THE JEST (1917), *JURGEN (1919), *FIGURES OF EARTH (1921), THE HIGH PLACE (1923), THE SILVER STALLION (1926), SOMETHING ABOUT EVE (1927), THE WAY OF ECBEN (1929), SMIRT (1934), SMITH (1935), SMIRE (1937), THE KING WAS IN HIS COUNTING HOUSE (1938), HAMLET HAD AN UNCLE (1940), FIRST GENTLEMAN OF AMERICA (1942), THERE WERE TWO PIRATES (1946).

Stories: THE LINE OF LOVE (1905), GALLANTRY (1907), CHIVALRY (1909), THE CERTAIN HOUR (1916), THE MUSIC FROM BEHIND THE MOON (1926), THE WHITE ROBE (1928).

EDITIONS AND REPRINTS

C's works were collected in the Storisende Edition in 18 volumes (1927-30) arranged as the Biography of the Life of Manuel. Each volume was revised and contains a special preface by C. BETWEEN DAWN AND SUNSET (New York, 1930), edited and introduced by John Macy, is an anthology selected from C's works. Two of C's works were issued by the Modern Library, BEYOND LIFE (1923), essays, and THE CREAM OF THE JEST (1927). There were seven editions of JURGEN and the work was set to music by Deems Taylor. FIGURES OF EARTH, JURGEN, THE SILVER STALLION, and THE HIGH PLACE are available in paperback editions. THE NIGHTMARE HAS TRIPLETS (1972) is a reprinting of SMIRT, SMITH, SMIRE.

BIOGRAPHY

C has yet to be the subject of a full-length biography, and meanwhile one must rely on fragmentary sources. J.L. Davis' JBC (see above) contains some biography, and the following articles are contributions to the life: Emmett Peter, "C: The Making of a Rebel," CAROLINA QUARTERLY 14 (1962): 74-81; Frank Durham, "Love as a Literary Exercise: Young JBC Tries His Wings," MissQ 18 (1964-65): 26-37; William Gotschalk, "JBC at William and Mary: The Education of a Novelist," WILLIAM AND MARY REVIEW 5 (No. 2, 1967): 1-10; Jerry Page, "The Man at Storisende: A Biographical Note," KALKI 2 (nos. 1, 2, 1968): 8-12. In William Manchester's DISTURBER OF THE PEACE (New York, 1951) there is an account of the JURGEN censorship case. Also

* Of Special Importance

48

C's publisher McBride issued a slender volume, JURGEN AND THE LAW (New York, 1923), which prints essential documents of the case. Irene and Allen Cleaton's BOOKS AND BATTLES (Boston, 1937) contains anecdotes about C. Also one should consult Carl Van Vechten's FRAGMENTS FROM AN UNWRITTEN AUTOBIOGRAPHY (New Haven, 1955) and Burton Rascoe's BEFORE I FORGET (New York, 1937). A recent letter collection deals in part with C: Gerald Langford, ed., INGENUE AMONG THE LIONS: THE LETTERS OF EMILY CLARK TO JOSEPH HERGESHEIMER (Austin, Tex., 1965).

C has written about himself in AS I REMEMBER IT (New York, 1955) and in these quasi-autobiographical volumes: THESE RESTLESS HEADS (1932), SPECIAL DELIVERY (1933), and QUIET, PLEASE (1952). There also is a letter collection, Padraic Colum and Margaret Freeman Cabell, eds., BETWEEN FRIENDS: LETTERS OF JBC AND OTHERS (New York, 1962). Other letters appear in "Letters of George Sterling to JBC," AL 44 (1972): 146-53. Other bits of biographical data may be gleaned from the issues of THE CABELLIAN and KALKI.

CRITICISM

Davis' volume in the Twayne series is the best brief analysis and summary of C's entire corpus. Davis argues that C's work should be placed in Northrop Frye's "romance-anatomy" classification, not in the usual socio-realistic category, and in this context C ranks "among the major rather than the minor authors of the twentieth century." Another useful book that appeared with Davis' is Arvin Wells' JESTING MOSES: A STUDY IN CABELLIAN COMEDY (Gainesville, Fla., 1962). This is an intelligent, competent study of C's comic vision with particular attention to JURGEN, FIGURES OF EARTH, and SOMETHING ABOUT EVE. There is a more recent book-length study, Desmond Tarrant's JBC: THE DREAM AND THE REALITY (Norman, Okla., 1967), but this work is an aggressive defense of C's work and seems more for the true-believers than the disinterested scholars. Tarrant thinks that C is "almost alone in twentieth-century literature in presenting man as, if not master of his fate, at least equal to it."

C's literary reputation has undergone more than the usual vicissitudes since he began publishing in 1904. For the first two decades he was simply ignored, but in the 1920's his books suddenly caught on and he became a celebrity. John Bellamy's dissertation, "JBC: A Critical Study of His Reputation," DA 14 (1954): 825-26, reports that his books "were looked upon as products of a stupendous genius." During the 1930's and 1940's C's reputation plummeted again to near zero, and at the time Bellamy wrote C's rediscovery had not yet taken place. Since C's death in 1958 and spurred perhaps by the excellent bibliographies published by the University Press of Virginia, C's rehabilitation has taken place. The huge C collection now is available at the University of Virginia, and between 1954 and 1968 ten dissertations and three books (discussed above) were written. The two periodicals devoted to C, KALKI and THE CABELLIAN, appeared in the late-1960's, but the flurry of interest of the 1960's appears in the 1970's to be falling back to a more modest concern.

There is space here only to post a few milestones along the road of C criticism. Vernon Parrington's "The Incomparable Mr. C," PACIFIC REVIEW 2 (1921): 359-70; repr. in MAIN CURRENTS IN AMERICAN THOUGHT, vol. 3 (New York, 1930), praised C extravagantly as a creator of great literature and a prose master. Other early admirers were Hugh Walpole and H.L. Mencken, who published pamphlets praising C during the 1920's, and Carl Van Doren, who wrote a small book. Louis Untermeyer, another champion of that era, also wrote several pieces (see Brewer's bibliography). The detractors began during C's decade of greatest acclaim, however, with Paul Elmer More's attack in THE DEMON OF THE ABSOLUTE (Princeton, 1928), which accused C of affectations, false notes, cheap smartness, and superficiality. Granville Hicks in THE GREAT TRADITION (New York, 1935) thought C a double "fraud, for neither his romanticism nor his pessimism is genuine." The attack was continued by Peter Monro Jack in Malcolm Cowley, ed., AFTER THE GENTEEL TRADITION (New York, 1937; Carbondale, Ill., 1964) and Oscar Cargill in INTELLECTUAL AMERICA (New York, 1941), who thought C "the most tedious person who has achieved high repute."

After World War II the balance began to be redressed by Edward Wagenknecht in "C: A Reconsideration," CE 9 (1948): 239-46, who sees C's work as not insincere or affected but genuinely reflecting the metaphysical dilemma of the modern age. Raymond Himelick in "C, Shelley, and the 'Incorrigible Flesh,'" SAQ 47 (1948): 88-95, followed somewhat the same line. A well-known re-evaluation of the next decade was Edmund Wilson's "The JBC Case Reopened," NY 32 (21 April 1956): 129-56; repr. in THE BIT BETWEEN MY TEETH (New York, 1956). Wilson thought C a master at "rendering the unstable aspects of life." Still later estimates include E.W. Parks in "JBC," MissQ 20 (1967): 97-102, who believes that C is the best writer we have had of philosophical romances but that he has lost popularity because his demands on the reader are too great.

Section 8

ERSKINE CALDWELL (1900-   )

Erskine Caldwell (hereafter EC or C) was born in Georgia, the son of a presbyterian minister. He had very little formal schooling, except for three years at
the University of Virginia, but he lived in various parts of the South as a boy
and as a young man worked as farm hand, mill worker, cook, waiter, stage-
hand, and reporter. His fiction reflects this varied experience as well as his
interest in social and economic problems. He has been a prolific writer, most
at home with the short story, since his first novelette appeared in 1929. His
books have sold millions of copies in paperback editions, but the critics do not
rank him very high in the pantheon of contemporary Southern writers.

BIBLIOGRAPHY AND MANUSCRIPTS

A bibliography of C's works and the writings about him is badly needed. He
has written 30 novels, over 150 short stories contained in 18 collections, 13
non-fiction works, and several screen plays plus the many fugitive pieces of a
busy writer's lifetime, but the task of describing these works has yet to be done.
The same is true of the secondary sources, but AAL yields three dozen articles,
and there also is bibliographical material in these sources: D.R. Noble's list
in Louis Rubin, ed., BIBLIOGRAPHICAL GUIDE TO THE STUDY OF SOUTHERN
LITERATURE (Baton Rouge, La., 1969); Louis Rubin and Robert Jacobs, eds.,
SOUTH: MODERN SOUTHERN LITERATURE IN ITS CULTURAL SETTING (Garden City, N.Y., 1961); James Korges' EC (UMPAW, 1969).

A large collection of MS material has been given to Dartmouth College, though
it is partially restricted. The collection includes literary MSS, correspondence,
personal papers, scrapbooks, mimeographed copies of screenplays. From this
collection has been published THE FINAL CHAPTER OF TOBACCO ROAD (Boston, 1972) with an introduction by E.C. Lathem. There are in addition significant holdings of MS material at the University of Chicago, Harvard, and there
are letters collections at the Viking Press, New York; the Wisconsin State Historical Society, Madison; the Minnesota Historical Society, St. Paul; the University of Oregon; the American Academy of Arts and Letters, New York; and
Yale.

51

WORKS OF FICTION

Novels: THE BASTARD (1929), POOR FOOL (1930), *TOBACCO ROAD (1932), *GOD'S LITTLE ACRE (1933), *JOURNEYMAN (1935), THE SACRILEGE OF ALAN KENT (1936), *TROUBLE IN JULY (1940), ALL NIGHT LONG (1942), *GEORGIA BOY (1943), TRAGIC GROUND (1944), A HOUSE IN THE UP-LANDS (1946), THE SURE HAND OF GOD (1947), THIS VERY EARTH (1948), PLACE CALLED ESTERVILLE (1949), EPISODE IN PALMETTO (1950), A LAMP FOR NIGHT FALL (1952), LOVE AND MONEY (1954), GRETTA (1955), CLAUDELLE INGLISH (1958), JENNY BY NATURE (1961), CLOSE TO HOME (1962), THE LAST NIGHT OF SUMMER (1963), *MISS MAMMA AIMEE (1967), SUMMERTIME ISLAND (1968), THE WEATHER SHELTER (1969), THE EARNSHAW NEIGHBORHOOD (1971).

Stories: AMERICAN EARTH (1930), WE ARE THE LIVING (1933), KNEEL TO THE RISING SUN (1935), SOUTHWAYS (1938), JACKPOT (1940), THE COURT-ING OF SUSIE BROWN (1952), GULF COAST STORIES (1956), CERTAIN WO-MEN (1957), WHEN YOU THINK OF ME (1959).

EDITIONS AND REPRINTS

C's stories and novels have been widely reprinted in inexpensive paperbound editions, and his stories have been extensively anthologized. There are too many reprints to list here, but some of the more interesting ones follow:

Stories: edited and introduced by Robert Cantwell, THE HUMOROUS SIDE OF EC (1951); H.S. Canby, STORIES BY EC (1944); Carvel Collins, MEN AND WOMEN (1961); also COMPLETE STORIES (1953).

Novels: GOD'S LITTLE ACRE appeared in The Modern Library in 1934, TO-BACCO ROAD in 1940; the former carried an introduction by C; THE BASTARD, POOR FOOL, and THE SACRILEGE OF ALAN KENT appeared in a single vol-ume (London, 1963); THREE (1960) contained in one volume TOBACCO ROAD, GEORGIA BOY, and THE SURE HAND OF GOD. There has been no collected edition of C, but some 22 of his novels and story collections are available in paperbound editions.

BIOGRAPHY

C's life has yet to be written. He has written about himself, however, and given frequent interviews. CALL IT EXPERIENCE: THE YEARS OF LEARNING HOW TO WRITE (1951) is autobiographic, but it was written in mid-career and focuses on C's literary life. DEEP SOUTH (1968) is a biography of C's father. C has written a good bit on writing, but this will be discussed under "Criticism" below. Also there is biographical information in C's various non-fiction works. Some interesting interviews: Carvel Collins, "EC at Work: A Conversation,"

* Of Special Importance

AtlM 202 (July 1958): 21-27; Alan Lelchuk and Robin White, "An Interview with EC," Per/Se 2 (Spring 1967): 11-20; Anon., "America's Most Censored Author; An Interview with EC," PUBLISHER'S WEEKLY 155 (1949): 1960-61. See also C's "My Twenty-Five Years of Censorship," ESQUIRE 50 (October 1958): 176-78. Some biographical material will be found in Korges' pamphlet (see above) and in the introduction to Cantwell's THE HUMOROUS SIDE OF EC. Beyond these meager sources one must go to the standard biographical reference works (see "Part one").

CRITICISM

Aside from one unpublished dissertation by Carlyle Cross, "EC as a Southern Writer," DA 24 (1964): 4696-97, there has been no full-length study of C in English. On the other hand there have been three dissertations in German, two published, dealing with C's style, language, art, and treatment of the share-cropper, and there was a Russian study published in Irkutsk in 1967. The best discussion of C in English is Korges' pamphlet, which is a brief but balanced and sensible survey. One could not begin to do justice to Faulkner in 46 pages, but with C the task is not so formidable. Korges believes that C, now in great disrepute among academic critics, will be "discovered" and that his reputation ultimately will rest solidly on a few books: TOBACCO ROAD, GOD'S LITTLE ACRE, JOURNEYMAN, GEORGIA BOY, MISS MAMMA AIMEE, and about 25 stories. His solid achievement now is obscured by the bulk of his output.

One should look at C's writings on writing in making any critical study of his work. He has written WRITING IN AMERICA (1967); a pamphlet, WORDS-MANSHIP: THE THEORY, PRACTICE AND REWARDS OF (1961); "The Art, Craft, and Personality of Writing," TQ 7 (1964): 37-43; "How to Live Like an Author," NEW WORLD WRITING, no. 15 (New York, 1959).

As suggested above, C has attracted more critical attention abroad than in America. GOD'S LITTLE ACRE alone has been translated into 21 languages. For a survey of C's impact in France, see Thelma Smith and W.L. Miner's TRANSATLANTIC MIGRATION: THE CONTEMPORARY AMERICAN NOVEL IN FRANCE (Durham, N.C., 1955) and Stewart Benedict, "Gallic Light on EC," SAQ (1961): 390-97. Prior to World War II American critics gave C much serious attention, but since that time he has been increasingly neglected at home while continuously discussed abroad. (A recent Italian bibliography lists more than six pages of articles on C published in Italy from 1945-55.)

Some of the early favorable discussions are found in Oscar Cargill's INTELLEC-TUAL AMERICA (New York, 1941); Leo Gurko's THE ANGRY DECADE (New York, 1947); J.W. Beach's AMERICAN FICTION: 1920-1940 (New York, 1941). Both Cargill and Gurko go so far overboard as to rank C above Faulkner, and Beach, while not so rash, devotes 30 pages to C's fiction. Another book of the period, which deals with C as a naturalistic writer, is Alfred Kazin's ON NATIVE GROUNDS (New York, 1942). An early unfavorable discussion is John Wade's "Sweet Are the Uses of Degeneracy," SoR 1 (1935-36): 449-66.

Although today C is infrequently discussed except in composite studies of Southern literature, the following more recent essays are recommended: Hugh Holman's "Southern Social Issues and the Outer World" in George Gore, ed. SOUTHERN FICTION TODAY (Athens, Georgia, 1969); Robert Cantwell's "C's Characters: Why Don't They Leave?" GaR 11 (1957): 252–64; Louise Grosset in VIOLENCE IN RECENT SOUTHERN FICTION (Durham, N.C., 1965); Kenneth Burke's "C: Maker of Grotesques" in his PHILOSOPHY OF LITERARY FORM, 2nd ed. (Baton Rouge, La., 1967).

Section 9

WILLA CATHER (1873-1946)

Willa Cather (hereafter WC or C) is best known for her stories and novels laid
in Nebraska where she grew up, but there is a great deal more to her work than
an exploitation of the Midwest. She was intensely interested in the place of
the artist in society, contrasts in social values, the moral and ethical relationships among people, and her work, while rooted in particular time and space,
deals with universal themes. As a stylist and craftsman, she ranks among the
best writers America has produced, and since her death her critical reputation
has steadily grown. Before publishing her first novel, she had a long career as
a journalist in Nebraska, Pittsburgh, and New York, but after 1912 she devoted
herself to fiction and lived mostly in New York. She traveled often, especially
to the Southwest where some of her most memorable fiction is laid, also Canada,
Europe, and New England.

BIBLIOGRAPHY AND MANUSCRIPTS

There is yet no definitive bibliography either of C's works or of secondary criticism. There is, however, a complete list of C's signed works and an extensive
annotated listing of criticism down to the mid-1950's in Phyllis Hutchinson, "The
Writings of WC: A List of Works by and About Her," BNYPL 60 (1956): 267-
88, 338-56, 378-400. Additional listings of her short fiction may be found in
Virginia Faulkner, ed., WC'S COLLECTED SHORT FICTION: 1892-1912 (Lincoln, Nebr., 1970). For C's extensive journalistic writings, many recently
identified, one should consult two sources: Bernice Slote, ed., THE KINGDOM
OF ART: WC'S FIRST PRINCIPLES AND CRITICAL STATEMENTS, 1893-1896
(Lincoln, 1967), and W.M. Curtin, ed., THE WORLD AND THE PARISH: WC'S
ARTICLES AND REVIEWS, 1893-1902 (Lincoln, 1970).

The place to begin any bibliographical study of C is with Slote's admirable essay in SMAA. This is authoritative, up-to-date, and covers in considerable
detail the topics treated here. Also useful but far briefer are the bibliographical notes accompanying James Schroeter, ed., WC AND HER CRITICS (Ithaca,
N.Y., 1967) and James Woodress, WC: HER LIFE AND ART (New York, 1970).

C's will forbade publication of her letters, but many of them have found their way into institutional collections. There are significant collections at the WC Pioneer Memorial in Red Cloud, Nebraska, Nebraska State Historical Society, Newberry Library, the University of Virginia, the University of Vermont, the Huntington Library, and a small but important group of letters at Harvard. C's MSS have not survived except for the revised typescripts of LUCY GAYHEART, SHADOWS ON THE ROCK, and MY MORTAL ENEMY, which are at the New York Public Library.

WORKS OF FICTION

Novels: ALEXANDER'S BRIDGE (1912), *O PIONEERS! (1913), THE SONG OF THE LARK (1915), *MY ANTONIA (1918), ONE OF OURS (1922), *A LOST LADY (1923), *THE PROFESSOR'S HOUSE (1925), MY MORTAL ENEMY (1926), *DEATH COMES FOR THE ARCHBISHOP (1927), SHADOWS ON THE ROCK (1931), LUCY GAYHEART (1935), SAPPHIRA AND THE SLAVE GIRL (1941).

Stories: THE TROLL GARDEN (1905), YOUTH AND THE BRIGHT MEDUSA (1920), *OBSCURE DESTINIES (1932), THE OLD BEAUTY AND OTHERS (1948).

EDITIONS AND REPRINTS

C's writings were collected in 13 volumes by Houghton Mifflin (Boston, 1937–41). Houghton Mifflin and Knopf (now Random House) have kept all of her works in print, and O PIONEERS!, MY ANTONIA, THE SONG OF THE LARK, ONE OF OURS, MY MORTAL ENEMY, DEATH COMES FOR THE ARCHBISHOP, and SHADOWS ON THE ROCK are available in paperback editions. There also is a Vintage paperback, FIVE STORIES. There is a bad text of THE TROLL GARDEN in a Signet edition, and ALEXANDER'S BRIDGE is available as a Bantam paperback. WC'S COLLECTED SHORT FICTION (see above) reprints all of C's known stories published down to 1912, and Bernice Slote, ed., UNCLE VALENTINE AND OTHER STORIES: WC'S UNCOLLECTED SHORT FICTION, 1915–1929 (Lincoln, 1973), rescues other tales from periodical files. All of C's known stories now are in print in book form.

BIOGRAPHY

The most recent and authoritative biography is Woodress, WC: HER LIFE AND ART (see above). This combines biography and criticism in equal portions and is based on the examination of more than 1,000 letters. It also makes use of the extensively exhumed journalistic writings in THE KINGDOM OF ART and THE WORLD AND THE PARISH (see above). It corrects errors and amplifies some areas of E.K. Brown, WC: A CRITICAL BIOGRAPHY, completed by Leon Edel (New York, 1953), which still is a valuable book and especially useful for critical insights. Before Brown's book appeared, C's biography was strewn with misinformation and false scents, many of which were deliberate efforts on

* Of Special Importance

C's part to guard her privacy and to deemphasize her literary apprenticeship. There are, however, some important memoirs and other studies available, all of which were drawn on in Woodress' biography. First is Edith Lewis, WC LIVING (New York, 1953), which was written for Brown's use by C's lifelong friend. Brown did not have available, however, an equally important work written by another friend, Elizabeth Sergeant's WC: A MEMOIR (New York, 1953; reissued with index, Lincoln, 1963). An important book that fits C into her Nebraska context is Mildred Bennett's THE WORLD OF WC (New York, 1951; rev. with notes, Lincoln, 1961). Other shorter memoirs by friends: Dorothy Canfield Fisher, "Daughter of the Frontier," NYHTBR (28 May 1933); George Seibel, "Miss WC from Nebraska," NEW COLOPHON 2 (1949): 195–208; Phyllis Hutchinson, "Reminiscences of WC as a Teacher," BNYPL 60 (1956): 263–66; Elizabeth Moorhead, THESE TWO WERE HERE (Pittsburgh, 1950). There is an excellent account of C's college years in the introduction to THE KINGDOM OF ART.

Finally, it should be noted that there is much autobiography in C's fiction, although the experience has passed through the prism of creative artistry: the first part of THE SONG OF THE LARK, MY ANTONIA, O PIONEERS!, OBSCURE DESTINIES, A LOST LADY, "The Best Years" from THE OLD BEAUTY AND OTHERS, and a good many stories from COLLECTED SHORT FICTION. Also C wrote about her friendships with Annie Fields, Sarah Orne Jewett, and her meeting with Flaubert's niece In NOT UNDER FORTY (1936). Her travel letters from Europe were published as WC IN EUROPE (New York, 1956), with introduction by G.N. Kates, and reprinted in a more accurate text in THE WORLD AND THE PARISH.

CRITICISM

C's reputation was slow in growing, and it was not until she won the Pulitzer Prize in 1922 for ONE OF OURS, which Is perhaps the least successful of her novels, that she began attracting a great deal of attention. Early critics were concerned with her use of Nebraska and her creation of indomitable heroines like Alexandra Bergson in O PIONEERS!, Thea Kronberg in THE SONG OF THE LARK, and Antonia Shimerda in MY ANTONIA. They also were interested in her contrasts of pioneer days on the prairie with more effete contemporary times. They wrote of her as realist and regionalist. During the 1930's the socially conscious Marxist criticism of that era often attacked C for writing escapist literature and for not joining the struggle to reform society. After she died the critics began to study her style and structure and to move away from interest in theme and ideas. She now is fair game for more formalist criticism and hunters of myth and symbol and seems in the 1970's more romantic than realist.

Although C has never generated as much criticism as Faulkner or Hemingway, there has been a modest but steady stream of books and essays about her during the past generation, and she is one of nine fiction writers included in SMAA. Only a fraction of the criticism can be discussed here, but a spendid 30-page review of it exists in Slote's essay in the above book. A good place to get a brief overview of C is in Dorothy Van Ghent's pamphlet, WC (UMPAW, 1964), a well-written summary which is short but sympathetic and perceptive. Of medium length is Woodress' critical biography (see above), which discusses all of the novels and most of the stories, puts C into the context of time and place, studies the relationship of her fiction to her life, and synthesizes much of the scholarship of recent decades. A short-cut to C criticism, though it includes items of dubious value, is WC AND HER CRITICS (see above), which contains 34 critical selections by 25 writers ranging from 1915 to 1965. The early selections are useful, as they trace the early growth of C's reputation and bring together some of the significant early criticism. These include H.L. Mencken's early enthusiastic reviews from SMART SET, reviews by Edmund Wilson, essays by T.K. Whipple, Sinclair Lewis, and Joseph Wood Krutch. Also there are two selections from the detractors of the 1930's: Granville Hicks and Lionel Trilling, and a good essay by Rebecca West, written in 1927 as C began to acquire her rather considerable European reputation.

One should not overlook C's own statements about her work, as she was a very conscious craftsman and knew what she was trying to do. Her writings about writing are not numerous, but they are available in WC ON WRITING (1949), with a foreword by a young friend, Stephen Tennant. This collection is essential and supplies answers to the critical problems that perplexed reviewers who often saw C's novels as structurally flawed. Her answer to the denigrators of the 1930's also appears in her essay, "Escapism," and the collection contains her most famous article, "The Novel Demeublé." In addition there are four prefaces to other people's books, the most important of which is the introduction to an edition of Sarah Orne Jewett's stories.

Besides the works already discussed, C has been the subject of nine other books beginning with René Rapin's WC (New York, 1930), a pioneering effort which displeased its subject. Rapin's book, however, is a good first effort. He reads C sympathetically and intelligently and concludes that her work is classical "because its innate romanticism is checked by realism and both are made subservient to an ardent love of life and a respect for truth." It is also classical because her preoccupations are of general and permanent interest, and because her style is classical. The only other book on C written during her lifetime was produced as a thesis at the University of Rennes and written in French. Although hardly known to C scholars, Yvonne Handy's L'OEUVRE DE WC (Rennes, 1940) is a very respectable piece of work, which after an outdated biographical chapter, takes up in separate sections competent analyses of C's novels, philosophy, psychology, and art. She seems to take some of her cues from Regis Michaud, who lectured on American literature at the Sorbonne and whose essay on C appears in THE AMERICAN NOVEL TODAY (New York, 1928), but it is an independent work that sees C as endowing with universal significance her use of particularities.

David Daiches' WC: A CRITICAL INTRODUCTION (Ithaca, N.Y., 1951) is a good medium-length study of C's entire corpus by a skillful reader and good critic whose views are worth listening to. Daiches is interested in C's novels as individual literary works rather than as expressions of a philosophy or point of view. He follows a chronological order, treats plot, theme, character, style, and cross references his discussions. This book is a pleasure to read and happily free from jargon and pomposity.

John Randall's THE LANDSCAPE AND THE LOOKING GLASS: WC'S SEARCH FOR VALUE (Boston, 1960) is less satisfactory. It is a thick book, heavily documented, that began as one of the 30 dissertations that have been written on C through 1971. Randall's interests are sociological and he revives the nagging tone of the critics in the 1930's who accused C, as Randall does, of a "refusal to face the contemporary world" and of escaping into the past. He thinks she failed to learn from experience and that "WC had no adequate concept of society." A better book is Edward and Lillian Bloom's WC'S GIFT OF SYMPATHY (Carbondale, Ill., 1962), a sensitive study of C's themes and artistry, which drew together several articles previously published. The best chapter deals with the sources of DEATH COMES FOR THE ARCHBISHOP.

A specialized but interesting and insightful study is Richard Giannone's MUSIC IN WC'S FICTION (Lincoln, 1968), which extracts from the body of C's work one significant strand. C's interest in music and musicians began in her journalistic period and provided material for character, theme, plot, and structure in her fiction. One would expect that specialized studies like this would be the rule in future C scholarship, and this probably will be true, but the last three books have been general studies. Barbara Bonham's WC (Philadelphia, 1970) is a pastiche of undocumented material used without acknowledgment from earlier works and has nothing new to say. WC: THE WOMAN AND HER WORKS by Marion Brown and Ruth Crone (New York, 1970) is an undocumented, rather short (160-page) book written for high school students. It is accurate, readable and well suited to its audience. Dorothy McFarland's WC (New York, 1972) is a critical study that breaks no new ground and begins by attacking the long-eclipsed critics who thought C was an escapist, in order to establish that C's main interest is the precedence of moral and spiritual values over material values—hardly a novel thesis in the 1970's.

Among the large number of books that have chapters containing general estimates of C only a few of the most significant may be cited. In chronological order, these should begin with A.H. Quinn's chapter in AMERICAN FICTION (New York, 1936), a careful, judicious review of the bulk of her fiction. Alfred Kazin in ON NATIVE GROUNDS (New York, 1942) discusses C in a trenchant chapter dealing also with Ellen Glasgow, and Maxwell Geismar in THE LAST OF THE PROVINCIALS (Boston, 1947) writes competently of C as "The Lady in the Wilderness." George Whicher's section on C in A.H. Quinn, et al., THE LITERATURE OF THE AMERICAN PEOPLE (New York, 1951), also is very good. Other worthwhile essays are Francis Connolly's in H.C. Gardiner, ed., FIFTY YEARS OF THE AMERICAN NOVEL (New York, 1952), and F.J. Hoffman's in THE TWENTIES: AMERICAN WRITING IN THE POST-WAR DECADE (New York, 1955).

Among the special aspects of C's work that have been treated, the bulk of the studies deal with C as a Western or frontier writer or discuss three of her twelve novels: MY ANTONIA, THE PROFESSOR'S HOUSE, and DEATH COMES FOR

THE ARCHBISHOP. One of the former is Howard Jones' THE FRONTIER AND AMERICAN FICTION: FOUR LECTURES IN THE RELATIONSHIP OF LAND-SCAPE TO LITERATURE (Jerusalem, 1956). Of the many good treatments of MY ANTONIA, Terence Martin's "The Drama of Memory in MY ANTONIA," PMLA 84 (1969): 304-11, is especially interesting. Leon Edel's chapter on THE PRO-FESSOR'S HOUSE in his LITERARY BIOGRAPHY (New York, 1959) is an in-triguing psychological reading of the novel. D.H. Stewart, "C's Mortal Come-dy," QQ 73 (1966): 244-59, compares DEATH COMES FOR THE ARCHBISHOP with the DIVINE COMEDY.

Other special studies that should be mentioned include A.M. Buchan, "OUR DEAR SARAH": AN ESSAY ON SARAH ORNE JEWETT, which treats percep-tively one of C's most important relationships; Bernice Slote's essay, "The King-dom of Art," in her edition of C's journalistic writings, a pioneering study of myth and symbol in C's work; Mildred Bennett's introductory essay to WC: COL-LECTED SHORT FICTION, 1892-1912, one of the few studies of the stories; to which should be added Curtis Bradford, "WC's Uncollected Short Stories," AL 26 (1955): 537-51, and the only dissertation on the stories: Margaret O'Con-nor, "WC and the Art of the Short Story," DAI 32 (1972): 5240A.

Section 10

RAYMOND CHANDLER (1888-1959)

Raymond Chandler (hereafter RC or C) was the author of hard-boiled detective novels and stories with a Los Angeles setting. He was perhaps the best of his contemporaries in this genre, which included W.H. Wright (S.S. Van Dine), Erle Stanley Gardner, and Dashiell Hammett, and the forerunner of, though much superior to, the currently popular Mickey Spillane.

BIBLIOGRAPHY AND MANUSCRIPTS

See Matthew Bruccoli, RC: A CHECKLIST (Kent, Ohio, 1968), and Philip Durham, DOWN THESE MEAN STREETS A MAN MUST GO: RC'S KNIGHT (Chapel Hill, N.C. 1963). UCLA has a special collection including many MSS, letters, and editions.

WORKS OF FICTION

Novels: THE BIG SLEEP (1939), FAREWELL, MY LOVELY (1940), THE HIGH WINDOW (1942), THE LADY IN THE LAKE (1943), THE LITTLE SISTER (1949), THE LONG GOODBY (1953), PLAYBACK (1958).

Short Stories: FIVE MURDERERS (1944), FIVE SINISTER CHARACTERS (1945), RED WIND: A COLLECTION OF SHORT STORIES (1946), FINGER MAN AND OTHER STORIES (1946), SPANISH BLOOD: A COLLECTION OF SHORT STORIES (1946), TROUBLE IS MY BUSINESS (1950), THE SIMPLE ART OF MURDER (1950), PICK-UP ON NOON STREET (1952), PEARLS ARE A NUISANCE (1953).

EDITIONS AND REPRINTS

THE RC OMNIBUS (London, 1953), reprints C's first four novels; THE SECOND C OMNIBUS (London, 1962); THE RC OMNIBUS: FOUR FAMOUS CLASSICS, foreword L.C. Powell (New York, 1964); KILLER IN THE RAIN, intro. Philip Durham (Boston, 1964), reprints stories; THE SMELL OF FEAR (London, 1965),

61

reprints stories; THE MIDNIGHT RC, intro. Joan Kahn (Boston, 1971), reprints C's essay "The Simple Art of Murder," four stories, and two novels: THE LITTLE SISTER and THE LONG GOODBY. There have been innumerable foreign editions and translations of C's fiction; and eight novels plus the 1964 OMNIBUS are currently in print.

BIOGRAPHY

Durham's book (see above) combines both biography and criticism. In addition, there is a considerable amount of material in Dorothy Gardiner and Kathrine Walker, eds., RC SPEAKING (Boston, 1962; repr. Freeport, N.Y., 1971). This contains many letters and some reprinted essays in which C writes about himself.

CRITICISM

In the past decade interest has developed in C as a serious social commentator. Durham's book is a careful, informative study and the most extensive discussion available. Herbert Ruhm, "RC: From Bloomsbury to the Jungle--and Beyond" in David Madden, ed., TOUGH GUY WRITERS OF THE THIRTIES (Carbondale, Ill., 1968), calls THE LITTLE SISTER "the best of Hollywood novels," and R.W. Lid, "Philip Marlowe Speaking," KR 31 (1969): 153-78, has written a perceptive and important article separating the voice of C from that of his character. In another long article, "On RC," SoR 6 (1970): 624-50, F.R. Jameson studies form and content of C's fiction and believes the current interest in C derives from nostalgia for the 1930's and 1940's. In R.H. Miller, "The Publication of RC's THE LONG GOODBY," PBSA 53 (1969): 279-90, C's revisions of one novel are carefully studied. Some earlier studies of C: Ian Fleming, "RC," LonM 6, xii (1959): 43-54; Derek Sington, "RC on Crime and Punishment," TC 165 (1959): 502-04; Harold Orel, "RC's Last Novel: Some Observations on the Private Eye Tradition," JCMVASA 2 (1961): 59-63.

Section 11

WALTER VAN TILBURG CLARK (1909-1971)

Walter Van Tilburg Clark (hereafter WVC or C) was born in Maine but educated in Nevada, where he lived and taught for many years. He writes about the West, but not the West of romance and stereotypes, and although he wrote only three novels and one collection of stories (none after 1950), his critical reputation continues to grow. He is best known for one fine novel, THE OX-BOW INCIDENT (1940), a psychological story about a lynching in the Nevada cattle country.

BIBLIOGRAPHY AND MANUSCRIPTS

The most recent compilation which is "meant to be an exhaustive bibliography," is Richard Etulain, "WVC: A Bibliography," SDR 3, i (1965): 73-77; but there also is J.R. Kuehl, "WVC: A Bibliography," BB 22 (1956): 18-20. Bibliography is included in Herbert Wilner, "WVC," WR 22 (1956): 103-22, and in Max Westbrook, WVC (TUSAS, 1969). The Alan Swallow Papers at Syracuse University contain letters. The Library of Congress has the MSS of THE CITY OF TREMBLING LEAVES and THE TRACK OF THE CAT.

WORKS OF FICTION

Novels: *THE OX-BOW INCIDENT (1940), THE CITY OF TREMBLING LEAVES (1945), THE TRACK OF THE CAT (1949).

Stories: THE WATCHFUL GODS (1950).

EDITIONS AND REPRINTS

Both THE OX-BOW INCIDENT and THE TRACK OF THE CAT are Signet paperbacks. C has been translated into French, Portuguese, German, and Italian.

*Of special importance

BIOGRAPHY

Biographical information is included in Westbrook (see above); another full-length study, an unpublished dissertation, Jean Malloy, "The World of WVC," DA 29 (1969): 4008A, begins with biography. A long autobiographical essay appeared as "The Writer and the Professor," CHRYSALIS REV. 2 (Spring 1962): 60-107; but a briefer, more accessible interview on the same topic is Richard Diers, "Are Writers Made, Not Born?" SatR 48 (12 June 1965): 52-53. Also see John Hermann, "The Death of the Artist as Hero," SDR 4, ii (1966): 51-55, an essay by a friend.

CRITICISM

Westbrook's study, one of the better volumes in the Twayne series, is the most detailed source available for the study of C's entire canon. Westbrook argues that C has been misread by people expecting formula fiction in Westerns and that C's central concern is "the bifurcation of the conscious self from the unconscious self and not the corruption of the frontier."

Although Edmund Wilson wrote a flattering review of THE CITY OF TREMBLING LEAVES (NY 21 [26 May 1945]: 75-77), critical attention to C began after he published his third and last novel. Vernon Young wrote two articles: "The American Dream and Its Parody" and "Gods Without Heroes: The Tentative Myths of WVC," ArQ 6, 7 (1950, 1951): 112-23, 110-19. These were followed by a general survey: F.I. Carpenter, "The West of WVC," CE 13 (1952): 243-48. Later in the decade C attracted more attention in a variety of studies: John Portz, "Idea and Symbol in WVC," ACCENT 17 (1957): 112-28; Alan Swallow, "The Mavericks," Crit 2, iii (1959): 74-92, which extolled several Western novelists; J.R. Milton, "The Western Attitude: WVC," Crit 2, iii (1959): 27-73, which saw C writing on two levels--psychological relations and nature symbolism; C.E. Eisinger, "The Fiction of WVC: Man and Nature in the West," SWR 44 (1959): 214-26, a rather unsympathetic analysis.

As might be expected, THE OX-BOW INCIDENT has been the most studied of C's works. Westbrook probed "The Archetypal Ethic of THE OX-BOW INCIDENT," WAL 1 (1966): 105-18; B.W. Bates contributed "C's Man for All Seasons: The Achievement of Wholeness in THE OX-BOW INCIDENT," WAL 3 (1968): 37-49; Kenneth Anderson examined form and character in "Character Portrayal in THE OX-BOW INCIDENT," WAL 4 (1970): 287-98, comparing C's characters to those of Hawthorne and Melville, and "Form in WVC's OX-BOW INCIDENT," WR 6, i (1969): 19-25, discussing structural devices of sound and light.

Other discussions of C include: L.L. Lee, "WVC's Ambiguous American Dream," CE 26 (1965): 382-87; Max Westbrook, "Internal Debate As Discipline," WAL 1 (1966): 153-66; E.H. Cohen, "C's 'The Portable Phonograph,'" Expl 28 (1970): item 69. Finally, an interesting discussion of the film version of THE OX-BOW INCIDENT is in George Bluestone, NOVELS INTO FILM (Baltimore, 1957).

Section 12

JAMES GOULD COZZENS (1903-   )

James Gould Cozzens (hereafter JGC or C) was born in Chicago, raised on Staten Island, and educated at the Kent School and Harvard, where he began his literary career by publishing a novel when he was a sophomore. He then took a leave of absence from college and wrote another novel, and his subsequent career has been a slow, quiet succession of increasingly well-written novels. He lives in the country in New Jersey and shuns publicity and other writers. He won a Pulitzer Prize for GUARD OF HONOR (1948), and the publication of BY LOVE POSSESSED (1957) thrust him reluctantly into the public eye. His career proves that one can in the midst of change and experimentation go on writing the traditional social novel with considerable success.

BIBLIOGRAPHY AND MANUSCRIPTS

James Meriwether's JGC: A CHECKLIST (Detroit, 1972) is a thorough listing of primary materials: first printings of all books, all printings in English, and essays, poems, and stories still uncollected. Also it has an introduction by C. Pierre Michel's JGC: AN ANNOTATED CHECKLIST (Kent, Ohio, 1971), lists first American and British editions of C's books, and gathers up his stories, essays and other non-fiction, and poems in chronological order. It also contains a section on secondary material, although it does not list dissertations, of which there had been six down through 1971. These checklists supersede James Meriwether's "A JGC Check List," Crit 1 (Winter 1958): 57-63, and Richard Ludwig's "JGC: A Review of Research and Criticism," TSLL 1 (1959): 123-36. There are selected bibliographies in books on C by Bracher, Mooney, and Maxwell (see below).

C has given a large collection of his MSS and papers to Princeton, a gift which has been described by Richard Ludwig in "A Reading of the JGC Manuscripts," PULC 19 (1957): 1-14. This collection includes 11 literary MSS, many letters to and from C, galley proofs, documents, and even an unpublished novel. In addition to these papers at Princeton, Harvard has significant holdings of MS material, and there are a few letters at the University of Rochester, the American Academy of Arts and Letters, the University of Texas, Syracuse University, and Yale.

WORKS OF FICTION

Novels: CONFUSION (1924), MICHAEL SCARLETT (1925), COCKPIT (1928), SON OF PERDITION (1929), *S.S. SAN PEDRO (1931), THE LAST ADAM (1933), CASTAWAY (1934), *MEN AND BRETHREN (1936), ASK ME TOMORROW (1940), *THE JUST AND THE UNJUST (1942), *GUARD OF HONOR (1948), *BY LOVE POSSESSED (1957), MORNING, NOON, AND NIGHT (1968).

Stories: CHILDREN AND OTHERS (1964).

EDITIONS AND REPRINTS

There has been no collected edition of C's works, but all of his novels since S.S. SAN PEDRO have been kept in print, and at least six of them are available in paperback editions: BY LOVE POSSESSED, GUARD OF HONOR, THE JUST AND THE UNJUST, THE LAST ADAM; S.S. SAN PEDRO and CASTAWAY have been reprinted in a single volume.

BIOGRAPHY

There is no biography of C and until BY LOVE POSSESSED rocketed to the best-seller lists the general public was unaware of his existence. Some biographical material may be gleaned from the standard biographical sources (see "Part one"), and the following items are useful: "The Hermit of Lambertville," TIME 70 (2 September 1957): 72-78; "Recluse," NYTBR, 25 August 1957, p. 8. Since C does not give interviews and his desire for privacy seems to inhibit reminiscences by friends, one will probably have to study C through his works alone until such time in the future as the restricted C Papers at Princeton are opened for use by scholars. On one occasion C was quoted as saying that his social preference was to be left alone and that people had always seemed willing, even eager to gratify his inclination.

CRITICISM

If there is a dearth of biographical material on C, there is no lack of critical opinion. The criticism, however, all dates from the publication of GUARD OF HONOR (1948); it reached a great crescendo after the appearance of BY LOVE POSSESSED (1957), and in recent years it has diminished to a modest but continuing interest. Before 1948 there were only book reviews. The first serious article was Granville Hicks' "The Reputation of JGC," CE 11 (1950): 177-83. Hicks also is the author of the pamphlet JGC (UMPAW, 1964), which is the best short discussion available and the obvious place to begin any study of C's work.

* Of Special Importance

The first full-length study was James Parrish's unpublished dissertation, "C: A Critical Analysis," DA 15 (1955): 1856, which tried to evaluate C's achievement, put him in his proper place in American fiction, and to explain the relative neglect he had suffered. Parrish's view was that C's well-constructed fictions presented normal characters struggling through life in the old-fashioned social novel, and thus C gave the critics nothing they could get their hooks into. Perhaps so, but at the end of the 1950's Frederick Bracher produced a good study, THE NOVELS OF JGC (New York, 1959), which traced C's evolution from S.S. SAN PEDRO through BY LOVE POSSESSED, studying themes and techniques and evaluating results.

There have been two other general books on C: H.J. Mooney's JGC: NOVELIST OF INTELLECT (Pittsburgh, 1963) and D.E.S. Maxwell's C (London, 1964). The former, in his survey of the novels, finds that no other novelist of our time has made such an extreme commitment to reason, and he is among the extravagant praisers of BY LOVE POSSESSED. The latter is an excellent, sympathetic study which sees C as a successful and realistic portrayer of the complexity and ambiguity of man's place in society. Maxwell is sympathetic to C's conservatism and thinks he has a firm grasp on the nature of reality and uses the traditional novel form with imagination.

As one of our important minor novelists, C has been treated often in surveys of the novel from general or special points of view. Some significant studies: Michael Millgate, AMERICAN SOCIAL FICTION: JAMES TO C (New York, 1964); Arthur Mizener, THE SENSE OF LIFE IN THE MODERN NOVEL (Boston, 1964); Allen Guttman, THE CONSERVATIVE TRADITION IN AMERICA (New York, 1967). Three other good brief studies are Francis Duggan, "Facts and All Man's Fiction," THOUGHT 33 (1958-59): 604-16; Robert Scholes, "The Commitment of JGC," ArQ 16 (1960): 129-44, and J.W. Ward, "JGC and the Condition of Modern Man," ASch 27 (1957-58): 92-99.

Some of C's most-esteemed novels have been the subject of worthwhile articles: R.W. Lewis' "The Conflicts of Reality: C's THE LAST ADAM" in T.B. Whitbread, ed., SEVEN CONTEMPORARY AUTHORS (Austin, Tex., 1966); Horton Davies' A MIRROR OF THE MINISTRY IN MODERN NOVELS (New York, 1959), which deals with MEN AND BRETHREN; J.A. Parrish's "JGC Fights a War," ArQ 18 (1962): 35-40, which discusses GUARD OF HONOR; David Weimar's "The Breath of Chaos in THE JUST AND THE UNJUST," Crit 1 (Winter, 1958): 30-40. The last article was part of an entire issue of Crit devoted to C's work, which appeared while BY LOVE POSSESSED was gathering huzzahs and catcalls.

The controversy over this novel is worth reporting briefly. The same issue of Crit carried George Garrett's "BY LOVE POSSESSED: The Pattern and the Hero," pp. 41-47, which viewed the work favorably as the summation of C's chief themes. Earlier John Fischer in HM 215 (September 1957): 14-15, 18, 20, had nominated C for a Nobel Prize on the basis of the novel, to which Dwight Macdonald made a furious rebuttal: "By C Possessed," COMMENTARY 25 (January 1958): 36-47. Irving Howe in "JGC: Novelist of the Republic," NR 138 (20 January 1958): 15-19, also took a dim view of the novel.

Section 13

EDWARD DAHLBERG (1900-)

Although Dahlberg (hereafter ED or D) was one of the angry proletarian writers of the 1930's along with Farrell, Caldwell, and others, he had to wait until the 1960's to be recognized as a significant figure. Among the 219 bio-bibliographies in Fred Millett's CONTEMPORARY AMERICAN AUTHORS (New York, 1940) D is not to be found, and in Lewis Leary's AAL, 1900-1950 (Durham, N.C., 1954) there are no references at all. Born the illegitimate son of the owner of the Star Lady Barbershop of Kansas City, Dahlberg spent a miserable childhood in a Jewish orphanage in Cleveland, managed a college education at the University of California and Columbia University, and joined the American expatriates in Europe in the 1920's. He has not been a prolific writer, but his works have been sharply critical of American society.

BIBLIOGRAPHY AND MANUSCRIPTS

The indispensable guide is Harold Billings, A BIBLIOGRAPHY OF ED (Austin, Tex., 1971), which is up-to-date, accurate, thorough, and includes illustrations of title pages. There also is a bibliography in Billings' ED: AMERICAN ISH-MAEL OF LETTERS (see below).

WORKS OF FICTION

Novels: BOTTOM DOGS (1929), FROM FLUSHING TO CALVARY (1932), THOSE WHO PERISH (1934).

BIOGRAPHY

Although no one yet has written D's biography, two autobiographical volumes are available: BECAUSE I WAS FLESH: THE AUTOBIOGRAPHY OF ED (New York, 1964); THE CONFESSIONS OF ED (New York, 1971). Also D has issued a letter collection: EPITAPHS OF OUR TIMES: THE LETTERS OF ED (New York, 1967). There are more letters, besides essays, in Paul Carroll, ed., THE ED READER (New York, 1967) and some biographical material (reminiscences, tributes, correspondence) in a special issue of TriQ 20 (Fall 1970) edited by Jonathan Williams as FOR ED and also reprinted as ED: A TRIBUTE (New York: David Lewis, Inc., 1970). There are two interesting exchanges of letters between D and Herbert Read, the first more like essays than informal letters: TRUTH IS MORE SACRED (New York, 1961) and Reginald Terry, ed., "ED and Sir Herbert Read (1893-1968): A Memorial Symposium," MALAHAT REVIEW 9 (1969): special issue.

For a writer like D, whose life is inseparable from his ideas, one should approach his biography through his essay collections: DO THESE BONES LIVE? (New York, 1941), pub. as SING O BARREN (London, 1947), and as CAN THESE BONES LIVE? (New York, 1960); THE FLEA OF SODOM (1950); THE SORROWS OF PRIAPUS (1957; reissued with THE CARNAL MYTH and an intro. by D, 1973); ALMS FOR OBLIVION (1964; paperback ed., 1966); REASONS OF THE HEART (1965); CIPANGO'S HINDER DOOR (1966); THE LEAFLESS AMERICAN (1967); THE CARNAL MYTH: A SEARCH INTO CLASSICAL SEN- SUALITY (1968; paperback ed., 1970). Most of these volumes have been kept in print. Also see Fred Moramarco, "An Interview with ED," WHR 20 (1966): 249-53.

CRITICISM

Although D was "discovered" in the 1960's, there was no book on him until Jonathan Williams edited ED: A TRIBUTE (New York, 1972), which contained contributions from Kay Boyle, Allen Tate, Karl Shapiro, Jack Kerouac, Anthony Burgess, and others; and Fred Moramarco published ED (TUSAS, 1972), which was the outgrowth of his dissertation (Utah, 1969), the first on D. Earlier esti- mates worth noting are Ford Madox Ford, "The Fate of the Semi-classic," FORUM 97 (1937): 126-28; and James T. Farrell, "In Search of the Image," NEW MASSES 13 (4 December 1934): 21-22; repr. in THE LEAGUE OF FRIGHT- ENED PHILISTINES (New York, 1945). Alfred Kazin, who knew his work, made only a few references to him in ON NATIVE GROUNDS (New York, 1942), and Walter Rideout in THE RADICAL NOVEL IN THE UNITED STATES, 1900-1954 (Cambridge, Mass., 1956) wrote a few perceptive paragraphs.

The recent wave of interest in D began with Allen Tate, "A Great Stylist: The Prophet as Critic," SR 69 (1961): 314-17, which greeted warmly the revision of CAN THESE BONES LIVE? and Daniel Aaron, WRITERS ON THE LEFT (New York, 1961), who summed up D skillfully though briefly. These essays were followed by Jonathan Williams, "ED's Book of Lazarus," TQ 6, ii (1963): 35- 49, who compared BOTTOM DOGS with HUCK FINN; and Ihab Hassan, "The Sorrows of ED," MR 5 (1964): 457-61, who introduced several essays and poems by D. The next year saw the best general introduction that had appeared so far, by an Italian scholar, Lina Unali, "Introduzione a ED," SA 11 (1965): 271-308, and Josephine Herbst's thoughtful review article, "ED'S BECAUSE I WAS FLESH," SoR 1 (1965): 337-51. Three years later it was time for stock- taking and Harold Billings edited ED: AMERICAN ISHMAEL OF LETTERS (Aus- tin, Tex., 1968), a collection of critical essays including pieces by D.H. Lawrence, who originally had written an introduction for the 1929 edition of

BOTTOM DOGS, Allen Tate, Alfred Kazin, and William Carlos Williams. In the same year Jules Chametzky wrote a retrospective essay, "ED: Early and Late," in David Madden, ed., PROLETARIAN WRITERS OF THE THIRTIES (Carbondale, Ill., 1968). Finally, Fred Moramarco has written "Make Him a Legend in His Own Time," UPLL 1 (1969): 21–32.

That D's reputation now is spreading beyond the borders of the United States is attested to by the translation of his autobiography into both Italian and German (Turin, 1966; Munich, 1968) and a second long and probing article in Italian: Bonalda Stringher, "ED e la ricerca del mito," SA 14 (1968): 309–38.

Section 14

FLOYD DELL (1887-1969)

Floyd Dell (hereafter FD or D) was a Midwestern novelist who was born in Illinois and began his career as a journalist. He was one of the group that included Carl Sandburg, Theodore Dreiser, and Sherwood Anderson in Chicago before World War I. He grew up in poverty, had to leave high school to work in a factory, but fought his way up through reporting to become editor of the FRIDAY LITERARY REVIEW. Later he moved to New York, became a political radical and editor of MASSES, wrote plays and took part in the Bohemian life of Greenwich Village. During the 1930's he dropped his radicalism, became a liberal, and stopped writing.

BIBLIOGRAPHY AND MANUSCRIPTS

There is no complete bibliography. There is a selected bibliography, however, in John Hart, FD (TUSAS, 1971), and while not very accessible there is a list of all D's published works through 1958 in an unpublished dissertation by G.T. Tanselle, "Faun at the Barricades: The Life and Work of FD," DA 20 (1959): 2304-05. The standard sources, AAL and Gerstenberger, will yield additional items. If bibliography is scanty, the opposite is true of MSS. There are numerous significant collections, and these are useful for the study of the other more important writers whom D knew and corresponded with. The Library of Congress, the Wisconsin State Historical Society, the New York Public Library, Harvard, and the University of Chicago all have extensive holdings. The Newberry Library has a special collection including MSS, letters, and correspondence. Yale and Indiana Universities both have substantial letter collections.

WORKS OF FICTION

Novels: *MOON-CALF (1920), *BRIARY-BUSH (1921), JANET MARCH (1923), THIS MAD IDEAL (1925), RUNAWAY (1925), AN OLD MAN'S FOLLY (1926), AN UNMARRIED FATHER (1927), SOUVENIR (1929), LOVE WITHOUT MONEY (1931), DIANA STAIR (1932), THE GOLDEN SPIKE (1934).

Short stories: LOVE IN GREENWICH VILLAGE (1926).

* Of Special Importance

EDITIONS AND REPRINTS

The only novel which has been reprinted is MOON-CALF, which is available as a Hill and Wang paperback. LOVE IN GREENWICH VILLAGE also is in print (Freeport, N.Y., 1970).

BIOGRAPHY

Only one book has been written on D, Hart's volume in the Twayne series (cited above), but it deals with biography only incidentally. Tanselle's dissertation (see above) also contains biography as well as criticism. While there has been no formal biography, most of what has been written about D is more or less biographical, reflecting his long life and many literary associations. The Chicago Renaissance and Greenwich Village Bohemia are perennially interesting topics, and D appears in these studies: Bernard Duffy, THE CHICAGO RENAISSANCE IN AMERICAN LETTERS: A CRITICAL HISTORY (East Lansing, Mich., 1953), the best of these books; Dale Kramer, CHICAGO RENAISSANCE: THE LITERARY LIFE IN THE MIDWEST, 1900-1930 (New York, 1966); Allen Churchill, THE IMPROPER BOHEMIANS: A RE-CREATION OF GREENWICH VILLAGE IN ITS HEYDAY (New York, 1959); Emily Hahn, ROMANTIC REBELS: AN INFORMAL HISTORY OF BOHEMIANISM IN AMERICA (Boston, 1967). In addition D has been treated in an excellent study of literary radicalism: Daniel Aaron, WRITERS ON THE LEFT: EPISODES IN AMERICAN LITERARY COMMUNISM (New York, 1961).

D also has written his own life: HOMECOMING: AN AUTOBIOGRAPHY (New York, 1933; repr. Port Washington, N.Y., 1969), and three shorter reminiscences: "A Literary Self-Analysis," ModQ 4 (1927): 147-49; "On Being Sherwood Anderson's Literary Father," NLB 5 (1961): 315-21; "My Friend Edna St. Vincent Millay," MTJ 12, ii (1964): 1-3. See also Francelia Butler and R.H. Dillard, eds., "Parnassus in the 1920's: FD Contemplates his Own Period," TSL 12 (1967): 131-48, an interview. Another item of interest is Sinclair Lewis, "FD," BOOKMAN 52 (1921): 245. Tanselle has written many articles on D and other writers including these: "Vachel Lindsay Writes to FD," JISHS 57 (1964): 366-79; "Realist or Dreamer: Letters of Sherwood Anderson and FD," MLR 58 (1963): 532-37; "Sinclair Lewis and FD: Two Views of the Midwest," TCL (1964): 175-84; "Ezra Pound and a Story of FD's," N&Q 8 (1961): 350-52. And finally there is material on D to be found in the memoirs and biographies of his literary friends such as Anderson, Dreiser, and Lewis.

CRITICISM

A generation ago D might well have seemed as important as these literary friends, but he never went beyond his first two novels, which, incidentally, still are worth reading, and his silence after THE GOLDEN SPIKE (1934) relegated him to a very minor role in the twentieth-century novel. There has been a mild recent revival of interest, as evidenced by Hart's book, Tanselle's dissertation, and two more recent dissertations: R.O. Horberg, "To the Twentieth Century and Back: A Round Trip with FD," DA 29 (1968): 871A; J.T. Smith, "Feminism in the Novels of FD," DAI 31 (1970): 1814A.

Most of the criticism, however, is concentrated in the era when D was flourishing as a practicing novelist. The following works, all by competent critics of their day, have material: Carl Van Doren, CONTEMPORARY AMERICAN NOVELISTS, 1900-1920 (New York, 1922); Harry Hansen, MIDWEST PORTRAITS (New York, 1923); Stuart Sherman, CRITICAL WOODCUTS (New York, 1926); Harlan Hatcher, CREATING THE MODERN AMERICAN NOVEL (New York, 1935). Another worthwhile monograph is Ima Herron Honaker, THE SMALL TOWN IN AMERICAN LITERATURE (Durham, N.C., 1939; repr. New York, 1959); and Frederick Hoffman, THE TWENTIES: AMERICAN WRITING IN THE POSTWAR DECADE (New York, 1955), is good on D's early novels. Finally John Hart has written "FD: Intellectual Vagabond," WHR 16 (1962): 67-75.

Section 15

JOHN DOS PASSOS (1896-1970)

John Dos Passos (hereafter JDP or DP) was born in Chicago, the son of a wealthy corporation lawyer who had been the son of a Portuguese immigrant. DP was educated partly in Europe, graduated from Harvard in 1916, and like Hemingway and E.E. Cummings served in World War I in a volunteer ambulance unit. His war experiences inspired his first two novels; then he turned to the American scene with MANHATTAN TRANSFER (1925) and his magnum opus, the U.S.A. trilogy (1938). The latter work, which contains interesting experiments in fictional technique, attempts to encompass the entire history of DP's era. His political and social views come through loud and clear in his works, though his opinions during his long career shifted diametrically from left to right.

BIBLIOGRAPHY AND MANUSCRIPTS

As there is no complete and up-to-date bibliography of DP, the following are the best available: Jack Potter, A BIBLIOGRAPHY OF JDP (Chicago, 1950), which includes both primary and secondary materials; Martin Kallich, "Bibliography of JDP," BB 19 (1949): 31-35; William White, "More DP Bibliographical Addenda," PBSA 45 (1951): 156-58, which supplements Potter and Kallich; Virginia Reinhart, "JDP Bibliography: 1950 1966," TCL 13 (1967): 167-78, which updates the previous listings; LHUS, BIBLIOGRAPHICAL SUPPLEMENT II (1972), which adds a few items and was compiled after DP died. In addition, there is a brief bibliography of criticism and a list of six dissertations in John Wrenn's JDP (TUSAS, 1961). However, at least eleven more dissertations were written between 1961 and 1971.

DP's MSS and letters are widely scattered. There are large holdings at the University of Chicago, Harvard, Princeton, Virginia, and the New York Public Library. Two publishers, Longmans, Green and Prentice Hall, have extensive collections, and there are small letter collections at Yale, Indiana, the State University of New York at Buffalo, and Pennsylvania.

WORKS OF FICTION

Novels: ONE MAN'S INITIATION--1917 (1920); *THREE SOLDIERS (1921);

* Of Special Importance

STREETS OF NIGHT (1923); *MANHATTAN TRANSFER (1925); *THE 42ND
PARALLEL (1930), *1919 (1932), *THE BIG MONEY (1936), collected as a
trilogy, *U.S.A. (1938); ADVENTURES OF A YOUNG MAN (1939), NUMBER
ONE (1943), THE GRAND DESIGN (1949), collected as a trilogy, DISTRICT
OF COLUMBIA (1952); THE PROSPECT BEFORE US (1950); MOST LIKELY TO
SUCCEED (1954); THE GREAT DAYS (1958); MIDCENTURY (1961).

EDITIONS AND REPRINTS

No effort has been made to collect DP's works, but Kenneth Lynn has edited a
volume of selections, THE WORLD IN A GLASS (1966). Much of DP's fiction
has been kept in print. The following titles are available both in hard covers
and paper: ONE MAN'S INITIATION--1917, THREE SOLDIERS, MANHATTAN
TRANSFER, MOST LIKELY TO SUCCEED and MIDCENTURY. The trilogies are
in print both as separate and single volumes. THREE SOLDIERS has been a
Modern Library title since 1922, and U.S.A. also is in the same series. The
latter has had many editions and printings, as has MANHATTAN TRANSFER.

BIOGRAPHY

A complete biography of DP has not yet appeared, but for his early career there
is Melvin Landsberg's DP'S PATH TO "U.S.A.": A POLITICAL BIOGRAPHY,
1912-1936 (Boulder, Colo., 1971). This is a very competent, well-documented
account of DP's life down to the publication of his trilogy. Also there is biographical material in Wrenn's study and in R.G. Davis' pamphlet JDP (UMPAW,
1962). Also useful is John Chamberlain's early pamphlet JDP: A BIOGRAPHY
AND CRITICAL STUDY (New York, 1939). Townsend Ludington, ed., THE
FOURTEENTH CHRONICLE (Boston, 1973) is a rich, essential collection of 643
pages of letters and diary entries covering DP's life from 1910 to 1970 and there
is some biographical information in George Knox and Herbert Stahl's DP AND
"THE REVOLTING PLAYWRIGHTS" (Upsala, Sweden, 1964), which deals with
the New Playwrights' Theater of the 1920's.

A few biographical articles are available: Charles Bernardin, "JDP's Harvard
Years," NEQ 27 (1954): 3-26; Michael Gold, "The Education of JDP," EJ
23 (1933): 87-97; Richard Whalen, "Conversation with DP," NeL 42 (23 February 1959): 20-21; David Sanders, "Interview with JDP," ClarQ 11 (1964):
89-100; Frank Gado, "An Interview with JDP," IDOL (Union College) 45 (1969):
5-25. In addition DP has written THE BEST TIMES: AN INFORMAL MEMOIR
(1966); "Ma vie d'artiste," NL (7 March 1968): 1, 7. As a prolific writer of
non-fiction, DP's views on life, art, society, politics, history may be gathered
from his many volumes of essays. See also DP's introduction to the 1969 edition of ONE MAN'S INITIATION.

CRITICISM

The best place to begin a study of DP is with Davis' excellent pamphlet, which
summarizes in 45 pages the disillusioned career of DP as Telemachus or Quixote

* Of Special Importance

on a "search that could have no terminus in space." Wrenn's book, which began as one of the 24 dissertations that DP has inspired, also is a very competent study. It tries to see DP whole and not through the stereotypes of DP as young rebel, disillusioned middle-aged novelist, and old-man reactionary. There also is a book-length study of DP's novels in J.D. Brantley's THE FICTION OF JDP (The Hague, 1968), which develops the thesis that DP gradually discovered in the course of his novels that what he was attacking was not specific institutions but organized power.

DP has not been a very fashionable writer since his political conservatism of the 1950's alienated many of the critics. Much of the criticism, therefore, must be found in articles and chapters in books; but DP seems to occupy a secure niche as one of the most important writers of the second magnitude. The early DP criticism is very favorable, and when MANHATTAN TRANSFER and the U.S.A. trilogy were current books, they were properly recognized as significant. One of the first important recognitions that DP received was Sinclair Lewis' enthusiastic review of MANHATTAN TRANSFER in SRL 2 (1925): 361; republished in expanded version as a pamphlet (1926). Some of the early interesting discussions are in Malcolm Cowley's EXILE'S RETURN (New York, 1934), Granville Hicks' THE GREAT TRADITION (New York, 1935), and Harlan Hatcher's CREATING THE MODERN AMERICAN NOVEL (New York, 1935). Cowley's second thoughts appear in AFTER THE GENTEEL TRADITION (New York, 1937; Carbondale, Ill., 1964).

During the 1940's DP continued to receive very careful attention. J.W. Beach's AMERICAN FICTION: 1920-1940 (1941) and more important "DP: 1947," SR 55 (1947): 406-18, Maxwell Geismar's WRITERS IN CRISIS (Boston, 1942), and Carl Van Doren's THE AMERICAN NOVEL: 1789-1939 (New York, 1940) all contain worthwhile discussions. Geismar also introduced a new edition of U.S.A. in 1946. Perhaps the most valuable treatment of this era is in Alfred Kazin's ON NATIVE GROUNDS (New York, 1942), which begins to see DP's accomplishments in perspective down to that watershed era of World War II. Edmund Wilson's chapter on DP in THE TRIPLE THINKERS (New York, 1938; rev. ed., 1948) should be consulted, as Wilson takes issue with the Marxist critics of the 1930's who had embraced DP as a fellow traveller. Wilson recognized him as a middle-class liberal. (Wilson's views of DP at the end of his first decade of work may be found in THE SHORES OF LIGHT [New York, 1952] in an essay originally written in 1929.) Another interesting article in this connection is Granville Hicks' "Politics and JDP," AR 10 (1950): 85-98.

Three books that deal with DP and others from special perspectives are worth noting: W.M. Frohock's THE NOVEL OF VIOLENCE IN AMERICA, 1920-1950 (Dallas, 1950); Blanche Gelfant's THE AMERICAN CITY NOVEL (Norman, Okla., 1954); Frederick Feied's NO PIE IN THE SKY (New York, 1964), which studies hobo culture in the works of London, Kerouac, DP, and others.

The best of the periodical criticism as well as some of the essays already cited above have been collected in Allen Belkind, ed., DP, THE CRITICS, AND THE WRITER'S INTENTION (Carbondale, Ill., 1971). This gathering of seventeen pieces, which spans thirty years, also includes an essay on the vicissitudes of DP criticism. Another brief (eight-page pamphlet) collection, this one more appreciative than critical, appeared as JDP: AN APPRECIATION (New York, 1954), in which Max Eastman and other friends paid tribute to DP's achievement.

Section 16

THEODORE DREISER (1871-1945)

Theodore Dreiser (hereafter TD or D) was born in Terre Haute, Indiana, the twelfth child of a poverty-stricken immigrant German weaver and a Moravian farmer's daughter. He spent his childhood in various Indiana towns before going to Chicago to work at the age of 16. He later managed one year at Indiana University, then became a newspaperman in Chicago and St. Louis and finally a magazine editor in New York. Even though his first novel SISTER CARRIE was published in 1900, D had to go on editing magazines until 1911 when JEN-NIE GERHARDT released him to full-time writing. D was always a controversial figure because of the powerful naturalism of his novels, but he eventually won a secure place among American novelists, and his reputation remains high.

BIBLIOGRAPHY AND MANUSCRIPTS

There is no definitive bibliography of D's works or the writings about him. A start has been made, however, by Donald Pizer in "The Publications of TD: A Checklist," PROOF: THE YEARBOOK OF AMERICAN BIBLIOGRAPHICAL AND TEXTUAL STUDIES (Columbia, S.C., 1971). This list supersedes all previous compilations, but it does not attempt to deal with foreign editions or translations. Also still needed is a descriptive bibliography of D's books. For writings about D there are no listings both complete and up-to-date, but the following are available: R.N. Miller, A PRELIMINARY CHECKLIST OF BOOKS AND ARTICLES ON TD (Kalamazoo, Mich., 1947), mimeographed by Western Michigan College Library; Alfred Kazin and Charles Shapiro, "A Selected Bibliography of D Biography and Criticism," in their THE STATURE OF TD (Bloomington, Ind., 1955); H.C. Atkinson, CHECKLIST OF TD (Columbus, Ohio, 1969), a pamphlet in the Merrill series, and TD: A Checklist (Kent, Ohio, 1971), pp. 49-104, which lists books, dissertations, and articles about D and a few reviews; Jack Salzman, "TD (1871-1945)," ALR 2 (1969): 132-38. The last item is a brief bibliographical essay which has been superseded by R.H. Elias in SMAA. Elias' excellent essay in SMAA has been reprinted in his TD: APOSTLE OF NATURE (Ithaca, N.Y., 1970). In 1970 a D NEWSLETTER, which publishes bibliographic material and an annual checklist of D scholarship, was started at Indiana State University.

The bulk of the D papers is at the University of Pennsylvania. This is a huge collection including notes, manuscripts, galley and page proofs of most of D's published works. There is much unpublished material, diaries, journals, photographs, letters by and to D, clippings, and reviews. Other much smaller collections may be found at Indiana, Cornell, the New York Public Library, and the Enoch Pratt Free Library in Baltimore. The Pennsylvania collection has been described: R.H. Elias, "The Library's D Collection," LCUP 17 (1950): 78-80; Neda Westlake, "TD's NOTES ON LIFE," LCUP 20 (1954): 69-75, and "TD Collection--Addenda," LCUP 25 (1959): 55-57.

WORKS OF FICTION

Novels: *SISTER CARRIE (1900), *JENNIE GERHARDT (1911), *THE FINANCIER (1912), THE TITAN (1914), THE "GENIUS" (1915), *AN AMERICAN TRAGEDY (1925), THE BULWARK (1946), THE STOIC (1947).

Stories: FREE (1918), CHAINS (1927), A GALLERY OF WOMEN, 2 vols. (1929).

EDITIONS AND REPRINTS

There never has been a collected edition of D's works, and little care has been taken with the texts of the many reprints of his novels. Only SISTER CARRIE has received adequate attention in recent editions: those edited by Donald Pizer for Norton, by Jack Salzman for Bobbs-Merrill (both 1969) and Claude Simpson for Houghton Mifflin (1959). The 1901 London edition of SISTER CARRIE has been reprinted (New York, 1968) with an introduction by Salzman. Both AN AMERICAN TRAGEDY and JENNIE GERHARDT are available in hardbound and paperback editions; THE FINANCIER, THE TITAN, and THE "GENIUS" all are in paperback editions; there are in all 12 editions of SISTER CARRIE in print. FREE, which recently was reprinted, was put into the Modern Library in 1925 with an introduction by Sherwood Anderson. The Modern Library edition of SISTER CARRIE carried an introduction by D giving D's version of the suppression of the original edition. James T. Farrell edited and introduced THE BEST STORIES OF TD (Cleveland, 1956). Philip Gerber introduced TRILOGY OF DESIRE (New York, 1972) containing THE FINANCIER, THE TITAN, THE STOIC.

BIOGRAPHY

W.A. Swanberg's D (New York, 1965) is the definitive life, excellently researched and written, full of new facts and corrected old ones. It is not likely that much new information will subsequently turn up; but Swanberg's biography makes no effort to deal with D as artist and writer. For this aspect one should read Elias' TD: APOSTLE OF NATURE (New York, 1949; rev. ed., Ithaca,

* Of Special Importance

N.Y., 1970), which does concern itself with the effects of D's reading, news-paper experiences, and social and political views on his literary works. Elias knew D in the last eight years of his life, had access to his papers, and his book is a careful, scholarly work.

Two newer books that complement Swanberg by providing interior biography are Ellen Moers' TWO DS (New York, 1969) and Richard Lehan's TD: HIS WORLD AND HIS NOVELS (Carbondale, Ill., 1969). Moers' study is a "biography" of SISTER CARRIE and AN AMERICAN TRAGEDY which probes deeply the myriad influences on D's work. Moers was the first scholar to have had access to D's letters to "Jug," his first wife, and the first to establish D's real debts to both Crane and Howells. There is an abundance of riches in this book. Lehan's work is more comprehensive, as it deals with all of D's work, and its aim is to consider "the genesis and evolution of the novels, their pattern, and their mean-ing." It is based on a careful study of the D Papers at Pennsylvania and is especially good in seeing overall design and recurring themes.

A different sort of book is Ruth Kennell's TD AND THE SOVIET UNION, 1927-1945: A FIRST-HAND CHRONICLE (New York, 1969). This work, by the woman who was D's secretary on his tour of Russia, is based on both her notes and D's and throws added light on D's long romance with the Soviet Union. It is not new light, however, as Swanberg also used this material. Still of some biographical value is the pioneering work of Dorothy Dudley's FORGOTTEN FRONTIERS: D AND THE LAND OF THE FREE (New York, 1932; repr. 1946). To this book should be added Helen Dreiser's memoir, MY LIFE WITH D (Cleve-land, 1951), and D's autobiographical volumes (which are factually unreliable): A TRAVELER AT FORTY (1913), A HOOSIER HOLIDAY (1916), A BOOK ABOUT MYSELF (1922), republished as NEWSPAPER DAYS (1931), and DAWN (1931). Two letter collections have appeared: R.H. Elias, ed., LETTERS OF TD, 3 vols. (Philadelphia, 1959), and Louise Campbell, ed., LETTERS TO LOUISE (Philadelphia, 1959). Since 1959 a few additional letters have been published: ELN 6 (1968): 122-24; ALR 3 (1970): 259-70. Another reminiscence inviting comparison with Helen Dreiser's book is Marguerite Tjader's TD: A NEW DI-MENSION (Norwalk, Conn., 1965), a book by the woman who was D's aman-uensis in his last years. This view of D also manages to add something to Swanberg's account.

Because D lived a long time and his life touched the lives of many writers, critics, and journalists, there are many accounts of him in books and articles and other people's memoirs. There isn't space here to list them, but Elias (SMAA, pp. 109-15) summarizes them ably.

CRITICISM

D's life and work are so closely allied that it is difficult to separate biography from criticism, and some of the books already discussed, such as those by Lehan, Moers, and Elias, also could be listed in this section. A large body of D criticism already has been produced, and there seems little likelihood now that readers and critics will lose interest in D. From the beginning the arguments over D's work were noisy and voluminous, and since his death he gradually has achieved the stature of a major novelist, though there still is controversy over how well he wrote.

For brief overviews of D at pamphlet length there are two reliable essays: W.M. Frohock's TD (UMPAW, 1972) and Charles Shapiro's GUIDE TO TD (Columbus, Ohio. 1969). Shapiro's longer work, TD: OUR BITTER PATRIOT (Carbondale, Ill., 1962), is a thematic study which grew out of his Indiana University dissertation (1954), and while it is overly schematized, it gives an informed reading of D's works. Another short book, which is perhaps better balanced and more judicious, is Philip Gerber's TD (TUSAS, 1964), a work that focuses on the things in D's life that went into the making of his novels. The best medium-length book is still F.O. Matthiessen's TD (New York, 1951). This work by one of the great critics of American literature treats D sensitively and perceptively without denying his blemishes. It probably played a significant role in establishing D's present high reputation. Twenty years after Matthiessen's book appeared, Robert Penn Warren published a study, HOMAGE TO TD (New York, 1972), which is likely to do much to consolidate and maintain the current high status of D's reputation. Warren's work is a highly personal reading by a distinguished novelist and critic who has felt the power of D's work for many years. He argues boldly that D's often clumsy prose style pales before the larger aspects of art. "Words, however, are not the only language of fiction. There is the language of the unfolding scenes" and in handling matters of "psychological veracity and subtlety, of symbolic densities and rhythmic complexities" D is an artist. Still another recent book is John McAleer's TD: AN INTRO-DUCTION AND INTERPRETATION (New York, 1968). This is not a pioneering work but it "clearly grasps D's concern with and rendering of the conflict between Nature and the American Dream and is able to provide a persuasive, fresh reading of the major works" (Elias, SMAA).

The controversy over D's work is one of the more interesting battles in American literature. Stephen Stepanchev's D AMONG THE CRITICS (New York, 1950) is an eight-page pamphlet summarizing his New York University dissertation (1950). It traces the vicissitudes of D's reputation from the early angry blast of Stuart Sherman in "The Naturalism of Mr. TD," NATION 101 (2 December 1915): 148-50, and the equally loud advocacy of H.L. Mencken in various places, one of which is in A BOOK OF PREFACES (New York, 1917), to the period immediately after his death, by which time his reputation was beginning to loom large. Two shortcuts exist for getting at the widely scattered D criticism: Alfred Kazin and Charles Shapiro, eds., THE STATURE OF TD (see above), and John Lydenberg, ed., D: A COLLECTION OF CRITICAL ESSAYS (Englewood Cliffs, N.J., 1971). Kazin's introduction to the former is illuminating, and the collection contains essays by Mencken and Sherman plus others by Sherwood Anderson, Sinclair Lewis, Randolph Bourne, Lionel Trilling, James T. Farrell, and T.K. Whipple. Among these are the attacks and defenses (cited above) of Sherman and Mencken. The Lydenberg collection contains 15 selections, some of which duplicate the contents of the earlier volume, but this gathering contains essays by Leslie Fiedler, Malcolm Cowley, Robert Penn Warren, Irving Howe, and Ellen Moers, and half of the book is given over to post-World War II contemporary appraisals.

SISTER CARRIE and AN AMERICAN TRAGEDY have been studied in depth, especially in Moers' book cited above. Lars Ahnebrink's "D's SISTER CARRIE and
Balzac," SYMPOSIUM 7 (1953): 306-22, documents an important influence;
Malcolm Cowley's "Sister Carrie's Brother" (repr. in Lydenberg and Kazin and
Shapiro) sees the novel as part of the disaster that hit American literature in the
1890's; Yoshinobu Hakutani in "SISTER CARRIE and the Problem of Literary Naturalism," TCL 13 (1967): 3-17, finds the determinism in the book only half-
hearted. Jack Salzman's New York University dissertation (DA 27 [1966]:
783A) was a history of the novel, and another dissertation by George Steinbrech-
er (Chicago, 1954) studied D's fictional method in SISTER CARRIE and JENNIE
GERHARDT.

Three unpublished dissertations have devoted themselves entirely to AN AMERI-
CAN TRAGEDY: J.F. Castle (Michigan, 1952), Marjorie Dustman (DA 26 [1965]:
367), E.G. Palmer (Syracuse, 1952). A considerable amount of attention has
been given to the Grace Brown-Chester Gillette murder case that D used, in-
cluding an entire book: Charles Samuels, DEATH WAS THE BRIDEGROOM (New
York, 1955). Stuart Sherman, who denounced D's early work, praised AN
AMERICAN TRAGEDY: "Mr. D in Tragic Realism," THE MAIN STREAM (New
York, 1927). Irving Howe summarizes ably the view of those who think this
novel D's greatest in "D and Tragedy"; another very favorable essay is Robert
Penn Warren's "An American Tragedy"; and a rebuttal is Charles Samuels' "Mr.
Trilling, Mr. Warren, and AN AMERICAN TRAGEDY" (all three repr. in Lyden-
berg).

Every book dealing with the twentieth-century novel contains a chapter on D,
some of which are excellent, but it is possible here to list only a few. I omit
critics whose works already have been cited in this essay: Charles Van Doren
in THE AMERICAN NOVEL, 1789-1939 (New York, 1940); Ludwig Lewisohn in
EXPRESSION IN AMERICA (New York, 1932); the two Marxist critics of the
1930's: Vernon Calverton in THE LIBERATION OF AMERICAN LITERATURE (New
York, 1932), and Granville Hicks in THE GREAT TRADITION (New York, 1935);
Edward Wagenknecht in CAVALCADE OF THE AMERICAN NOVEL (New York,
1952); R.E. Spiller in THE CYCLE OF AMERICAN LITERATURE (New York,
1955); C.C. Walcutt in AMERICAN LITERARY NATURALISM: A DIVIDED
STREAM (Minneapolis, 1956); Maxwell Geismar in REBELS AND ANCESTORS
(Boston, 1953); Vernon Parrington in Norman Foerster, ed., THE REINTERPRE-
TATION OF AMERICAN LITERATURE (New York, 1928); Donald Pizer in REAL-
ISM AND NATURALISM IN NINETEENTH-CENTURY AMERICAN LITERATURE
(Carbondale, Ill., 1966); Daniel Aaron in WRITERS ON THE LEFT: EPISODES
IN AMERICAN LITERARY COMMUNISM (New York, 1961); Blanche Gelfant in
THE AMERICAN CITY NOVEL (Norman, Okla., 1954).

D always has enjoyed a large reputation outside of the United States, and no
study of him is complete without an examination of studies written by foreign
scholars. An excellent Swedish study of D is included in Lars Ahnebrink's THE
BEGINNINGS OF NATURALISM IN AMERICAN FICTION, 1891-1903 (Upsala,
1950). There have been two books in German: Wolfgang Staab, DAS DEUTSCH-
LANDBILD TDS (Mainz, 1961); Karl-Heinz Winzberger, DIE ROMANEN TDS

(Berlin, 1955). There have been books on D published in Tokyo by Matsuo Takagaki (1933), in Budapest by Lenke Bizam (1963), and in Paris by Cyrille Arnavon (1956). D's romance with Russia was reciprocated, as three books, all by Yasen Zasurskij, appeared in Moscow between 1952 and 1964, and Valentina Libman's RUSSIAN STUDIES OF AMERICAN LITERATURE, ed. Clarence Gohdes (Chapel Hill, N.C., 1969), contains nine pages devoted to D.

Section 17

JAMES T(HOMAS) FARRELL (1903-)

James T. Farrell (hereafter JTF or F) was born in Chicago, the son of a team-ster and the grandson of Irish immigrants on both sides of his family. He grew up in lower middle-class surroundings, went to parochial schools, and attended but did not graduate from the University of Chicago. He began writing in Chicago, the locale of his most important fiction, but after marriage he took his bride to Paris for a year, and he was there when his first novel, YOUNG LONIGAN, was accepted for publication. F, a writer in the realist-naturalist tradition, has been a prolific author, but the critics do not take him very seri-ously. His early novels of the Studs Lonigan trilogy are treated respectfully, however, and his books have sold millions of copies in paperback editions.

BIBLIOGRAPHY AND MANUSCRIPTS

The best listing of primary works is Edgar Branch's A BIBLIOGRAPHY OF JTF'S WRITINGS (Philadelphia, 1959), updated by Branch's "A Supplement to the Bib-liography of JTF's Writings," ABC 11 (June 1961): 42-48; another supplement, ABC 17 (May 1967): 9-19; and the appendix to his JTF (TUSAS, 1971). There is no complete checklist of criticism of F, but there are selective lists in this book as well as in Branch's pamphlet JTF (UMPAW, 1963).

F has given his MSS and papers to the University of Pennsylvania and he con-tinues to add to the collection. For a description of this huge holding (234 boxes of MSS and 87 boxes of correspondence) see Neda Westlake, "The JTF Collection at the University of Pennsylvania," ABC 11 (June 1961): 21-24. The collection is partially restricted. There are also F collections at the Uni-versity of Kentucky, the New York Public Library, and Harvard. Additional material may be found at the University of Virginia, the American Academy of Arts and Letters in New York, Princeton, and the Asheville, N.C., Public Library.

WORKS OF FICTION

Novels: *YOUNG LONIGAN (1932), GAS-HOUSE MCGINTY (1933), *THE

*Of Special Importance

YOUNG MANHOOD OF STUDS LONIGAN (1934), *JUDGMENT DAY (1935),
*STUDS LONIGAN: A TRILOGY (1935), A WORLD I NEVER MADE (1936),
NO STAR IS LOST (1938), TOMMY GALLAHER'S CRUSADE (1939), FATHER
AND SON (1940), ELLEN ROGERS (1941), MY DAYS OF ANGER (1943),
BERNARD CLARE (1946), THE ROAD BETWEEN (1949), YET OTHER WATERS
(1952), THE FACE OF TIME (1953), BOARDING HOUSE BLUES (1961), THE
SILENCE OF HISTORY (1963), WHAT TIME COLLECTS (1964), LONELY FOR
THE FUTURE (1966), NEW YEAR'S EVE 1929 (1967), A BRAND NEW LIFE
(1968), JUDITH (1969), INVISIBLE SWORDS (1971).

Stories: CALICO SHOES (1934), GUILLOTINE PARTY (1935), CAN ALL THIS
GRANDEUR PERISH? (1937), $1000 A WEEK (1942), TO WHOM IT MAY CON-
CERN (1944), WHEN BOYHOOD DREAMS COME TRUE (1946), THE LIFE AD-
VENTUROUS (1947), AN AMERICAN DREAM (1950), FRENCH GIRLS ARE VI-
CIOUS (1955), A DANGEROUS WOMAN (1957), SIDE STREET (1961), SOUND
OF A CITY (1962), CHILDHOOD IS NOT FOREVER (1969).

EDITIONS AND REPRINTS

There has been no collected edition of F, and the reprints are too numerous to
mention. Some collections are worth noting, however. In 1938 the Modern
Library brought out the Studs Lonigan trilogy with an introduction by F. THE
SHORT STORIES OF JTF (1937) reprinted his first three volumes of stories with
an introduction by R.M. Lovett (see "Criticism" below); AN OMNIBUS OF
SHORT STORIES reprinted three of his next four collections of stories. The fol-
lowing are in print: THE FACE OF TIME, A DANGEROUS WOMAN, FRENCH
GIRLS ARE VICIOUS, INVISIBLE SWORDS, OMNIBUS OF SHORT STORIES.
STUDS LONIGAN is available both in hard covers and paper.

BIOGRAPHY

There has been no biography of F, though chapter 1 of Branch's Twayne volume
is a succinct account of F's life to 1971, and it is preceded by a chronology.
F has written about himself in several volumes: REFLECTIONS AT FIFTY (1954),
MY BASEBALL DIARY (1957), IT HAS COME TO PASS (1958), the last being
an account of a trip to Israel. Shorter autobiographical pieces: "A Novelist
Begins," AtlM 142 (1938): 330-34; "F Revisits Studs Lonigan's Neighborhood,"
NYTBR, 20 June 1954, pp. 4-5, 12; "The World I Grew Up In," COMMON-
WEAL 83 (1966): 606-07. In addition F has written a great deal of criticism,
literary as well as social, which contains his ideas on a wide variety of topics,
and STUDS LONIGAN is written out of F's own experience growing up in Chicago. Among the various interviews F has given, one might be cited: Haskel
Frankel, "Updating an Old Favorite," SatR 47 (20 June 1964): 32-34.

CRITICISM

The place to begin any study of F is with Branch's Minnesota pamphlet and his
Twayne volume (both cited above). These are the only separately published

* Of Special Importance

studies of F and are indispensable. Branch has used the huge F Collection at
the University of Pennsylvania and has talked and corresponded with F. He is
a defender of F as a significant writer who has created a large fictional world
populated with a gallery of living characters. He admits, however, that F has
limitations and that he never has been able to realize the full potential of his
vision. His judgments are balanced and based on a careful reading of F's rather enormous output.

As Branch points out, "very possibly F has been attacked in print more often
than any other American author of this century." The attacks began with the
publication of his first novel, although the early denigrations were drowned out
by the praises. During the 1930's F was regarded as a controversial but important writer and he was looked on as one of the rising young writers of proletarian fiction. As he continued writing novel after novel during the 1940's and
1950's without surpassing his achievement with the Studs Lonigan trilogy, however, the critics who damned him drowned out those who praised him. But for
the most part the critics have ignored him in recent years. There is space here
only to chart briefly his critical fortunes.

Although the NYTBR (1 May 1932) disparaged YOUNG LONIGAN, Horace
Gregory in the NATION 135 (20 July 1932): 61, found it "honest, unspectac-
ular realism clothed in a vigorous, well-rounded style." Gregory remained
faithful to F through the years and later wrote that F's work was continuing to
survive and placed him in the "major tradition of the realistic school of fiction":
"JTF: Beyond the Provinces of Art," NEW WORLD WRITING 5 (1954): 52-65.
Others who praised him (and they almost always also admitted his repetitiveness
and stylistic limitations) in the 1930's were R.M. Lovett, "JTF," EJ 5 (1937):
347-54 (repr. as intro. to the stories); Earle Birney, "The Fiction of JTF," CF
19 (1939): 21-24. Among the more important dissenters was Granville Hicks
in THE GREAT TRADITION (New York, 1935), who thought the Studs Lonigan
trilogy an "unimaginative, unselective sociological casebook study."

At the beginning of the 1940's J.W. Beach in AMERICAN FICTION: 1920-
1940 (New York, 1941) wrote a balanced and fair appraisal which treated F as
a significant and good novelist. Alfred Kazin in ON NATIVE GROUNDS (New
York, 1942), was less approving. He disliked F's "graceless style" and thought
his effects were the result not of art but of perfect literalness. Yet he admitted
the early work had power. Ruth Hatfield's "The Intellectual Honesty of JTF,"
CE 3 (1942): 337-46, was completely laudatory.

In the 1950's there were a number of significant essays on F included as chapters in books. Except for O'Malley, who is quite negative, the views of the
rest are middle of the road: Frank O'Malley, "JTF: Two Twilight Images," in
Harold Gardiner, ed., FIFTY YEARS OF THE AMERICAN NOVEL (New York,
1951); Blanche Gelfant, THE AMERICAN CITY NOVEL (Norman, Okla., 1954);
C.C. Walcutt, AMERICAN LITERARY NATURALISM: A DIVIDED STREAM (Minneapolis, 1956); Walter Rideout, THE RADICAL NOVEL IN THE UNITED STATES,
1900-1954 (Cambridge, Mass., 1956); W.M. Frohock, THE NOVEL OF VIO-
LENCE IN AMERICA, 1920-1950 (Dallas, 1957).

Of the more recent essays the following are significant: Richard Mitchell, "STUDS LONIGAN: Research in Morality," CR 6 (1962): 202-14; T.G. Rosenthal, "STUDS LONIGAN and the Search for an American Tragedy," BAASB 7 (December 1963): 46-54; Wallace Douglas, "The Case of JTF," TriQ 2 (1965): 105-23; G.T. Alexis, "F since our Days of Anger," CE 27 (1965): 221-26. Alexis charts F's decline and concludes, as do most of F's readers, that STUDS LONIGAN: A TRILOGY is F's best and most enduring work.

Although Branch's book is the only published full-length study of F, two of the seven unpublished dissertations should be mentioned: H.H. Dyer's "Studs Lonigan and Danny O'Neill Novels," DA 26 (1965): 3332, and Irene Reiter's "A Study of JTF's Short Stories and Their Relation to His Longer Fiction," DA 25 (1965): 5285.

Section 18

WILLIAM FAULKNER (1897-1962)

Since his death in 1962 William Faulkner (hereafter WF or F) has come to be regarded as America's most important twentieth-century writer. Born in Mississippi of an old southern family, he grew up in Oxford, to which the fictional Jefferson of his novels bears a strong resemblance, and except for a short period in the Royal Air Force in Canada during World War I, some newspaper work in New Orleans, and occasional travels, his career was closely associated with his native state. Beginning with SARTORIS (1929) and THE SOUND AND THE FURY (1929), he slowly created the world of Yoknapatawpha County in novel after novel, story after story. His total accomplishment is the making of a mythical and fictional world unparalleled in contemporary literature. Although his reputation grew slowly, it reached a climax in 1950 with the winning of the Nobel Prize.

BIBLIOGRAPHY AND MANUSCRIPTS

There has not yet been a comprehensive bibliography of primary and secondary materials, and one must get at F bibliography from a variety of sources. For the listing of F's own writings James Meriwether has done important pioneering work: WF: A CHECK LIST (Princeton, 1957), THE LITERARY CAREER OF WF: A BIBLIOGRAPHICAL STUDY (Princeton, 1961; rev. ed., Columbia, S.C., 1971). Meriwether also has published A CHECKLIST OF WF (Columbus, 1970), which includes secondary material, and "The Short Fiction of WF: A Bibliography," PROOF 1 (1971): 293-329. To these should be added Linton Massey's WF: MAN WORKING, 1919-1962: A CATALOGUE OF THE WF COLLECTIONS AT THE UNIVERSITY OF VIRGINIA (Charlottesville, 1968).

For secondary sources Meriwether's admirable essay in SMAA is the best starting point, and although out of date now Maurice Beebe's "Criticism of WF: A Selected Checklist," MFS 13 (1967): 115-61, remains useful, as does Olga Vickery's "Selective Bibliography" in F.J. Hoffman and Olga Vickery, eds., WF: THREE DECADES OF CRITICISM (East Lansing, Mich., 1960).

Partial or selected listings of criticism are to be found in the myriad books and dissertations written to date, casebooks on individual works, collections of reprinted criticism, etc. Indicative of F's worldwide stature are such compilations as Gordon Price-Stephens, "The British Reception of WF, 1929-1962," MissQ 18 (1965): 119-200; Stanley Woodworth, WF EN FRANCE (1931-1952) (Paris, 1959); Peter Makuck, "F Studies in France: 1953-1969," DAI 32 (1971): 3314A; Mario Materassi, "F Criticism in Italy," IQ 57 (1971): 47-85.

Specialized bibliographies are found in John Bassett, "WF's THE SOUND AND THE FURY: An Annotated Checklist of Criticism," RALS 1 (1971): 217-46, and Thomas Inge, "WF's LIGHT IN AUGUST: An Annotated Checklist of Criticism," RALS 1 (1971): 30-57. A review of F scholarship during its first important decade is in John Hagopian, "The Adyt and the Maze: Ten Years of F Studies in America," JA 6 (1961): 134-51.

Most of F's MSS, as described by Massey (see above), are at the University of Virginia, but there are additional papers at the University of Texas and small collections at Yale, Princeton, and Harvard.

WORKS OF FICTION

Novels: SOLDIERS' PAY (1926), MOSQUITOES (1927), SARTORIS (1929), *THE SOUND AND THE FURY (1929), *AS I LAY DYING (1930), SANCTUARY (1931), *LIGHT IN AUGUST (1932), PYLON (1935), *ABSALOM, ABSALOM! (1936), THE WILD PALMS (1939), *THE HAMLET (1940), *GO DOWN, MOSES (1942), INTRUDER IN THE DUST (1948), REQUIEM FOR A NUN (1951), A FABLE (1954), THE TOWN (1957), THE MANSION (1960), THE REIVERS (1962).

Stories: THESE 13 (1931), IDYLL IN THE DESERT (1931), MISS ZILPHIA GANT (1932), DR. MARTINO (1934), THE UNVANQUISHED (1938), KNIGHT'S GAMBIT (1949), BIG WOODS (1955).

EDITIONS AND REPRINTS

F's reputation and stature have insured the reprinting and availability of all his works. There are multiple editions both in hard covers and paper; but there is no collected edition, and there are many corrupt texts in existence. The older Modern Library editions and the New American Library Signet volumes are unreliable. F's publisher, Random House, however, has reissued by photo-offset the original editions of THE SOUND AND THE FURY, PYLON, THE UNVANQUISHED, and LIGHT IN AUGUST, all of which F had proofread fairly carefully. There have been new editions with editorial and authorial emendations of SANCTUARY and THE HAMLET and a reprinting from the MS of AS I LAY DYING. Studies made from the MS and galleys of two novels have been published by Gerald Langford: F'S REVISION OF "SANCTUARY": A COLLATION OF THE UNREVISED GALLEYS AND THE PUBLISHED BOOK (Austin, Tex., 1972) and F'S REVISION OF "ABSALOM, ABSALOM!": A COLLATION OF

* Of Special Importance

THE MANUSCRIPT AND THE PUBLISHED BOOK (Austin, Tex., 1971). [See Michael Millgate's strictures on the latter in ALS: 1971, pp. 115-16.] Douglas Day has edited FLAGS IN THE DUST (New York, 1973), which is the original uncut version of SARTORIS.

Other textual studies have been made as dissertation topics: Stephen Dennis, "The Making of SARTORIS: A Description and Discussion of the Manuscript and Composite Typescript of WF's Third Novel," DAI 31 (1970): 384A; Thomas McHaney, "WF's THE WILD PALMS: A Textual and Critical Study," DAI 30 (1969): 2540A-41A; Abner Butterworth, "A Critical and Textual Study of WF's A FABLE," DAI 31 (1971): 5390A; James Kibler, "A Study of the Text of WF's THE HAMLET," DAI 31 (1971): 5407A; Noel Polk, "A Textual and Critical Study of WF's REQUIEM FOR A NUN," DAI 32 (1971): 980A.

Various volumes of previously uncollected materials have been published: Carvel Collins, ed., NEW ORLEANS SKETCHES (New Brunswick, N.J., 1958; rev. ed., New York, 1968) and EARLY PROSE AND POETRY (Boston, 1962); James Meriwether, ed., ESSAYS, SPEECHES & PUBLIC LETTERS (New York, 1966); Malcolm Cowley, ed., THE F-COWLEY FILE: LETTERS AND MEMORIES, 1944-1962 (New York, 1966), which contains F's correspondence with Cowley when the latter was editing the Viking PORTABLE F (still an important text and in print). There also have been four collections of interviews, statements, colloquies: Robert Jeliffe, ed., F AT NAGANO (Tokyo, 1956, 1966); Frederick Gwynne and Joseph Blotner, eds., F IN THE UNIVERSITY (Charlottesville, Va., 1959); J.L. Fant and Robert Ashley, eds., F AT WEST POINT (New York, 1964); James Meriwether and Michael Millgate, eds., LION IN THE GARDEN (New York, 1968).

Besides the numerous editions of individual novels and story collections, there are available THREE FAMOUS SHORT NOVELS ("Spotted Horses," "The Old Man," and "The Bear"), THE F READER (A Modern Library Giant), and COLLECTED STORIES.

BIOGRAPHY

The long-awaited but often postponed "official" life finally made its appearance early in 1974. Written by Joseph Blotner, this biography had been in preparation since F died in 1962. It is a two-volume omnium gatherum of the life records and as a massive compilation of biographical data it probably will remain the definite treatment for many years. For students wishing a shorter but equally authoritative life, there is the long introductory chapter of Michael Millgate's THE ACHIEVEMENT OF WF (New York, 1966). This chapter, which sets the record straight, is an admirable piece of scholarship and draws on letters and unpublished material as well as previous research.

There are two volumes of family reminiscence by F's brothers: John Faulkner, MY BROTHER BILL (New York, 1963) and Murry C. Falkner [sic], THE FAULKNERS OF MISSISSIPPI (Baton Rouge, La., 1967). Both are undocumented but useful in presenting F's early years. Carvel Collins' prefaces to NEW ORLEANS SKETCHES and EARLY PROSE AND POETRY provide valuable information on F's early career down to 1925. F's early life and career down to SARTORIS also is the subject of H.E. Richardson's WF: THE JOURNEY TO SELF-DISCOVERY (Columbia, Mo., 1969). Various smaller aspects of F's career have been carefully studied: his military service in Michael Millgate, "WF: Cadet," UTQ 35 (1966): 117-32, and Gordon Price-Stephens, "F and the Royal Air Force," MissQ 17 (1964): 123-28; his Hollywood career in Joseph Blotner, "F in Hollywood" in W.R. Robinson and George Garrett, eds., MAN AND THE MOVIES (Baton Rouge, La., 1967), and George Sidney, "WF and Hollywood," ColQ 9 (1961): 67-88; his missions for the State Department and service on a writers' committee in Joseph Blotner, "WF: Roving Ambassador," INTERNATIONAL EDUCATIONAL AND CULTURAL EXCHANGE (U.S. Advisory Commission on International Educational and Cultural Affairs) (Summer, 1966): 1-22, and "WF: Committee Chairman," in Ray Browne and Donald Pizer, eds., THEMES AND DIRECTIONS IN AMERICAN LITERATURE: ESSAYS IN HONOR OF LEON HOWARD (Lafayette, Ind., 1971); his friendships in James Meriwether and Walter Rideout, "On the Collaboration of F and Anderson," AL 35 (1963): 85-87, and Emily Stone, "F Gets Started," TQ 8 (1965): 142-48.

For a writer who was as deeply rooted as F in his native earth, the relationship between his work and people and places is important. There has been much research on this topic, some of it wrong and now superseded. There is a dissertation on Col. William C. Falkner, the novelist's great-grandfather who was the model for Colonel Sartoris: Donald Duclos, DA 23 (1962): 233. Two articles assess the relationship between Oxford, Mississippi, and the fictional Jefferson: G.T. Buckley, "Is Oxford the Original of Jefferson in WF's Novels?" PMLA 76 (1961): 447-54, and Calvin Brown, "F's Geography and Topography," PMLA 77 (1962): 652-59. A collection of anecdotal material by friends and neighbors is in James Webb and A.W. Green, WF OF OXFORD (Baton Rouge, La., 1965), and an old hunting companion's (Cullen's) memories are enshrined in John Cullen and Floyd Watkins, OLD TIMES IN THE F COUNTRY (Chapel Hill, N.C., 1961). Another sort of F record is the collection of photographs taken in and around Oxford in Martin Dain, F'S COUNTRY: YOKNAPATAW-PHA (New York, 1964).

CRITICISM

Keeping up with F scholarship is nearly a fulltime occupation. There is a judicious winnowing of the superabundance of material in James Meriwether's SMAA essay, and since 1963 it has been possible to follow the yearly output in the Faulkner chapter of ALS. The quantity of F scholarship, nevertheless, is prodigious and has risen gradually from less than two dozen items listed in the annual MLA bibliography in 1952 to 114 items in the 1971 compilation. More than 80 books of criticism, biography, letters, uncollected writings, etc., have appeared in the twenty years between 1952 and 1972. During the same period F has been the subject of at least 144 dissertations, 34 of them completed in 1971 alone. Hence the following pages are intended only to be a very selective and brief introduction to the available writings about F.

Two scholarly tools useful for criticism should be mentioned first: Joseph Blotner's WF'S LIBRARY: A CATALOGUE (Charlottesville, Va., 1965) and the ongoing concordance project at West Point. As of 1973 concordances for THE HAMLET, the poetry, and Collins' edition of EARLY PROSE AND POETRY had been completed.

Two excellent general books appeared in the last decade: Michael Millgate's study (see above) and Cleanth Brooks' WF: THE YOKNAPATAWPHA COUNTRY (New Haven, 1963). Millgate's work is accurate, scholarly, reliable, and after the introductory chapter dealing with biography it devotes chapters to each of the novels and another to the stories. It sums up with what Meriwether calls "probably the best" short statement of F's literary achievement. Brooks' study is the work of a first-rate critical intelligence, and the essays are detailed and illuminating. Brooks deals with the background of F's fiction before treating the Yoknapatawpha novels. The paperback edition (1966) corrects some errors in the original printing. Another work, which attempts to provide a comprehensive view of Yoknapatawpha County both as a fictional creation and as a projection of Lafayette County, Mississippi, is Elizabeth Kerr's YOKNAPATAWPHA: F'S "LITTLE POSTAGE STAMP OF NATIVE SOIL" (New York, 1969), but it is too sociological and not entirely successful.

An earlier worthwhile general study is Olga Vickery's THE NOVELS OF WF (Baton Rouge, La., 1959; rev. ed., 1964). It examines all of F's novels with careful discrimination and may be consulted with confidence. A more specialized but still broad study is Hyatt Waggoner's WF: FROM JEFFERSON TO THE WORLD (Lexington, Ky., 1959), which examines F's artistic development with special attention to the Christian aspects of his work. Two more general books, still not superseded, are the pioneering works of Irving Howe, WF: A CRITICAL STUDY (New York, 1952; rev. ed., 1962), and William Van O'Connor, THE TANGLED FIRE OF WF (Minneapolis, 1954).

For the beginner there are a number of brief introductions to F's work: Millgate's early book, WF (New York, 1961); Lawrance Thompson's WF: AN INTRODUCTION AND INTERPRETATION (New York, 1963, 1967); Frederick Hoffman's WF (TUSAS, 1961, 1966); Walter Everett's F'S ART AND CHARACTERS (Woodbury, N.Y., 1969). The latter is a handbook for the study of F and includes a dictionary of characters. For the serious study of the 13 Yoknapatawpha novels and additional stories one needs a detailed glossary of characters, such as Robert Kirk and Marvin Klotz provide in F'S PEOPLE: A COMPLETE GUIDE AND INDEX TO CHARACTERS IN THE FICTION OF WF (Berkeley, 1963). There also is a list of characters appended to Brooks' study (see above). Three more guides to F's characters exist, but none is as accurate as the Kirk-Klotz work. These are Margaret Ford and Suzanne Kincaid, WHO'S WHO IN F (Baton Rouge, La., 1963); Harry Runyon, A F GLOSSARY (New York, 1964); Dorothy Tuck, CROWELL'S HANDBOOK OF F (New York, 1964). Another useful handbook type of work is Edmond Volpe's A READER'S GUIDE TO WF (New York, 1964), which contains detailed discussions of the novels and chronologies in an appendix.

There are some very good studies of partial aspects of F's work. John Hunt in
WF: ART IN THEOLOGICAL TENSION (Syracuse, 1965, 1972) analyzes THE
SOUND AND THE FURY, ABSALOM, ABSALOM!, and "The Bear" as works
that put in opposition the Christian and Stoic visions of life. Richard Adams
in F: MYTH AND MOTION (Princeton, 1968) and Walter Brylowski in F'S
OLYMPIAN LAUGH: MYTH IN THE NOVELS (Detroit, 1968) both examine
F's work from the view of myth criticism. Warren Beck's MAN IN MOTION:
F'S TRILOGY (Madison, 1961) is an impressive study of THE HAMLET, THE
TOWN, and THE MANSION, which draws interesting conclusions about F's
mind and art. The trilogy was studied again more recently in James Watson's
THE SNOPES DILEMMA: F'S TRILOGY (Coral Gables, Fla., 1970), but the
latter is inferior to the former. Sally Page's F'S WOMEN: CHARACTERIZA-
TION AND MEANING (Deland, Fla., 1972) is a careful study of the whole
range of F's female characters. It traces the development of F's women, his
beliefs about them, and his artistic uses of them. Joseph Reed's F'S NARRA-
TIVE (New Haven, 1973) examines the importance of narrative in F's work and
the narrative techniques he employed.

Less useful partial studies include Melvin Backman's F: THE MAJOR YEARS,
A CRITICAL STUDY (Bloomington, Ind., 1966), which surveys the fiction from
SARTORIS to GO DOWN, MOSES, and Joseph Gold's WF: A STUDY IN
HUMANISM FROM METAPHOR TO DISCOURSE (Norman, Okla., 1966), which
examines "The Bear" plus novels from INTRUDER IN THE DUST through THE
REIVERS. A study that focuses on some of the characters is John Longley's
THE TRAGIC MASK: A STUDY OF F'S HEROES (Chapel Hill, N.C., 1961).
James Early's THE MAKING OF "GO DOWN, MOSES" (Dallas, 1972) is a
disappointing attempt at an important subject, the genetic study of a major work.

Style and language, religion and philosophy, and race problems long have inter-
ested students of F. Walter Slatoff's QUEST FOR FAILURE: A STUDY OF WF
(Ithaca, N.Y., 1960; New York, 1972) examines at length F's syntax in order
to prove a thesis. Two other studies of this type are Irena Kaluza, THE FUNC-
TIONING OF SENTENCE STRUCTURE IN THE STREAM-OF-CONSCIOUSNESS
TECHNIQUE OF WF'S "THE SOUND AND THE FURY": A STUDY OF LIN-
GUISTIC STYLISTICS (Krakov, 1967), and Robert Weber, DIE AUSSAGE DER
FORM: SUR TEXTUR UND STRUKTUR DES BEWUSSTSEINSROMANS--DARGES-
TELLT AN WFS "THE SOUND AND THE FURY" (Heidelberg, 1969). There are
too many articles or chapters devoted to F's style to list here, but since 1969
ALS has devoted a special section to "Language and Style" in its annual survey
of F scholarship. A recent work that attempts to read F's work in the light of
Kierkegaard's thought is George Bedell's KIERKEGAARD AND F: MODALITIES
OF EXISTENCE (Baton Rouge, La., 1972), while J.R. Barth has edited a sym-
posium of ten essays entitled RELIGIOUS PERSPECTIVES IN F'S FICTION:
YOKNAPATAWPHA AND BEYOND (Notre Dame, Ind., 1972). Two books
which survey the race subject are competent studies, though they sometimes
confuse issues by identifying F with his characters: Charles Nilon, F AND THE
NEGRO (Boulder, Colo., 1965) and Charles Peavy, GO SLOW NOW: F AND
THE RACE QUESTION (Eugene, Ore., 1971).

In addition to the more than four score books on F in the last two decades, hundreds of articles and chapters from other books have treated every conceivable aspect of his work. Many of these essays are available in special issues of journals or in volumes of reprinted criticism. For a few years in the 1950's a special periodical, F STUDIES, was published at the University of Minnesota. Both volumes 2 (1956) and 13 (1967) of MFS contain special issues devoted to F, as do volumes 22, 23, 24 (1969, 1970, 1971) of MissQ. The pioneer volume of reprinted criticism was edited by Frederick Hoffman and Olga Vickery as WF: TWO DECADES OF CRITICISM (East Lansing, Mich., 1951) and revised as WF: THREE DECADES OF CRITICISM (East Lansing, Mich., 1960). Robert Penn Warren edited F: A COLLECTION OF CRITICAL ESSAYS (Englewood Cliffs, N.J., 1966), and more recently appeared D.M. Schmitter, ed., WF: A COLLECTION OF CRITICISM (New York, 1973).

Besides these general collections there have been specialized gatherings: Thomas Inge, ed., THE MERRILL STUDIES IN "LIGHT IN AUGUST" (Columbus, 1971), John Vickery, ed., "LIGHT IN AUGUST" AND THE CRITICAL SPECTRUM (Belmont, Calif., 1971), and David Minter, ed., TWENTIETH-CENTURY INTERPRETATIONS OF "LIGHT IN AUGUST" (Englewood Cliffs, N.J., 1969); James Meriwether, ed., STUDIES IN "THE SOUND AND THE FURY" (Columbus, 1970); Michael Cowan, ed., TWENTIETH-CENTURY INTERPRETATIONS OF "THE SOUND AND THE FURY" and Arnold Goldman, ed., TWENTIETH-CENTURY INTERPRETATIONS OF "ABSALOM, ABSALOM!" (Englewood Cliffs, N.J., 1968, 1971). Also there are two casebooks: F.L. Utley, Lynn Bloom, and Arthur Kinney, eds., BEAR, MAN, AND GOD: SEVEN APPROACHES TO WF'S "The Bear" (New York, 1964), and Thomas Inge, ed., WF: "A Rose for Emily" (Columbus, 1970).

F's reputation is great throughout the world, and he is a prophet honored at home and abroad. He has attracted major attention in France, as attested by R.N. Raimbault, F (Paris, 1963); Monique Nathan, F PAR LUI-MEME (Paris, 1963); Edgar Coindreau, THE TIME OF WF: A FRENCH VIEW OF MODERN AMERICAN FICTION (Columbia, S.C., 1971), this last by a distinguished French critic who has been F's translator; and two more recently translated studies: Francois Pitavy, F'S "LIGHT IN AUGUST," and Andre Bleikasten, F'S "AS I LAY DYING" (both Bloomington, Ind., 1973). Also there are good German and Italian studies: Heinrich Straumann, WF (Frankfurt, 1968), and Hans Bungert, WF UND DIE HUMORISTISCHE TRADITION DES AMERIKANISCHEN SUDENS (Heidelberg, 1971); Mario Materassi, I ROMANZI DI WF (Rome, 1968). In addition, in the last decade there have been books on F published in Chile, Brazil, Japan, Russia, and Rumania.

Section 19

VARDIS FISHER (1895-1968)

Vardis Fisher (hereafter VF or F) was born in Idaho where he lived most of his life. He began his career as a professor of English, earning his Ph.D. at the University of Chicago and teaching at the University of Utah and New York University. His subjects were the West, his own experience, and the human condition. He wrote both historical novels and contemporary ones, including a tetralogy centering on a character much like himself, and a cycle of 12 novels on the development of civilization.

BIBLIOGRAPHY AND MANUSCRIPTS

There is an up-to-date compilation in George Kellogg, "VF: A Bibliography," WAL 5 (1970): 45-64, which expanded the same writer's list published by the University of Idaho Library as a supplement to the BOOKMARK (13, iii, 1961). It lists both primary and secondary materials. Also see Johnson. There are significant MSS holdings in the Swallow Collection at Syracuse University, and at Harvard; Yale and Washington State University have special collections of MS material.

WORKS OF FICTION

Novels: TOILERS OF THE HILLS (1928); DARK BRIDWELL (1931); Vridar Hunter tetralogy: *IN TRAGIC LIFE (1932), *PASSIONS SPIN THE PLOT (1934), *WE ARE BETRAYED (1935), *NO VILLAIN NEED BE (1936); APRIL: A FABLE OF LOVE (1937); FORGIVE US OUR VIRTUES (1938); CHILDREN OF GOD (1939); CITY OF ILLUSION (1941); THE MOTHERS: AN AMERICAN SAGA OF COURAGE (1943); THE TESTAMENT OF MAN: DARKNESS AND THE DEEP (1943), THE GOLDEN ROOMS (1944), INTIMATIONS OF EVE (1946), ADAM AND THE SERPENT (1947), THE DIVINE PASSION (1948), THE VALLEY OF VISION (1951), THE ISLAND OF THE INNOCENT (1952), A GOAT FOR AZAZEL (1957), MY HOLY SATAN (1958), ORPHANS IN GETHSEMANE (1960), PEMMICAN (1956); TALE OF VALOR (1958), MOUNTAIN MAN (1965).

Stories: LOVE AND DEATH (1959).

* Of Special Importance

EDITIONS AND REPRINTS

The Vridar Hunter tetralogy was published simultaneously by Doubleday and Caxton Printers of Caldwell, Idaho. MOUNTAIN MAN is available in a paperback and was reissued in hard covers by Alan Swallow (Denver, 1971). Ten other novels are still in print.

BIOGRAPHY

F's biography has yet to be written, but there is biographical material in Joseph Flora, VF (TUSAS, 1965) and George Kellogg, "First Man of Idaho Letters," BOOKMARK 13 (1961): 93-95. Two essays by F are somewhat biographical: THOMAS WOLFE AS I KNEW HIM AND OTHER ESSAYS (Denver, 1963) (F and Wolfe were instructors at New York University together); "The Western Writer and the Eastern Establishment," WAL 1 (1967): 244-59. Also see three articles by Flora: "VF and James Branch Cabell: An Essay on Influence and Reputation," THE CABELLIAN 2, i (1969): 12-16; "VF and James Branch Cabell: A Postscript," ibid. 3, i (1970): 7-9; "VF and Wallace Stegner, Teacher and Student," WAL 5 (1970): 121-28. There is a lengthy interview with F in J.R. Milton, ed., THREE WEST: CONVERSATIONS WITH VF, MAX EVANS, MICHAEL STRAIGHT (Vermillion, S. Dak., 1970), and "VF Memorial" (CABELLIAN 3 [1970]: 25-26) by Opal [Mrs. Vardis] Fisher.

CRITICISM

F began to attract attention after writing his Vridar Hunter tetralogy in the 1930's. There were two studies: David Rein, VF: CHALLENGE TO EVASION (Chicago, 1938), a negligible piece of Marxist criticism with an introductory essay in refutation by F himself; and J.P. Bishop, "The Strange Case of VF," SoR (1937): 348-59; reprinted in Bishop's COLLECTED ESSAYS (New York, 1948). This essay compares F with Faulkner, Wolfe, and Caldwell. F's own views of that decade may be examined in his essay collection, THE NEUROTIC NIGHTINGALE (1935). F was the forgotten man of American letters during the 1940's and 1950's, though he kept on writing steadily. At the end of the 1950's, however, his friend and publisher Alan Swallow hailed him as one of the Western writers soon to come into his own: "The Mavericks," Crit 2, iii (1959): 74-92.

Then between 1963 and 1970 four dissertation writers discovered him: Joseph Flora, whose study of the Vridar Hunter novels (Michigan, 1962) later was revised to make the Twayne study (see above); G.F. Day, "The Uses of History in the Novels of VF," DA 29 (1968): 1225A; A.K. Thomas, "The Epic of Evolution, Its Etiology and Art: A Study of VF's TESTAMENT OF MAN," DA 29 (1968): 277A-78A; Dorys Grover, "A Study of the Poetry of VF," DAI 30 (1970): 3009A.

Other work includes a special number of ABC (14, i, 1963), which contains four articles on F's work plus two statements by F himself; F.C. Robinson, "The Donner Party in Fiction," UNIVERSITY OF COLORADO STUD. 10 (1966): 87-93, on F's THE MOTHERS; K.L. Duncan, "William Golding and VF: A Study in Parallels and Extensions," CE 26 (1965): 480-82; R.W. Taber, VF: New Directions for the Historical Novel," WAL 1 (1967): 285-96. The most recent contribution is Wayne Chatterton's VF: THE FRONTIER AND REGIONAL WORKS (Boise, Ida., 1972), a fifty-page pamphlet.

Section 20

F. SCOTT FITZGERALD (1896-1940)

F. Scott Fitzgerald (hereafter FSF, SF, or F) seems secure in his present reputation as one of the major voices in American fiction of the first half of the century. As F was one of the most characteristic figures of the "Jazz Age" of the 1920's, his novels and stories continue to attract a wide audience. He was born in St. Paul, was educated at Princeton, and served briefly in the army at the end of World War I. His first novel appeared in 1920, and his reputation was made. Subsequently, he and his attractive wife Zelda cut a glittering swath across America and Europe until insanity overtook Zelda and the Depression, failing creative power, and alcoholism crippled F. His death at the age of 44 seemed a tragic waste of creative talent.

BIBLIOGRAPHY AND MANUSCRIPTS

Matthew Bruccoli's FSF: A DESCRIPTIVE BIBLIOGRAPHY (Pittsburgh, 1972) now provides an up-to-date and complete descriptive bibliography of F's works, and this part of F bibliography should not have to be done again. Lists of the writings about F, however, will have to be updated periodically, as the critical exegesis continues its annual torrent, but for material about F through 1966, there is Jackson Bryer's THE CRITICAL REPUTATION OF FSF (Hamden, Conn., 1967), which includes some 2,100 items, almost all annotated. The reviews and articles are listed chronologically so that one may follow F's critical fortunes. For the years after 1966 there is the F NEWSLETTER (1958-68), now reprinted in book form as a single volume (Washington, 1972). This has been succeeded by the F-HEMINGWAY ANNUAL (1969-   ), ed. by Bruccoli and C.E.F. Clark, Jr. The place to begin any bibliographical study of F, however, is with Bryer's excellent essay in SMAA, which represents an expert winnowing of the biographical and critical wheat from the chaff. A handy recent listing both of primary and secondary materials is M.J. Bruccoli's 39-page CHECKLIST OF FSF (Columbus, 1970).

Most of F's MSS are at Princeton, which also has many letters to and from F, photographs, first editions, corrected galley proofs, F's personal library, and a scrapbook. The MSS include holograph copies of all five novels. For a description, not complete, see Arthur Mizener, PULC 12 (1951): 190-96, and since 1951 other materials have been added to the collection. Smaller collections may be found at Yale, the Lilly Library of Indiana University, and The University of Virginia. The F NEWSLETTER has published accounts of these holdings.

WORKS OF FICTION

Novels: THIS SIDE OF PARADISE (1920), THE BEAUTIFUL AND THE DAMNED (1922), *THE GREAT GATSBY (1925), *TENDER IS THE NIGHT (1934), THE LAST TYCOON (1941).

Stories: FLAPPERS AND PHILOSOPHERS (1920), TALES OF THE JAZZ AGE (1922), ALL THE SAD YOUNG MEN (1926), TAPS AT REVEILLE (1935).

EDITIONS AND REPRINTS

THE GREAT GATSBY appeared in the Modern Library (1934) with an introduction by F. After F died Scribner's, publishers of all his works, issued THE LAST TYCOON (unfinished when F died), with GATSBY, five stories and an introduction by Edmund Wilson. New Directions issued THE CRACK-UP (1945), which is essays, letters, and notebook entries. The Viking PORTABLE F appeared in 1945, and in 1951 Malcolm Cowley edited a revised version of TENDER IS THE NIGHT. Scribner's has issued all of F's books in recent years and also put out most of them in paperback. Hardcover editions in print include THREE NOVELS (GATSBY, TENDER, TYCOON) and the F READER, edited by Mizener. The latter is also available in paper, as is BABYLON REVISITED AND OTHER STORIES. The closest thing to a collected edition is the BODLEY HEAD SF (6 vols., London, 1958-63), including all the novels and many essays and stories.

In the 1950's and 1960's interest in F led to the search for uncollected and unpublished material. Mizener gathered 20 stories and essays in AFTERNOONS OF AN AUTHOR (1957). Scribner's issued THE PAT HOBBY STORIES (1962), 17 short pieces from F's last years previously published in ESQUIRE. John Kuehl edited THE APPRENTICE FICTION OF FSF, 1909-1917 (1965) and the THOUGHT-BOOK OF FSF (1965). The former is 15 stories and two plays written in high school and college, and the latter is F's diary at age 14. Bruccoli and Bryer have edited FSF IN HIS OWN TIME: A MISCELLANY (Kent, Ohio, 1972), and Bruccoli has brought out a MS facsimile edition of GATSBY (Washington, 1972).

BIOGRAPHY

There are two good complementary biographies: Arthur Mizener's THE FAR SIDE OF PARADISE (Boston, 1951; rev. ed., 1965) and Andrew Turnbull's SF (New York, 1962). The former is based on a careful use of the extensive Princeton

* Of Special Importance

papers, is scholarly, documented, readable, and deals ably with the literary works. The latter concerns itself with the man behind the books and stories, is an expert journalist's account, and is based on a friendship plus scores of interviews over a period of years. Turnbull also is the editor of THE LETTERS OF FSF (New York, 1963), a large collection which is indispensable for the study of F's life. Another letter collection, which in part duplicates Turnbull's, is John Kuehl and Jackson Bryer, eds., DEAR SCOTT/DEAR MAX: THE F-PERKINS CORRESPONDENCE (New York, 1971). Also available is Matthew Bruccoli, ed., AS EVER, SCOTT FITZ--: LETTERS BETWEEN FSF AND HIS LITERARY AGENT, HAROLD OBER, 1919-1940 (Philadelphia, 1972).

There are many essays, parts of books, and reminiscences by friends on portions of F's life, but only a few may be cited here. Kuehl's introduction to THE APPRENTICE YEARS contains material on the early years, as does H.D. Piper's FSF: A CRITICAL PORTRAIT (New York, 1965). The files of PULC during the 1940's and 1950's contain a good bit of material on F's Princeton years. A reminiscence of F in the army is A.F. Meyers, "Lieutenant FSF," PELL 1 (1965): 167-76. F's relations with his wife are treated fully and well in Nancy Milford's best-selling ZELDA (New York, 1970). In addition one should consult the section in Piper's book on Zelda's novel SAVE ME THE WALTZ and Sara Mayfield's composite biography, EXILES FROM PARADISE, ZELDA AND SF (New York, 1971). For memories of F in Paris in the 1920's, see Morley Callaghan's THAT SUMMER IN PARIS (New York, 1963). Also noteworthy is Hemingway's vicious sketch of F on a motor trip in France in A MOVEABLE FEAST (New York, 1964), and Calvin Tomkins' LIVING WELL IS THE BEST REVENGE (New York, 1971), an account of Gerald and Sarah Murphy, who were the models for Nicole and Dick Diver. A good picture of F in his sad last years is Sheilah Graham's autobiography, BELOVED INFIDEL (New York, 1958), written with Gerold Frank. The PAT HOBBY stories also record in fiction these years, and Budd Schulberg's novel, THE DISENCHANTED (New York, 1950), though denied, is a roman à clef of F in Hollywood. An overview of this period is Arnold Latham's CRAZY SUNDAYS: FSF IN HOLLYWOOD (New York, 1971), a study based on F's screen writing. Finally, the recently published facsimile LEDGER, ed. M.J. Bruccoli (Washington, 1972) and covering the years 1919-1936, makes available more previously unpublished material. Arthur Mizener's SF AND HIS WORLD (New York, 1972) is a picturebook with a short narrative.

CRITICISM

Because F is one of the most fashionable writers among academic critics, it is impossible here to list more than a fraction of the studies, long and short. The 1970 MLA INTERNATIONAL BIBLIOGRAPHY alone listed 23 items on F, not counting the 122 pages of material in the F-HEMINGWAY ANNUAL for that year. Between 1950 and 1970 27 dissertations were written on F. Five of the dissertations have eventuated in books, but to these studies have been added another six books, two pamphlets, and five collections of reprinted criticism. To thread his way through this maze, the neophyte would be well advised to start with Charles Shain's pamphlet (UMPAW, 1961) or Kenneth Eble's brief study (TUSAS, 1963).

It was ten years after F's death before the first dissertation was written (James Miller, University of Chicago, 1950), and eleven before Mizener's fine biography appeared. Mizener's work is also a distinguished piece of criticism. Miller's thesis, the first book-length study, was published as THE FICTIONAL TECHNIQUE OF FSF (The Hague, 1957) and later expanded into FSF: HIS ART AND TECHNIQUE (New York, 1964). Miller focuses on F's literary influences and how they shaped his fiction. He reads the works carefully and perceptively. William Goldhurst in FSF AND HIS CONTEMPORARIES (Cleveland, 1963) studies the influence of F's friends, Mencken, Wilson, Hemingway, and Lardner, but with inconclusive results. Sergio Perosa in THE ART OF FSF (Ann Arbor, 1965), a study originally published in Italian (Rome, 1961), ably analyzes all of F's fiction, stories as well as novels, from a thematic standpoint, pointing out links between the works and trying to see F's development as an artist.

Piper's FSF: A CRITICAL PORTRAIT (see above), besides dealing with biography, also concerns itself with sources and influences and in Frederick Hoffman's view (ALS 1964) is "a major contribution to the understanding of F's life and his work." Bryer, however, finds much of it "rendered redundant by other scholarship" and "unreasonably overrated" (SMAA). Another book that followed Piper's is Richard Lehan's FSF AND THE CRAFT OF FICTION (Carbondale, Ill., 1966), an excellent study that links F with his literary antecedents and contemporaries and supplies good readings of the novels. A more recent book is Robert Sklar's FSF: THE LAST LAOCOON (New York, 1967), which argues that F was the last of the Romantics, who grew up believing in genteel nineteenth century values, and had to discard his beliefs in the course of his creative life. Two of the latest contributions to the F bookshelf are Milton Hindus' FSF: AN INTRODUCTION (New York, 1968), short but useful, and Milton Stern's THE GOLDEN MOMENT: THE NOVELS OF FSF (Urbana, Ill., 1970), which Piper (AL 43:469) calls a pedestrian book yet one that gives careful readings to each novel. It defends the revised text of TENDER IS THE NIGHT that Malcolm Cowley edited. F is approached from another angle in John Callahan's THE ILLUSIONS OF A NATION: MYTH AND HISTORY IN THE NOVELS OF FSF (Urbana, Ill., 1972).

For students who wish to know what F's contemporaries thought of him, there is Bruccoli and Jackson Bryer's FSF IN HIS OWN TIME (see above), half of which contains articles about F from 1915-40. But the fact is that F did not attract much attention during his lifetime. The early novels appeared without much fanfare, and even GATSBY was not rated high by most reviewers. One of the few early essays of value is Edmund Wilson's piece in THE BOOKMAN in 1922 (repr. in THE SHORES OF LIGHT [1952] and in Mizener's, Hoffman's, and Kazin's collections [see below]). One should see Mencken's discerning review of GATSBY from the BALTIMORE SUN (repr. in Kazin) and a significant essay by Paul Rosenfeld written just before the novel appeared (repr. in Hoffman and Kazin). TENDER IS THE NIGHT, however, evoked much discussion pro and con, and there was no agreement about its merits or defects. For a consideration of this controversy, see M.J. Bruccoli, "TENDER IS THE NIGHT and the Reviewers," MFS 7 (1961): 49-54.

After F's death his critical reputation began to grow, and he now is the subject of an ever-increasing volume of criticism. Many of the best essays have been culled from books and journals for the following collections of reprinted criticism: Alfred Kazin, ed., FSF: THE MAN AND HIS WORK (Cleveland, 1951), mostly essays from the 1940's; Arthur Mizener, ed., FSF: A COLLECTION OF CRITICAL ESSAYS (Englewood Cliffs, N.J., 1963), mostly articles from after 1945; Ernest Lockridge, ed., TWENTIETH-CENTURY INTERPRETATIONS OF "THE GREAT GATSBY" (Englewood Cliffs, N.J., 1968); F.J. Hoffman, ed., "THE GREAT GATSBY": A STUDY (New York, 1962); Marvin LaHood, ed., "TENDER IS THE NIGHT": ESSAYS IN CRITICISM (Bloomington, Ind., 1969); Kenneth Eble, ed., FSF: A COLLECTION OF CRITICISM (New York, 1973). Although there is a good deal of duplication among these volumes, they provide more than three dozen essays on the two novels and other aspects of F's work. In addition eight more articles appeared in a special F issue of MFS 7, i (1961).

Because GATSBY now is generally considered F's most important novel and a modern classic, it gets the lion's share of critical attention. The early novels have not been examined as thoroughly, though they are treated in most of the recent book-length studies. There is an unpublished dissertation, however, on the early works: R.E. Long, "The Hero and Society in the Earlier Novels of FSF: A Study in Literary Milieu," DA 29 (1969): 2715-16A. GATSBY, it would seem, has been adequately treated. Hoffman's "THE GREAT GATSBY": A STUDY is a casebook approach to the novel, very well done, which also ends with four pages of bibliography. Hoffman does not reprint contemporary reviews, however. An important article dealing with the writing of the novel is Kenneth Eble, "The Craft of Revision: THE GREAT GATSBY," AL 36 (1964): 315-26.

Next to GATSBY, TENDER IS THE NIGHT receives the most attention. Bruccoli's dissertation (Virginia, 1961), later published as THE COMPOSITION OF "TENDER IS THE NIGHT" (Pittsburgh, 1963), examines exhaustively the 17 drafts and three versions of the novel that F worked on over a period of nine years. This detailed study makes clear that F was a self-conscious craftsman and not the happy-go-lucky natural writer that he often appeared to be. In studying this novel one also should look at Malcolm Cowley's edition of the novel republished "With the Author's Final Revisions" and an introduction (1951) and Tomkins' book on the Murphys (see under biography). Among the numerous essays on this novel listed in the various checklists one might be cited: Arthur Mizener's chapter in his TWELVE GREAT AMERICAN NOVELS (New York, 1967).

There are a great many chapters devoted to F in books that have appeared since his death, but only a few may be cited: Kazin's ON NATIVE GROUNDS (New York, 1942), Oscar Cargill's INTELLECTUAL AMERICA (New York, 1941), and Maxwell Geismar's THE LAST OF THE PROVINCIALS (Boston, 1947) all treat F favorably and seriously, Geismar's chapter being the most extensive and in Bryer's opinion "not only the first extensive review and evaluation of the entire F canon but also one of the best" (SMAA). There have been dissenters among the F critics, however, one of whom is Edward Dahlberg; see a 1951 essay reprinted in his ALMS FOR OBLIVION (Minneapolis, 1964). Other essays of significance include Richard Chase's discussion in THE AMERICAN NOVEL

AND ITS TRADITION (New York, 1957); Frederick Hoffman's THE MODERN
NOVEL IN AMERICA, 1900-1950 (Chicago, 1951); W.M. Frohock's STRANGERS
TO THIS GROUND (Dallas, 1961); Wright Morris' THE TERRITORY AHEAD (New
York, 1958).

F's stories (about 160) have received much less attention than his novels. But
this lack is being filled by two recent studies: J.A. Higgins' FSF: A STUDY
OF THE STORIES (New York, 1971), which is the definitive study, at least so
far; and R.M. Prigozy's dissertation, "The Stories and Essays of FSF," DAI 30
(1969): 2544-45A.

Foreign scholars and readers never have found F as fascinating as Americans, and
he has attracted much less attention abroad than many lesser authors. Perosa's
book in Italian (cited above) was a notable exception, but lately F has been
attracting more European interest. A study in French now is available by Bernard Poli et al: FSF: THE GREAT GATSBY [and] TENDER IS THE NIGHT
(Paris, 1969), and recently a book appeared in German: Hans Schitter, DIE
DREI LETZEN ROMANE FSFS (Bonn, 1968), which focuses on the same pair of
novels plus THE LAST TYCOON.

Section 21

ELLEN GLASGOW (1873-1945)

Ellen Glasgow (hereafter EG or G) was born into a prominent Virginia family that on her mother's side was related to the Randolphs. Outwardly her life was uneventful, for she lived and died in her native Richmond. She never married, and from 1897 when she published her first novel until she died nearly half a century later her career was a succession of novels, some of them distinguished works of art, and a growing critical reputation. She rebelled in her early fiction against the sentimental romance of Southern tradition and exemplified in her work her belief that what the South needed was "blood and irony." Her strength lay in her steadfast use of the material she knew best, the social and cultural history of her region and Virginia character, and a tough, disciplined mind.

BIBLIOGRAPHY AND MANUSCRIPTS

William Kelly's EG: A BIBLIOGRAPHY (Charlottesville, Va., 1964), ed. by Oliver Steele, is the most important bibliographical source available, supersedes earlier listings, and needs only to be supplemented by writing about G since its publication. Kelly covers exhaustively the primary materials, both separate publications and contributions to periodicals, lists secondary materials, including reviews and dissertations, and describes MSS in the EG Collection at the University of Virginia, which is the largest single holding of G material. Kelly's work may be supplemented by a recent bibliographical essay by Edgar MacDonald in RALS (1972): 131-56, which is a good evaluative summary of the entire range of G scholarship. (For some strictures on the listing of primary works in Kelly's bibliography, see this essay, pp. 132-33). Two other books, Blair Rouse's EG (TUSAS, 1962) and Frederick McDowell's EG AND THE IRONIC ART OF FICTION (Madison, Wisc., 1960), also evaluate the scholarship to the time of their publication.

Besides the MSS at Virginia described in Kelly's bibliography, there are many letters in the EG and other Virginia collections. G was an indefatigable letter writer and there are in addition many letters in various institutional collections: Smith College, the Universities of Florida, Pennsylvania, Illinois, and North Carolina, Duke University, the Joint Libraries of Nashville, the Library of Congress, Yale, Harvard, Princeton, and the New York Public Library. There are additional MSS at the American Academy of Arts and Letters in New York.

WORKS OF FICTION

Novels: THE DESCENDANT (1897), PHASES OF AN INFERIOR PLANET (1898), *THE VOICE OF THE PEOPLE (1900), *THE BATTLE-GROUND (1902), THE DELIVERANCE (1904), THE WHEEL OF LIFE (1906), THE ANCIENT LAW (1908), THE ROMANCE OF A PLAIN MAN (1909), THE MILLER OF OLD CHURCH (1911), VIRGINIA (1913), LIFE AND GABRIELLA (1916), THE BUILDERS (1919), ONE MAN IN HIS TIME (1922), *BARREN GROUND (1925), *THE ROMAN- TIC COMEDIANS (1926), THEY STOOPED TO FOLLY (1929), THE SHELTERED LIFE (1932), *VEIN OF IRON (1935), *IN THIS OUR LIFE (1941).

Stories: THE SHADOWY THIRD AND OTHER STORIES (1923).

EDITIONS AND REPRINTS

There are two collected editions, published with G's introductions for each nov- el, the Old Dominion Edition (Garden City, N.Y., 1929-33) and The Virginia Edition (New York, 1938). Neither is complete, however, as the first contains eight novels and the second twelve. G's last work, unpublished in her lifetime, BEYOND DEFEAT, was edited and annotated by Luther Gore (Charlottesville, Va., 1966). Richard Meeker collected and introduced THE COLLECTED STORIES OF EG (Baton Rouge, La., 1963), which includes the eleven stories issued during G's lifetime plus one posthumously published tale. Most of G's novels are not in print, but those that are include: THE VOICE OF THE PEOPLE, THE BATTLE-GROUND, BARREN GROUND, VEIN OF IRON, and IN THIS OUR LIFE. These also are available in paperback editions. BARREN GROUND, perhaps G's best-known novel, was issued by the Modern Library in 1936.

BIOGRAPHY

The most accessible biography of EG is E.S. Godbold's EG AND THE WOMAN WITHIN (Baton Rouge, 1972), a good and useful work but not the definitive biography. G's formative years are treated more extensively in Raper (see be- low), but Godbold makes use of the notes that Marjorie Kinnan Rawlings made for her projected biography of G, and the later years are covered thoroughly. An excellent portrait of G appears in Monique Parent's EG: ROMANCIERE (Paris, 1962), a French dissertation which unfortunately has not been translated. There also is some biographical material and a useful chronology of G's life in Blair Rouse's EG. J.R. Raper's WITHOUT SHELTER: THE EARLY CAREER OF EG (Baton Rouge, 1971) treats at some length G's early years and influences.

Essential for any biographical study is G's autobiography, THE WOMAN WITH-

* Of Special Importance

IN (New York, 1954), published by G's literary executors nearly a decade after her death. Although G was a novelist and approached the writing of her own life as a creative artist, her emotional life and her career paralleled each other, and thus while the facts may be handled loosely, the general thrust of this work is true. Besides the autobiography there have been a good many letters published: Blair Rouse, ed., LETTERS OF EG (New York, 1958); James Colvert, ed., "Agent and Author: EG's Letters to Paul Revere Reynolds," SB 14 (1961): 177-96; FIVE LETTERS FROM EG CONCERNING CENSORSHIP (Richmond, 1962), note by Louis Rubin; Douglas Day, ed., "EG's Letters to the Saxtons," AL 35 (1963): 230-36.

There are numerous reminiscences available, and G gave interviews (see Kelly's bibliography) without much reluctance. The most important of the former is James Branch Cabell's chapter in his AS I REMEMBER IT (New York, 1955), the memoir of an old friend. But also see Hamlin Garland's essays in his ROADSIDE MEETINGS and MY FRIENDLY CONTEMPORARIES (New York, 1930, 1932); Carl Van Vechten's FRAGMENTS FROM AN UNWRITTEN AUTOBIOGRAPHY (New Haven, 1955); Douglas Freeman's "EG: Idealist," SRL 12 (1935): 11-12; Julian Meade's I LIVE IN VIRGINIA (New York, 1935); H.S. Canby's "EG: A Personal Memory," SRL 28 (22 December 1945): 13.

CRITICISM

Although G enjoyed a large amount of critical acclaim during her lifetime, especially after the mid-1920's, the first book about her did not appear until 1960, but since then there have been six books and a pamphlet. A good study of the growth of her reputation is found in Kelly's dissertation, "Struggle for Recognition" (Duke, 1957), which deals with the criticism during her life. This material is summarized in the introduction to his bibliography. The place to begin a study of G is with Louis Auchincloss' pamphlet EG (UMPAW, 1964), an admirable brief essay by a novelist, which was reprinted in Auchincloss' PIONEERS AND CARETAKERS (Minneapolis, 1965). Another useful short study is Rouse's volume in the Twayne series, but Rouse is a very partial champion and rates G higher perhaps than she deserves.

Essential to any critical study is A CERTAIN MEASURE (1943, 1969), which is a revised collection of the prefaces G published with the Virginia edition of her works. She writes perceptively about her own work in a manner reminiscent of Henry James' prefaces. She said she had read every book on the art of writing, and she certainly had read many of the major novelists. See C.C. Tutwiler, Jr., A CATALOGUE OF THE LIBRARY OF EG (Charlottesville, Va., 1969).

The first book on G to appear was Frederick McDowell's (see above), which analyzes carefully all of the works and studies the relationship between G's theory and practice. Parent's work (see above) appeared two years later and besides having a good biographical section devotes a third of its space to a close examination of the novels. Joan Santas' EG'S AMERICAN DREAM (Charlottesville, 1965) was the next book-length contribution. It began as a Cornell dissertation that in MacDonald's view (see "Bibliography" above) was rushed into print too quickly. While it is a competent book, it does not add anything to the McDowell, Rouse, and Parent studies.

The three most recent books include Godbold's biography and Raper's WITHOUT SHELTER (see above), and Marion Richards' EG'S DEVELOPMENT AS A NOVEL-IST (The Hague, 1971; New York, 1971). Raper's work, the outgrowth of a Northwestern dissertation, is a significant examination of G's early work with a particular eye towards the Darwin influence. Raper throws more light than anyone else yet has done on G's formative years. Richards' study, one of the 29 dissertations written on G through 1971, was completed in 1961, but when published in 1971 it already had been superseded. It studies the novels in light of G's own statements (which need careful scrutiny) in A CERTAIN MEASURE and THE WOMAN WITHIN.

G is the subject of many chapters in books dealing with the novel, literary history, or special topics. Only a few may be cited: Alfred Kazin's ON NATIVE GROUNDS (New York, 1942); Edward Wagenknecht's CAVALCADE OF THE AMERICAN NOVEL (New York, 1952); Maxwell Geismar's REBELS AND AN-CESTORS (Boston, Mass., 1953); Jay B. Hubbell, THE SOUTH IN AMERICAN LITERATURE (Durham, N.C., 1954). A particularly good discussion by a leading Southern scholar is in Hugh Holman's THREE MODES OF SOUTHERN FIC-TION (Athens, Ga., 1966), a study of Faulkner, Wolfe, as well as G. Also one should examine the work of another important scholar who knew G: Howard Mumford Jones's JEFFERSONIANISM AND THE AMERICAN NOVEL (New York, 1966), which links Cather, Wharton, and G. Also significant is Louis Rubin's NO PLACE ON EARTH: EG, JAMES BRANCH CABELL AND RICHMOND-IN-VIRGINIA (Austin, Tex., 1969).

G's work generates continuing interest, and there are good recent articles dealing with specific aspects of her work. For comparisons with other writers see George Marshall's "Hardy's Tess and EG's BARREN GROUND," TSLL 1 (1960): 517-21, and Robert Holland's "Miss G's 'Prufrock,'" AQ 9 (1957): 435-40. For G as social historian see an article carved from Daniel Patterson's dissertation, "EG's Plan for a Social History of Virginia," MFS 5 (1959-60): 353-60, which produced as a rejoinder Oliver Steele's "EG, Social History, and the 'Virginia Edition,'" MFS 7 (1961): 173-76. More light on this topic, plus the G-Cabell relationship, appears in Edgar MacDonald's "The G-Cabell Enten-te," AL 41 (1969): 76-91. Other articles worth noting are by two of the seven dissertation writers who have published books on G: Allen Becker, "EG and the Southern Literary Tradition," MFS 5 (1959-60): 295-303; Luther Gore, "Literary Realism or Nominalism," AL 34 (1962): 72-79.

There are two slender volumes of earlier criticism, both reprinted in 1969: EG by Dorothea Mann (Garden City, N.Y., 1928) with reviews by Cabell, Joseph Collins, and Carl Van Vechten, besides an essay by Mann; EG: CRITICAL ES-SAYS (Garden City, N.Y., 1929) with essays by Stuart Sherman, Sara Haardt, and Emily Clark.

Section 22

CAROLINE GORDON (1895-)

Caroline Gordon (hereafter CG or G) is a Southern novelist and short story writer whose critical reputation is still gathering momentum. She grew up in Todd County, Kentucky, near the Tennessee border, the setting for much of her fiction, and became an associate of the Nashville Agrarians, one of whom, Allen Tate, she married. Although coming from the South, much of her adult life has been spent as writer and teacher in northern institutions, Columbia University among others. Converted to Catholicism in the 1940's, G is a writer much concerned with order, stability, and spiritual values.

BIBLIOGRAPHY AND MANUSCRIPTS

There is no complete bibliography of G, but one must make do with Joan Griscom, "Bibliography of CG," Crit 1 (1956): 74-78, and the selective bibliographies in Frederick McDowell, CG (UMPAW, 1966), and W.J. Stuckey, CG (TUSAS, 1972). As for MSS, there is a collection at Princeton University.

WORKS OF FICTION

Novels: PENHALLY (1931), *ALECK MAURY, SPORTSMAN (1934), *NONE SHALL LOOK BACK (1937), THE GARDEN OF ADONIS (1937), *GREEN CENTURIES (1941), THE WOMEN ON THE PORCH (1944), THE STRANGE CHILDREN (1951), THE MALEFACTORS (1956), *THE GLORY OF HERA (1972).

Stories: THE FOREST OF THE SOUTH (1945), OLD RED AND OTHER STORIES (1963).

EDITIONS AND REPRINTS

In 1972 Cooper Square Publishers reprinted in uniform format G's first seven novels and OLD RED AND OTHER STORIES.

*Of Special Importance

BIOGRAPHY

G's biography has yet to be written, and until this happens, one must rely on fragmentary sources: Stanley Kunitz and Howard Haycraft, TWENTIETH-CEN-TURY AUTHORS, WHO'S WHO, McDowell's UMPAW pamphlet, Stuckey's TUS-AS volume, and scattered data that comes out of critical essays. A useful summary is Donald Stanford, "CG: From PENHALLY to A NARROW HEART," SoR 7 (1971): xv-xx. A short reminiscence is Mary O'Connor, "On CG," SoR 7 (1971): 463-66. Also see David Ragan, "Portrait of a Lady Novelist," MTQ 8 (Winter 1947): 18-20. Since G's life as teacher, critic, and writer is well integrated, there is much of her family, background, and experience in her fiction and to study her literary work and opinions is to study her life.

CRITICISM

G's critical views, which are illustrated in her fiction, may be examined in THE HOUSE OF FICTION: AN ANTHOLOGY OF THE SHORT STORY (1950), which she edited with her husband Allen Tate, and in her study HOW TO READ A NOVEL (1957). Both books are in print. A good background study for Southern agrarianism, which deals only in passing with G, is John L. Stewart, THE BURDEN OF TIME: THE FUGITIVES AND AGRARIANS (Princeton, 1965).

That G's critical reputation is gathering momentum is attested to by two volumes both appearing in 1972: Stuckey's Twayne volume and T.H. Landess, ed., THE SHORT FICTION OF CG: A CRITICAL SYMPOSIUM (Irving, Tex.). The latter consists of six essays by University of Dallas faculty and students. Although Ford Madox Ford (a writer she is indebted to) noticed her as early as 1931 (BOOKMAN 74: 371-76), and Robert Penn Warren wrote about her work in 1934 (SWR 20: 5-10), her first important critical attention came in a special issue of Crit 1 (Winter 1956) which carried articles by Andrew Lytle, Louise Cowan, Frederick Hoffman, William Van O'Conner, Morgan Blum, and Danforth Ross. In the same year Willard Thorp wrote "The Way Back and the Way Up: The Novels of CG," BuR 6, iii: 1-15, and Vivienne Koch published "Companions in the Blood," SR 64: 645-51. During the next 15 years G's reputation spread, and in 1958 Samuel Brown, Jr., wrote a dissertation at Vanderbilt, "CG and the Impressionist Novel," DA 18: 1795, and James Rocks did another at Duke: "The Mind and Art of CG," DA 27 (1966): 1835A. The same author has followed up with articles: "The Mind and Art of CG," MissQ 21 (1968): 1-16; "The Christian Myth as Salvation: CG's THE STRANGE CHILDREN," TSE 16 (1968): 149-60; "The Short Fiction of CG," TSE 18 (1970): 115-35.

In 1971 G was honored again when the SOUTHERN REVIEW devoted a major part of an issue to her work, including in its coverage a chapter from a forthcoming novel and critical articles, besides those already cited, by C.B. Baum and F.C. Watkins, Radcliffe Squires, Ashley Brown, and T.H. Landers. Brown previously had written "The Achievement of CG," SHR 2 (1968): 279-90, and "The Novel as Christian Comedy" in REALITY AND MYTH: ESSAYS IN AMERICAN LITERATURE IN HONOR OF RICHARD CROOM BEATTY, W.E. Walker and R.L. Welker, eds. (Nashville, 1964).

At the present time G is likely to be discussed in any serious study of Southern fiction. She was treated in two articles in Louis Rubin and Robert Jacobs, eds., SOUTHERN RENASCENCE (Baltimore, 1953): Vivienne Koch's "The Conservatism of CG" and Walter Sullivan's "Southern Novelists and the Civil War." She also was the subject of "Art and Miss G" in William Van O'Connor, THE GROTESQUE: AN AMERICAN GENRE AND OTHER ESSAYS (Carbondale, Ill., 1962), and chapters in John Bradbury, RENAISSANCE IN THE SOUTH: A CRITICAL HISTORY OF THE LITERATURE, 1920–1960 (Chapel Hill, N.C., 1963), and Chester Eisinger, FICTION OF THE FORTIES (Chicago, 1964).

Other recent articles worth noting are Brainard Cheney, "CG's THE MALEFACTORS," SR 79 (1971): 360–72; Marie Fletcher, "The Fate of Women in a Changing South: A Persistent Theme in the Fiction of CG," MissQ 21 (1968): 17–28; Larry Rubin, "Christian Allegory in CG's 'The Captive'," SSF 5 (1968): 283–89.

Section 23

ERNEST HEMINGWAY (1898-1961)

As we move into the last quarter of the twentieth century, Ernest Hemingway (hereafter EH or H) emerges with William Faulkner as one of the two most important American writers of the decades following World War I. Born the son of an Oak Park, Illinois, doctor, H after high school served his literary apprenticeship as a reporter on the KANSAS CITY STAR before joining an ambulance unit in Europe during World War I. After the war he was a newspaper foreign correspondent until he began publishing novels and stories in the mid-twenties. His fiction is shaped by his interest in his own war experiences and his interest in big game hunting, deep-sea fishing, bullfighting, prizefighting. He lived strenuously himself, but as an artist he worked slowly and carefully.

BIBLIOGRAPHY AND MANUSCRIPTS

Students of H owe a great debt to Audre Hanneman, whose EH: A COMPREHENSIVE BIBLIOGRAPHY (Princeton, N.J., 1967) is a model of its kind, full, accurate, and complete down through 1966, and it supersedes earlier listings. It is organized into two main parts: a descriptive, enumerative bibliography of H's work and an enumerative bio-bibliography of books, parts of books, and articles on H. The first part is an exhaustive compilation, which includes not only books, articles, and stories by H but also lists reprints, translations, anthologies, and 110 letters that have been published in whole or in part. The secondary listings in part two arrange the books on H (more than 60 through 1966) and parts of books in alphabetical order and the articles in newspapers and journals chronologically. Supplemental to this bibliography is Hanneman's "Hanneman Addenda," FITZGERALD-H ANNUAL 1970 (Washington, D.C., 1970).

Next to Hanneman's excellent bibliography the most useful bibliographical tool for the study of H is Frederick Hoffman's acute summary and evaluation of H scholarship down to 1967 in SMAA. In an admirably succinct 25 pages Hoffman reduces the mountain of writing about H to a manageable pile. This is the obvious place to begin any serious study of H's life and works.

Other bibliographical items that should be mentioned as useful because they are fairly up-to-date are William White's CHECKLIST OF EH (Columbus, Ohio,

1970) and the checklist of criticism by Maurice Beebe and John Feaster in the special H number of MFS 14 (iii, 1968). Finally, the FITZGERALD-H ANNUAL, which began in 1969, will provide a yearly source of articles and current bibliography.

Hanneman devotes a section to "Library Holdings of Manuscripts and Letters," which shows that Dartmouth, Harvard, Princeton, Yale, the New York Public Library, and the Universities of Virginia, Indiana, Southern Illinois, and Texas have small holdings of MSS. There are modest letter collections at Virginia, the Library of Congress, Princeton, and Yale. H left instructions to his executors that none of his letters was ever to be published. The great bulk of MSS is still owned by Mrs. Hemingway, who plans to give her collection to the John F. Kennedy Library in Cambridge. This collection is described by Philip Young and Charles Mann in THE H MANUSCRIPTS: AN INVENTORY (University Park, Pa., 1969). This inventory reports that there are about 19,500 pages of MSS in the holdings, of which some 3,000 remained unpublished in 1969. Since this survey was taken, however, ISLANDS IN THE STREAM (a 435-page novel) and a collection of eight previously unpublished NICK ADAMS STORIES, Philip Young, ed., have been published from this material.

WORKS OF FICTION

Novels: THE TORRENTS OF SPRING (1926), *THE SUN ALSO RISES (1926), *A FAREWELL TO ARMS (1929), TO HAVE AND HAVE NOT (1937), *FOR WHOM THE BELL TOLLS (1940), ACROSS THE RIVER AND INTO THE TREES (1950), *THE OLD MAN AND THE SEA (1952), ISLANDS IN THE STREAM (1970).

Stories: THREE STORIES AND TEN POEMS (1923), IN OUR TIME (1925), MEN WITHOUT WOMEN (1927), WINNER TAKE NOTHING (1933), THE FIFTH COLUMN AND THE FIRST FORTY-NINE STORIES (1938).

EDITIONS AND REPRINTS

Since 1926 Charles Scribner's has been H's publisher, and all of his books have been kept in print both in hardbound and paper editions. There is no collected works, however, although there have been many editions and reprintings. Malcolm Cowley edited a Viking PORTABLE H (1944), which includes all of THE SUN ALSO RISES and stories and excerpts from longer works. The same selection is found in the ESSENTIAL H (London, 1947). The only anthology now in print is Scribner's THE H READER (1953), which contains THE TORRENTS OF SPRING and THE SUN ALSO RISES as the only complete longer works. Scribner's issued THREE NOVELS OF EH (1962) with introductions by Cowley, Robert Penn Warren, and Carlos Baker, which included THE SUN ALSO RISES, A FAREWELL TO ARMS, and THE OLD MAN AND THE SEA. Sinclair Lewis wrote

* Of Special Importance

an introduction to an edition of FOR WHOM THE BELL TOLLS (Princeton, N.J., 1942) and Edmund Wilson introduced the second American edition of IN OUR TIMES (1930). Since H's death three volumes of previously unpublished material have appeared: A MOVEABLE FEAST (1964), ISLANDS IN THE STREAM (1970), and THE NICK ADAMS STORIES (1972); and the following collections of reprinted essays and articles: G.E. Hanrahan, ed., THE WILD YEARS: TORONTO "STAR" ARTICLES (New York, 1962), a Dell paperback containing 73 articles originally published between 1920 and 1924; William White, ed., BY-LINE EH: SELECTED ARTICLES AND DISPATCHES OF FOUR DECADES (New York, 1967), a larger collection containing newspaper and magazine articles published between 1920 and 1956; M.J. Bruccoli, ed., EH: CUB REPORTER: "KANSAS CITY STAR" STORIES (Pittsburgh, 1970); M.J. Bruccoli, ed., EH'S APPRENTICESHIP: OAK PARK, 1916-1917 (Washington, D.C., 1971), a collection of H's writings in school publications at Oak Park High School. J.M. Howell has edited H'S AFRICAN STORIES: THE STORIES, THEIR SOURCES, THEIR CRITICS (New York, 1969).

BIOGRAPHY

Carlos Baker's EH: A LIFE STORY (New York, 1969), is the authorized life and probably will be the definitive one. It does not include criticism with biography, which disturbed some reviewers, but Baker already had treated H critically in his EH: THE WRITER AS ARTIST. This biography is a monumental source of the facts of H's life from his birth in Oak Park to his death in Idaho. It is a balanced, fair account, well written and impeccably researched.

Although Baker's work subsumes all the previously published biographical material, there are some milestone works published before Baker's book appeared which should be mentioned. John McCaffery, ed., EH: THE MAN AND HIS WORK (Cleveland, 1950), began what has since become a long shelf of books on H. This work begins with biographical selections and continues with 18 other critical pieces, many of which contain biographical information. Since H is one of the most autobiographical of writers, it is impossible to divorce a discussion of his work from a consideration of the man. Thus the separation of this essay into biographical and critical sections is somewhat arbitrary, and one must read both parts in researching H the man. While separating H the author from some of his characters is a job for experts, even A MOVEABLE FEAST, which is intended to be non-fiction, must be read cautiously. It is cast in the form of a memoir, but it is highly colored by nostalgic memories, and the portraits of Fitzgerald, Gertrude Stein, Ford Madox Ford, and others are downright malicious.

Charles Fenton's THE APPRENTICESHIP OF EH (New York, 1954) was the first detailed examination of H's early writing on his high school newspaper, the Kansas City STAR, and his post-World War I journalism down to 1924. G.-A. Astre's H PAR LUI-MEME (Paris, 1959) was an effort to present the man through a selection of his own writings. Soon after H died Leicester Hemingway published MY BROTHER, EH (Cleveland, 1962), and this was followed by a sister's memoir, Marceline Hemingway Sanford, AT THE HEMINGWAYS: A FAMILY

PORTRAIT (Boston, 1962). To these should be added Constance Montgomery's H IN MICHIGAN (New York, 1966). Other reminiscences include J.G. Kiley, H: AN OLD FRIEND REMEMBERS (New York, 1965), which recalls H in Paris in the 1920's and Bimini and Key West later; Morley Callaghan, THAT SUMMER IN PARIS: MEMOIRS OF TANGLED FRIENDSHIPS WITH H, FITZGERALD, AND SOME OTHERS (New York, 1963); Robert McAlmon, BEING GENIUSES TO-GETHER (London, 1938); Gertrude Stein, THE AUTOBIOGRAPHY OF ALICE B. TOKLAS (New York, 1933).

Since Baker's biography appeared, there have been other retrospective accounts: William Seward, MY FRIEND, EH: AN AFFECTIONATE REMINISCENCE (Bruns-wick, N.J., 1969), contributes little and if read alone gives a badly distorted, though very favorable, picture of H; Lloyd Arnold, HIGH ON THE WILD WITH EH (Caldwell, Ida., 1968) is a memoir by a Sun Valley public relations man who knew H from 1939 on. There are many fine photographs in this book, but if one wants H's life recorded in pictures, the best source is Leo Lania's H: A PICTORIAL BIOGRAPHY (New York, 1961).

Two more biographical items, both rather notorious efforts to cut H down to size, should be mentioned. Lillian Ross's NEW YORKER profile, originally published in 1950, was reprinted in book form as PORTRAIT OF H (New York, 1961). This book exploits a rather vulnerable personality, but it is not nearly as nasty a portrait as A.E. Hotchner produced in PAPA H: A PERSONAL MEM-OIR (New York, 1966). Hotchner, who played a Boswell to H's Johnson in the author's late agonizing years, followed the master with pen and tape recorder; but the result was a grotesque Boswellian account, the image of a great writer breaking down and moving towards the ultimate suicide in 1961.

It is beginning to seem that everyone who knew H eventually will write about me and H. The reminiscences were further augmented in 1972 by Vernon (Jake) Klimo's memories, taken down by Will Oursler in H AND JAKE. Klimo was a drifter, pirate, arms-smuggler, and jailbird who knew H in the 1930's and after, but his recollection of things past adds little either to H the man or H the leg-end.

CRITICISM

There is space in this essay only to indicate a fragment of the vast amount that has been written about H. Hanneman's bibliography contains 252 pages of items, including 60 books written down through 1966. Since Hanneman published her listings another 30 books of all sorts have appeared: unpublished writings, fugi-tive pieces, reprinted criticism, biographical and critical studies. Thus in a little over 20 years some 90 books have come out, and to add to the books is an annual flood of scholarly articles, many of minute value certainly, that in-undate the serial bibliographies. Between 1967 and 1970 the annual MLA bib-liography listed another 200-plus items and counted as one item only the FITZ-GERALD-H ANNUAL which contains hundreds of additional pages of material. The flood also is reflected in H's popularity as a subject for dissertations: 32

written down through 1966; 28 more produced between 1967 and 1971. The end is not in sight.

Confronted with this problem, the bewildered student might well begin his study of H criticism with Earl Rovit's EH (TUSAS, 1963), a competent brief study, or pamphlets by William White (MERRILL GUIDE TO EH [Columbus, Ohio, 1969]) and Philip Young (UMPAW, 1959). A longer and significant study is Young's book, EH (New York, 1952; rev. ed., 1966), which is an excellent work by a knowledgeable scholar who has been pursuing H ever since he wrote his dissertation at Iowa in 1948. Carlos Baker also has been studying H for a long time, and his EH: THE WRITER AS ARTIST (Princeton, N.J., 1952), which is full of excellent criticism, was revised and enlarged in 1956 and again in 1963 and 1972. The final version deals with all of H's writing published during his lifetime and provides a critical companion to his biography. Two other general works also are available: John Atkins, THE ART OF EH: HIS WORK AND PERSONALITY (London, 1952; New York, 1953; rev. ed., London, 1964), a book not so good as either Young's or Baker's; Sheridan Baker, EH (New York, 1967), one of the best short studies.

H's popularity among teachers of contemporary fiction has resulted in the reprinting of much critical material. It is possible now to lay one's hands on an abundance of criticism without ever going to the original sources of publication in books and journals. The original collection of this sort was McCaffery's (see above), which came out in 1950 and reprinted some of the well-known early essays: pieces from the 1930's by Lincoln Kirstein, J. Kashkeen (Russian editor and scholar), and Delmore Schwartz; pieces from the 1940's by Alfred Kazin, James T. Farrell, Edmund Wilson, and John Peale Bishop. Carlos Baker has edited two volumes: H AND HIS CRITICS: AN INTERNATIONAL ANTHOLOGY (New York, 1961), which added another 20 essays including different pieces by Wilson and Kashkeen and others by such well-known critics as Lionel Trilling, Mario Praz, Mark Spilka, Harry Levin, and Joseph Warren Beach. The collection was truly international, with contributions from French, Italian, German, Russian, Spanish, and Japanese critics, although more than half were by Americans. Baker followed this volume with EH: CRITIQUES OF FOUR NOVELS (New York, 1962), which included four essays on THE SUN ALSO RISES, five on A FAREWELL TO ARMS, six on FOR WHOM THE BELL TOLLS, and five on THE OLD MAN AND THE SEA. The same year also saw the appearance of R.P. Weeks' collection for the Prentice-Hall Twentieth Century Views series: H: A COLLECTION OF CRITICAL ESSAYS (Englewood Cliffs, N.J., 1962). This volume added 16 more essays or selections from books. The most recent collection is Arthur Waldhorn, ed., EH: A COLLECTION OF CRITICISM (New York, 1973). Finally, there have been in recent years individual novels treated this way: William White, THE MERRILL STUDIES IN "THE SUN ALSO RISES" (Columbus, Ohio, 1969), which gathers 15 contemporary reviews and later critical evaluations; Jay Gellens, TWENTIETH CENTURY INTERPRETATIONS OF "A FAREWELL TO ARMS" (Englewood Cliffs, N.J., 1970), which reprints 17 more essays; Katharine Jobes' edition of the same series' companion volume on THE OLD MAN AND THE SEA (1968) with another 17 essays. There is a fair amount of duplication in all these books, but among them one now has easy access to dozens of critical essays. To these volumes of reprinted criticism one also should add two special issues of MFS (1, iii, 1955; 14, iii, 1968) and a special issue of RENDEZVOUS 5 (ii, 1970). A special study of THE SUN ALSO RISES, which links the real people to H's characters, is Bertram Sarason's H AND THE SUN SET (Washington, 1972).

Since approximately the time of H's death, scholarship has turned towards the specialized study which illuminates in great detail one facet of the subject's life and work. There have been three studies of H's heroes and heroism: Joseph De Falco, THE HERO IN H'S SHORT STORIES (Pittsburgh, 1963), which is preoccupied with mythic interpretations; D.E. Wylder, H'S HEROES (Albuquerque, N.M., 1969); Leo Gurko's EH AND THE PURSUIT OF HEROISM (New York, 1968), a more satisfactory study that concludes: "It is H's search for a relevant and sustainable heroism that lies at the heart of his work." H also has been studied from the standpoint of philosophy, religion, and love. John Killinger's H AND THE DEAD GODS (Lexington, Ky., 1960) fits H's unsystematized philosophic views into the framework of existentialism; Julanne Isabelle's H'S RELIGIOUS EXPERIENCE (New York, 1964) tries rather unsuccessfully to make a man of faith out of her subject; R.W. Lewis' H ON LOVE (Austin, Tex., 1965) employs psychoanalysis and the "Tristan-Iseult syndrome" to approach H in a way that F.J. Hoffman (SMAA) called "stifling."

Other books on H in the late 1960's included some good ones: Richard Hovey's H: THE INWARD TERRAIN (Seattle, 1968); Jackson Benson's H: THE WRITER'S ART OF SELF-DEFENSE (Minneapolis, 1969); Richard Peterson's H: DIRECT AND OBLIQUE (The Hague, 1969). Hovey makes a psychological study of what caused H to write as he did, connecting H's life and art, as Young did in his pioneering study. Benson argues a thesis that H was a deadly serious writer who searched for the bedrock of experience and contributed much to fighting the bankruptcy of our language and superficiality of our literature. Peterson's book is concerned with relating H's themes, ideas, and attitudes to his style, imagery, and technique.

Another solid study, the only attempt so far to study H's nonfiction, is R.O. Stephens' H'S NONFICTION: THE PUBLIC VOICE (Chapel Hill, N.C., 1968). This is a thorough account of H's newspaper and magazine work which shows him, despite his self-image as a lonely man working outside the mainstream of American life, to be a very public figure. A good account of H's interest and possible use of art is Emily Watts' EH AND THE ARTS (Urbana, Ill., 1971), a study which shows how "the poetry and prose of H might have been enriched and deepened by the painting and sculpture and architecture which he saw being created around him." A compact study of H's art is Sheldon Grebstein's H'S CRAFT (Carbondale, Ill., 1973).

A curious addition to the H bookshelf is the work of an Indian scholar, Chaman Nahal, whose THE NARRATIVE PATTERN IN EH'S FICTION (Rutherford, N.J., 1971) argues that H's ingenuity in technique lies in "his taking aesthetic note of moments of passivity as an essential component of any given total action." Nahal believes that we have in H "the projection of a passive hero" who finds greater fulfillment in passivity than in action. The most useful addition to the recent spate of books is Arthur Waldhorn's A READER'S GUIDE TO EH (New

York, 1972), a handy volume which contains straightforward chronological sum-
maries of H's work and life and the criticism.

At the time he won the Nobel Prize in 1954, H was already known and widely
read throughout the world. Hanneman's bibliography lists 382 translations into
33 languages, including Albanian, Estonian, Burmese, and Icelandic. Hans
Benz' EH IN UBERSETZUNGEN (Frankfurt, 1963) lists translations of H's work
into 45 languages, breaking down, as Hanneman does not, the regional languages
of countries like India and Yugoslavia. His great popularity in Europe is summarized in Roger Asselineau, ed., THE LITERARY REPUTATION OF H IN EUROPE
(Paris, 1965). H has been translated complete in eight-volume editions in both
France and Japan, and the Russians have been reading H since the 1930's. See
Deming Brown, SOVIET ATTITUDES TOWARD AMERICAN WRITING (Princeton,
N.J., 1962), chap. 12, and Yuri Prizel, "H in Soviet Literary Criticism," AL
44 (1972): 445-56. In many of the countries in which H has been translated
there also have been studies published by foreign scholars. Books on H have
appeared in Russian, Polish, Hungarian, Japanese, Danish, Flemish, Malay,
and a considerable body of critical exegesis now exists in French, Italian, and
German.

Section 24

JOSEPH HERGESHEIMER (1880-1954)

Joseph Hergesheimer (hereafter JH or H) came from a middle-class Pennsylvania German background. He grew up in a Philadelphia suburb, studied art, traveled and studied in Europe, and then turned to writing. His apprenticeship was long, and he was 34 when his first novel was published. His work covers a wide range--realistic novels and romance, historical and contemporary fiction--with settings in various parts of the Eastern United States and Latin America. His work is uneven, but his earliest novels are his best.

BIBLIOGRAPHY AND MANUSCRIPTS

Herbert Swire, A BIBLIOGRAPHY OF THE WORK OF JH (Philadelphia, 1923); Jacob Schwartz, 1100 OBSCURE POINTS: BIBLIOGRAPHIES OF 25 ENGLISH AND 21 AMERICAN AUTHORS (London, 1931); W.F. Taylor, A HISTORY OF AMERICAN LETTERS, with Bibliographies by Harry Hartwick (Boston, 1936); J.J. Napier, "JH: A Selected Bibliography, 1913-1945," BB 24 (1963-64): 46-48, 52, 69-70. Also equipped with bibliography is R.E. Martin, THE FICTION OF JH (Philadelphia, 1965).

The following libraries have large collections of MSS: Harvard, New York Public, and Princeton; also the Wisconsin State Historical Society, University of California at Berkeley, and Yale have significant holdings of letters. The University of Texas has an extensive collection, which has been described in a dissertation by H.L. Stappenbeck: "A Catalog of the JH Collection at the University of Texas at Austin," DA 29 (1969): 3621-2A. An earlier account is J.E. Slate, "The JH Collection," LCUT 7 (1961): 24-31.

WORKS OF FICTION

Novels: THE LAY ANTHONY (1914), MOUNTAIN BLOOD (1915), *THE THREE BLACK PENNIES (1917), LINDA CONDON (1919), *JAVA HEAD (1919), CYTHEREA (1922), THE BRIGHT SHAWL (1922), BALISAND (1924), TAMPICO (1926), THE PARTY DRESS (1930), THE LIMESTONE TREE (1931), THE FOOLS-

* Of Special Importance

CAP ROSE (1934).

Stories: GOLD AND IRON (1918), THE HAPPY END (1919), QUIET CITIES (1928), TRIALL BY ARMS (1929), SWORDS AND ROSES (1929), LOVE IN THE UNITED STATES AND THE BIG SHOT (1932), TROPICAL WINTER (1933).

EDITIONS AND REPRINTS

Only three of H's books have been reprinted: THE THREE BLACK PENNIES (1930, 1961), JAVA HEAD (1946), and SWORDS AND ROSES (1972). The first reprinting of the former contains an introduction by the author. Both novels are in print.

BIOGRAPHY

Two early studies contain biographical information: Llewellyn Jones, JH: THE MAN AND HIS WORK (New York, 1920), a 33-page pamphlet, and James Branch Cabell, JH: AN ESSAY IN INTERPRETATION (Chicago, 1921). H has written two autobiographical works: FROM AN OLD HOUSE (New York, 1925), and THE PRESBYTERIAN CHILD (New York, 1923). There are two letter collections: Gerald Langford, ed., INGENUE AMONG THE LIONS: THE LETTERS OF EMILY CLARK TO JH (Austin, Tex., 1965); J.J. Napier, "Letters of Sinclair Lewis to JH, 1915-1922," AL 38 (1966): 236-46.

In addition there are various reminiscences by other writers: Burton Rascoe, "Contemporary Reminiscences," ARTS AND DECORATION 21 (August 1924): 36, 66-67, and BEFORE I FORGET (New York, 1937); Carl Van Vechten, "How I Remember JH," YULG 22 (1948): 87-92; A.A. Knopf, "Reminiscences of H, Van Vechten, and Mencken," YULG 24 (1950): 145-64; Ernest Boyd, "JH," PORTRAITS REAL AND IMAGINARY (New York, 1924); George Jean Nathan, "Hergy," THE BORZOI 1925 (New York, 1925). See also Jerome Gray, "An Author and His Town," BOOKMAN 67 (1928): 159-64.

CRITICISM

There has been a good bit written about H in the past 50 years, especially in the 1920's when he seemed a more important writer than he does today. His reputation has faded badly, however, but there has been a minor revival of interest since J.J. Napier made him the subject of a doctoral dissertation: "JH: A Critical Study," DA 20 (1959): 301, and R.S. Leever followed with another unpublished dissertation: "JH: Historical Romancer," DA 22 (1962): 3667. Still a third dissertation has been published as a book: R.E. Martin, THE FIC-TION OF JH (Philadelphia, 1965). This work is the most comprehensive study, though it suffers from indecisive conclusions.

Too much has been written about H to allow for more than a brief selection here. Almost any general work on American fiction written after 1920 can be expected to devote a section to H, and he was a frequent topic for literary journalists in the 1920's. Some of the more interesting discussions: Carl Van Doren in CONTEMPORARY AMERICAN NOVELISTS (New York, 1922), Charles Baldwin, in THE MEN WHO MAKE OUR NOVELS (New York, 1924), H.L. Mencken in PREJUDICES: FIFTH SERIES (New York, 1926), J.W. Beach in THE OUTLOOK FOR AMERICAN PROSE (Chicago, 1926), Percy Boynton in MORE CONTEMPORARY AMERICANS (Chicago, 1927), J.B. Priestly in John Squire, ed., CONTEMPORARY AMERICAN AUTHORS (New York, 1928).

H was still frequently treated in the 1930's. Beach dealt with "Point of View: H" in THE TWENTIETH CENTURY NOVEL (New York, 1932); F.L. Pattee discussed him in THE NEW AMERICAN LITERATURE (New York, 1930); Geoffrey West in VQR 8 (1932): 95-108; Ludwig Lewisohn in EXPRESSION IN AMERICA (New York, 1932); Leon Kelley, "America and Mr. H," SR 40 (1932): 171-93; Granville Hicks in THE GREAT TRADITION (New York, 1935).

More recent estimates are Alfred Kazin in ON NATIVE GROUNDS (New York, 1942), B.R. Niles, "Flight from the Puritanic" in JOURNEYS IN TIME (New York, 1946); J.T. Fain, "H's Use of Historical Sources," JSH 18 (1952): 497-504; Conrad Aiken in A REVIEWER'S ABC (New York, 1958); J.J. Napier, "Conrad's Praise of JH," N&Q 6, vi (1959): 210; Phyllis Franklin, "The Influence of JH upon MOSQUITOES," MissQ 22 (1969): 207-13.

Section 25

ROBERT HERRICK (1868-1938)

Robert Herrick (hereafter RH or H) came from an affluent, middle-class New England family. The son of a lawyer, he had relatives who were Congregational ministers and one who was a professor. He went to private schools, graduated from Harvard, and taught English for most of his career at the University of Chicago. He belonged to the school of literary realists and produced a shelf of novels dealing with contemporary American society. He was always interested in the individual as moral agent and in the conflicts between social pressures and personal integrity. He never became a writer of first magnitude despite a great deal of craftsmanship in his fiction, and he seems likely to remain a minor figure.

BIBLIOGRAPHY AND MANUSCRIPTS

Charles Genthe, "RH (1868-1938)," ALR 1, i (1967): 56-60; Douglas Carlson, "RH: An Addendum," ALR 1, iii (1968): 67-68. In addition to these compilations there are bibliographies in Blake Nevius, RH: THE DEVELOPMENT OF A NOVELIST (Berkeley, 1962), and Louis Budd, RH (TUSAS, 1971). There are extensive holdings of MS materials at Harvard, the University of Chicago, and the New York Public Library. Also the University of California at Berkeley has a large number of letters.

WORKS OF FICTION

Novels: THE GOSPEL OF FREEDOM (1898), *THE WEB OF LIFE (1900), THE REAL WORLD (1901), THE COMMON LOT (1904), *THE MEMOIRS OF AN AMERICAN CITIZEN (1905), TOGETHER (1908), A LIFE FOR A LIFE (1910), THE HEALER (1911), HIS GREAT ADVENTURE (1913), *ONE WOMAN'S LIFE (1913), CLARK'S FIELD (1914), *HOMELY LILLA (1923), WASTE (1924), CHIMES (1926), *THE END OF DESIRE (1932), SOMETIME (1933).

Stories and Novellas: THE MAN WHO WINS (1897), LITERARY LOVE LETTERS AND OTHER STORIES (1897), LOVE'S DILEMMAS (1898), THEIR CHILD (1903),

* Of Special Importance

THE MAKING (New York, 1917); "The New Novel," NR 30 (12 April 1922): 17-20.

H's work generated a lively criticism, pro and con, from the start. Two articles by fellow Harvardians: Swinburne Hale, "Mr. RH and His Realism," HarM 36 (May 1903): 105-11 [favorable], and G.V. Seldes, "The American Novel," HarM 56 (March 1913): 1-11 [unfavorable]. Extravagant praise from a Danish critic appeared in Harald Nielsen, "RH," POET LORE 19 (1908): 337-63, while R.A. Holland, "'Together': A Nietzschean Novel," SR 16 (1908): 495-504, mounted an attack. A landmark in the favorable growth of H's reputation came with W.D. Howells' essay "The Novels of RH," NAR 189 (1909): 812-20. Two other significant evaluations appearing during H's lifetime are Newton Arvin, "Homage to RH," NR 82 (6 March 1935): 93-95, and H. Ludeke, "RH: Novelist of American Democracy," ES 18 (1936): 49-57.

In the past 20 years there has been little interest in H in the academic journals. Two important articles and one chapter in a book, however, should be noted: W.F. Taylor, "The Humanism of RH," AL 28 (1956): 287-301; Tom Towers, "Self and Society in the Novels of RH,": JPC 1 (1967); 141-57; Henry Nash Smith, "The Search for a Capitalist Hero: Businessmen in American Fiction," in E.F. Cheit, ed., THE BUSINESS ESTABLISHMENT (New York, 1964).

H was one of the group of Chicago writers who flourished early in the century and for discussions of the Chicago background, see Floyd Dell, "Chicago in Fiction," BOOKMAN 38 (1913): 274-75; Bernard Duffey, "Realism and the Genteel in RH's Chicago Novels," WHR 6 (1952): 261-71, and "RH" in Duffey's THE CHICAGO RENAISSANCE IN AMERICAN LETTERS (East Lansing, Mich., 1954); K.A. Jackson, "RH's Use of Chicago," MASJ 5 (1964): 24-32.

Studies of the novel or of American literature for the past 50 years have usually included chapters on H. Beginning with E.A. Bjorkman in his VOICES OF TOMORROW (New York, 1913), they continue with Carl Van Doren, CONTEMPORARY AMERICAN NOVELISTS (New York, 1922); Harry Hansen, MIDWEST PORTRAITS (New York, 1923); F.L. Pattee, THE NEW AMERICAN LITERATURE, 1890-1930 (New York, 1930); Charles Baldwin, THE MEN WHO MAKE OUR NOVELS (New York, 1924); Granville Hicks, THE GREAT TRADITION (New York, 1935); Oscar Cargill, INTELLECTUAL AMERICA (New York, 1941); Alfred Kazin, ON NATIVE GROUNDS (New York, 1942); Edward Wagenknecht, CAVALCADE OF THE AMERICAN NOVEL (New York, 1952); Grant Knight, THE STRENUOUS AGE IN AMERICAN LITERATURE (Chapel Hill, N.C., 1954); Kenneth Lynn, THE DREAM OF SUCCESS (Boston, 1955); Warner Berthoff, THE FERMENT OF REALISM (New York, 1965).

Section 26

(JAMES) LANGSTON HUGHES (1902-1967)

Langston Hughes (hereafter LH or H) is associated with the Harlem Renaissance
of the 1920's, but he was born in Joplin, Missouri, and grew up in the Midwest.
He experienced both urban and rural poverty before he graduated from high
school In Cleveland in 1920. He knocked about Europe and America for half
a dozen years, then went to college and began his literary career as a poet.
He wrote poetry throughout his life, but after 1950 eight of his books were fiction. He also was a notable playwright and a prolific and important writer of
books about black culture and history.

BIBLIOGRAPHY AND MANUSCRIPTS

The most extensive listing, including primary and secondary materials, is in
Donald Dickinson, A BIO-BIBLIOGRAPHY OF LH, 1902-1967 (Hamden, Conn.,
1967, 1972). Therman O'Daniel also has published "LH: A Selected Classified
Bibliography," CLAJ 11 (1968): 349-66, and his collection of essays, LH,
BLACK GENIUS: A CRITICAL EVALUATION (New York, 1971), contains bib-
liography. See also Ernest Kaiser, "Selected Bibliography of the Published
Writings of LH, " FREEDOMWAYS 8 (1968): 185-91. The major MS Collection is
at Yale, which has 500 MSS, 500 letters, and 2,000 pieces of correspondence to
H. There also are extensive holdings at the University of Chicago, Harvard, New
York Public Library; and Fisk University has a special collection. H's MS poems
are at the State University of New York (Buffalo).

WORKS OF FICTION

Novels: NOT WITHOUT LAUGHTER (1930), TAMBOURINES TO GLORY (1958).

Stories: THE WAYS OF WHITE FOLKS (1935), LAUGHING TO KEEP FROM
CRYING (1952), SOMETHING IN COMMON AND OTHER STORIES (1963),
which reprints most of the stories in the preceding volume plus nine others.

The Simple Books: [classified separately because they are blends of essays,
sketches, stories, vignettes, folklore] SIMPLE SPEAKS HIS MIND (1950), SIMPLE

TAKES A WIFE (1953), SIMPLE STAKES A CLAIM (1957), THE BEST OF SIMPLE (1961), SIMPLE'S UNCLE SAM (1965).

EDITIONS AND REPRINTS

H lived long enough to see a good part of his fiction reprinted, collected, and anthologized. His work appears in many anthologies (see Dickinson above, pp. 150-58), and a thick volume of his writing is THE LH READER (New York, 1958). THE BEST OF SIMPLE was reprinted in 1963 and 1968. THE WAYS OF WHITE FOLKS (1963), NOT WITHOUT LAUGHTER (1963), AND TAMBOURINES TO GLORY (1970) all have been reissued. These last three titles plus SIMPLE'S UNCLE SAM are available in paperback.

BIOGRAPHY

H has been adequately served biographically for a writer who died only in 1967. The first effort was Dickinson's work (see above), pp. 9-120, which is informative but not exhaustive. Next was Milton Meltzer's LH: A BIOGRAPHY (New York, 1968), which is directed at a young audience and is undocumented, but it has the added interest of having been written by a friend. There also is biography in J.A. Emanuel, LH (TUSAS, 1967). Charlemae Rollins, BLACK TROUBADOUR: LH (Chicago, 1970), is another juvenile biography by a friend. Additional biographical material may be found in Edwin Embree, 13 AGAINST THE ODDS (New York, 1944), and Therman O'Daniel, "Lincoln's Man of Letters," LUB 67 (July 1964): 9-12.

H has written two autobiographical volumes: THE BIG SEA: AN AUTOBIOGRAPHY (New York, 1940; repr. 1963); I WONDER AS I WANDER: AN AUTOBIOGRAPHICAL JOURNEY (New York, 1956; repr. 1964). To these works should be added several articles by H: "Harlem Literati in the Twenties," SRL 22 (22 June 1940): 13-14; "Simple and Me," PHYLON 6 (1945): 349-52; "The Negro Artist and the Racial Mountain," NATION 122 (1926): 692-94; "My Early Days in Harlem," FREEDOMWAYS 3 (1963): 312-14. Also see James Presley, "LH: A Personal Farewell," SWR 44 (1969): 49-84; Richard Rive, "Taos in Harlem: An Interview with LH," CONTRAST 14 (1967): 33-39; Fraser Drew, "LH and My Students," TRACE 32 (1959), 22-25; Woodie King, Jr., "Remembering Langston: A Poet of the Black Theater," NegroD 18, vi (1969): 27-32, 95-96.

CRITICISM

Of the book-length studies, O'Daniel's edited essays (see above) are the most important. About half of these essays originally appeared in a special H issue of CLAJ (June 1968). Emanuel's volume in the Twayne series, however, is useful and compact and follows his earlier study, "The Short Stories of LH," an unpublished Columbia University dissertation. To these may be added Rollins' book (previously cited). Among the articles and chapters from books treating H there are frequent discussions of his poetry and drama, none of which fall within the scope of the following paragraphs.

Critical interest in H has in general been a recent development. LHUS (1948) and THE LITERATURE OF THE AMERICAN PEOPLE (1950) barely mention H, though the former includes him in its bibliographies. Alfred Kazin in ON NATIVE GROUNDS (1942) and Oscar Cargill in INTELLECTUAL AMERICA (1941) do not discuss him. Most of the work on H has been done by black scholars in periodicals published by blacks, but the growing interest in Afro-American literature in the 1950's and 1960's has enhanced H's reputation. The only early article worth noting is John Chamberlain, "The Negro as Writer," BOOKMAN 70 (1930): 603-11, but there are various accounts of the Harlem Renaissance in which H is included. See, for example, James Weldon Johnson, BLACK MANHATTAN (New York, 1930), and Arna Bontemps, "The Awakening: A Memoir," in THE HARLEM RENAISSANCE REMEMBERED (see below). See also "Negro" in AAL, 1900-50, 1950-67.

Some significant general articles: James Presley, "The American Dream of LH," SWR 48 (1963): 380-86; Arthur Davis, "The Tragic Mulatto Theme in Six Works of LH," PHYLON 16 (1955): 195-204; J.A. Emanuel, "'Soul' in the Works of LH," NegroD 16, xi (1967): 25-30, 74-94, and "The Literary Experiments of LH," CLAJ 11 (1968): 335-44.

H's creation of a black folk hero in Jesse B. Simple has received a considerable amount of attention: Blyden Jackson, "A Word about Simple," CLAJ 11 (1968): 310-18, notes that H reached his widest audience with his stories of a Negro Everyman; Lawrence Mintz, "LH's Jesse B. Simple: The Urban Negro as Wise Fool," SNL 7 (1969): 11-21; Arthur Davis, "Jesse B. Semple [sic]: Negro American," PHYLON 15 (1954): 21-28; anon., "LH and the Example of Simple," BlackW 19, viii (1970): 35-38; B.R. Hampton, "On Identification with Negro Tricksters," SFQ 31 (1968): 55-65.

Among the composite studies in which H appears, these should be noted: Rebecca Barton, WITNESSES FOR FREEDOM (New York, 1948); H.M. Gloster, NEGRO VOICES IN AMERICAN FICTION (Chapel Hill, N.C., 1948); Robert Bone, THE NEGRO NOVEL IN AMERICA (New Haven, 1958); W.E. Turpin, "Four Short Fiction Writers of the Harlem Renaissance: Their Legacy of Achievement," CLAJ 11 (1967): 59-72; David Britt, "The Image of the White Man in the Fiction of LH, Richard Wright, James Baldwin, and Ralph Ellison," DA 29 (1968): 1532A; Wilfred Cartey, "Four Shadows of Harlem," NegroD 18, x (1969): 22-25, 83-92; Patricia Taylor, "LH and the Harlem Renaissance" in Arna Bontemps, ed., THE HARLEM RENAISSANCE REMEMBERED (New York, 1972).

H is well known outside the United States, and among the articles listed in AAL, 1950-67 one-third are written in languages other than English. A representative article appeared in the special H number of CLAJ 11 (1968): 331-34, as "A Danish Tribute to LH."

Section 27

RING LARDNER (1885-1933)

Ring Lardner (hereafter RL or L) was born in Michigan and educated as an engineer, but he began his career as a reporter and acquired his early reputation as a sportswriter. He turned to writing baseball stories while he was conducting a sports column for the CHICAGO TRIBUNE and for the rest of his life combined sports reporting and writing. A master of irony and humor, L wrote some of the best short stories of his era. His work is disarmingly funny, but under the veneer of humor there are sharp, satiric barbs In his portraits of baseball players, boxers, brokers, barbers, salesmen, and others. L's fiction is a rich vein of Americana between World War I and his death in 1933.

BIBLIOGRAPHY AND MANUSCRIPTS

There is no definitive bibliography, but a start was made on his published works in R.H. Goldsmith, "RL: A Checklist of All His Published Work," BB 21 (1954): 104-06, which lists not only his magazine and book publications but also his contributions to books by other people. There is in addition a bibliographical appendix of primary works in Donald Elder's RL (New York, 1953) and a selected list of both primary and secondary material in W.R. Patrick's RL (TUSAS, 1963). The latter lists and annotates 38 essays and three unpublished studies.

The largest collection of MSS, given by L's son, is at the Newberry Library. It consists of MSS of poems, stories, essays, and 740 letters from L to his fiancee. L was remarkably cavalier about his MSS and usually did not save them, as he had trouble thinking of himself as writing "literature." When HOW TO WRITE SHORT STORIES was being published, stories that went into that volume had to be photographed from the magazines in which they originally appeared. There are some MSS, however, in the possession of Bobbs-Merrill, L's publisher from 1917 to 1921.

WORKS OF FICTION

Novels: *YOU KNOW ME AL (1916), THE BIG TOWN (1921).

* Of Special Importance

Stories: GULLIBLE'S TRAVELS (1917), TREAT 'EM ROUGH (1918), OWN YOUR OWN HOME (1919), THE REAL DOPE (1919), HOW TO WRITE SHORT STORIES (1924), *THE LOVE NEST AND OTHER STORIES (1926), ROUND UP (1929), LOSE WITH A SMILE (1933).

EDITIONS AND REPRINTS

Scribner's issued THE WORKS OF RL, 4 vols. (1925); ROUND UP (1929) was in part a reprinting of earlier stories with some new ones. RL'S BEST STORIES (1938), introduction by William McFee, combined ROUND UP with THE BIG TOWN, and Gilbert Seldes edited and introduced THE PORTABLE RL (1946), a generous selection of L's fiction and other work. The Modern Library issued THE COLLECTED SHORT STORIES OF RL (1948); THE BEST SHORT STORIES OF RL (1957) is a retitled version of ROUND UP. Scribner's brought out a new edition of YOU KNOW ME AL (1960) and HAIRCUT AND OTHER STORIES (1961). Maxwell Geismar edited and introduced THE RL READER (1963), and Josephine Herbst introduced a University of Chicago Press edition of GULLIBLE'S TRAVELS (1965).

BIOGRAPHY

The best life of L is Donald Elder's RL (1953), which gives the fullest account and prints many letters, but it is not documented, though it does deal to some extent with the relation of L's life and works. Walton Patrick's RL (1963) contains a biographical first chapter and a chronology. Seldes includes biographical information in THE PORTABLE RL, and Geismar's RL AND THE PORTRAIT OF FOLLY (New York, 1972) creates the 1920's for a young audience, making L a central figure of the era.

There are a number of interesting reminiscences: Ring Lardner, Jr., "RL and Sons," ESQUIRE 77 (March 1972): 99-103; Walter Tittle, "Glimpses of Interesting Americans," CENTURY 110 (1925): 313-17; Grant Overton, "RL's Bell-Lettres," BOOKMAN 62 (September 1925): 44-49; F. Scott Fitzgerald, "Ring," NR (1933): 254-55; Sherwood Anderson, "Meeting RL," NO SWANK (Philadelphia, 1934).

Besides the letters previously mentioned in Elder's book, Clifford Caruthers has edited RING AROUND MAX: THE CORRESPONDENCE BETWEEN RL AND MAXWELL PERKINS (DeKalb, Ill., 1972). L's THE STORY OF A WONDER MAN, subtitled "Being the Autobiography of RL," actually is fiction, a parody of autobiography, but L did write about himself in "Autobiographical Sketch" in T.L. Masson's OUR AMERICAN HUMORISTS (New York, 1922) and in a series of essays in the SEP (14, 21 November 1931; 9, 23 January, 20 February, 16 April 1932).

* Of Special Importance

CRITICISM

The best general critical introduction is Patrick's book, which while brief looks at L's themes, characters, language, and craftsmanship and closes with a summary of L's reputation. Seldes' introduction to THE PORTABLE RL is even briefer but insightful and tries to make the distinction between L the writer and L the pot-boiler. There is an unpublished dissertation that surveys all of L's work: Richard Frakes, "RL: A Critical Survey," DA 13 (1953): 807-8, and Otto Friedrich's pamphlet RL (UMPAW, 1965) is useful.

One of the noteworthy aspects of L's work was his acute ear for American speech, and this topic has engaged a good many students of language. H.L. Mencken used material that L supplied in THE AMERICAN LANGUAGE, second and subsequent editions (1921-   ), and regarded L as a master of the vernacular. A long study of L's language is Isaac Clark's M.A. thesis (University of Texas), "An Analysis of RL's American Language, or Who Learnt You Grammar Bud?" Carl Van Doren's "Beyond Grammar: RL: Philologist among the Low-Brows," CENTURY 106 (1923): 471-75, and Robert Littell's "RL," NR (3 September 1924): 25-26, both praise L's speech while deploring his characters and plots. A 1924 essay by Seldes, "Mr. Dooley Meet Mr. L" (repr. and rev. in THE SEVEN LIVELY ARTS [New York, 1957]), originally urged L to emulate Finley Peter Dunne as satirist in dialect, but In the revision Seldes years later concluded that L was more durable because he used dialect for artistic ends.

L often has been compared with Mark Twain as user of the vernacular. See "Copies and Misfires" in Richard Bridgman's THE COLLOQUIAL STYLE IN AMERICA (New York, 1966); Howard Webb's "Mark Twain and RL," MTJ 11 (Summer 1960): 13-15; James Cox's "Toward Vernacular Humor," VQR 46 (1970): 311-30. Bridgman believes L was the unconscious heir of Twain but vernacular was a limitation because he only used it to depict characters he detested. Webb and Cox note that Twain learned vernacular English as a child while L learned proper English, and they trace the ramifications of this difference. Webb also treats L's language in "The Development of a Style: The L Idiom," AQ 12 (1960): 482-92.

L as a chronicler of America in the 1910's and 1920's has occupied the attention of many critics. Virginia Woolf in "American Fiction," MOMENTS AND OTHER ESSAYS (London, 1952), saw games, especially baseball, as providing L with material in the way that society did for English writers. James T. Farrell in "RL's Success Mad World" (NYTBR, 18 June 1944, p. 3) described L's characters as victims of "the terrible cost of success" in American life. Delmore Schwartz in "RL: Highbrow in Hiding," REPORTER 15 (9 August 1956): 52-54, analyzed L's use of games and marriage as vehicles of his disillusionment. A similar discussion is Howard Webb's "RL's Idle Common Man," JCMVASA 1 (1958): 6-13. Two unpublished dissertations deal generally with L's social criticism and depiction of the American scene: Stewart Rodnon, "Sports, Sporting Codes, and Sportsmanship in the Works of James T. Farrell, RL, Ernest Hemingway, and William Faulkner," DA 23 (1961): 634; Howard Webb's "RL's Conflict and Reconciliation with American Society," DA 13 (1953): 1202.

A good discussion of L's character types and characters is found in Norris Yates'
THE AMERICAN HUMORIST (Ames, Iowa, 1964) under the chapter heading
"The Isolated Man of RL." Webb also treats L's isolated characters in a significant essay, "RL's Fiction: A Re-evaluation," AL 31 (1960): 434-45, finding
as a dominant theme the inability of people to communicate with one another.

L's place in American literature has occasioned considerable debate. Early
critics saw him as he did himself, a not very serious artist. Also his humor was
regarded as genial and lowbrow and inconsequential. Sherwood Anderson, however, thought he was capable of writing another HUCK FINN (NR, 11 October
1922); so did Edmund Wilson (DIAL, July 1924), though Wilson thought he
lacked "artistic seriousness." Harry Salpeter in "The Boswell of New York,"
BOOKMAN 71 (1930): 384, quoted L's own opinion of his work: "I ain't no
satirist. I just listen." Clifton Fadiman attacked L as a misanthrope in two
articles in the NATION (1 May 1929; 22 March 1933). Maxwell Geismar in
WRITERS IN CRISIS (Boston, 1942) tried to explain L's hatred of mankind as a
result of his self-identification with his satirized characters. John Berryman in
an attempt at summary believed that L failed as artist because he lacked courage, selflessness and ambition to push his talent: "The Case of RL: Art and
Entertainment," COMMENTARY 22 (1956): 416-23. A recent assessment describes L as humorist in his first period, satirist in mid-career, and a pessimistic
nihilist in his last phase: Louis Hasley, "RL: The Ashes of Idealism," ArQ
26 (1970): 219-32.

Section 28

SINCLAIR LEWIS (1885-1951)

Sinclair Lewis (hereafter SL or L) was born in Sauk Center, Minnesota, which
is the Gopher Prairie of his novel MAIN STREET. He graduated from Yale,
tried newspaper work and hack writing, worked for a publisher for a time, and
then brought out his first novel in 1912. It was not until 1920, however, that
MAIN STREET appeared; but after that date Lewis was a celebrity and a popular
though controversial author. He wrote 23 novels altogether, the last appearing
in the year he died. He had a good eye for detail, a talent for mimicry, and
a sharp sense of satire. He examined with his scalpel one aspect after another
of American life in the 1920's, producing in succession MAIN STREET, BABBITT,
ARROWSMITH, ELMER GANTRY, DODSWORTH, all novels that help define and
characterize that decade. In 1930 he won the Nobel Prize, the first American
to be so honored, but his best work had been done and the last 20 years of his
life were an anticlimax.

BIBLIOGRAPHY AND MANUSCRIPTS

There is a need for a definitive bibliography of primary and secondary materials,
but until one is prepared lesser compilations will have to serve. The most recent listing is James Lundquist's CHECKLIST OF SL (Columbus, 1970), which
lists both works by and about L but is highly selective (36 pages) and unannotated. The most complete bibliography of L's works is in the appendix to Mark
Schorer's SL: AN AMERICAN LIFE (New York, 1961), where L's writings are
tabulated year by year. For an annotated secondary bibliography one may consult Sheldon Grebstein's SL (TUSAS, 1962).

Documenting L's considerable reputation abroad are several bibliographies in
the following works: Bernice Matlowsky's pamphlet SL (Washington, 1951) for
L's reception in Spanish; Carl Anderson, THE SWEDISH ACCEPTANCE OF AMER-
ICAN LITERATURE (Philadelphia, 1957); Anne Springer, THE AMERICAN NOVEL
IN GERMANY (Hamburg, 1960); Valentina Libman, RUSSIAN STUDIES OF
AMERICAN LITERATURE: A BIBLIOGRAPHY (Chapel Hill, N.C., 1969).

L willed his correspondence and papers to Yale, but this huge collection does
not contain the typescripts of most of his novels, which apparently were lost.

Less important MS collections include the Dorothy Thompson papers at Syracuse University and the material at the University of Texas described in SL: AN EXHIBITION FROM THE GRACE HEGGER LEWIS-SL COLLECTION (Austin, Tex., 1960). The University of California at Berkeley has an extensive gathering of material used by Schorer in writing his biography, and there are letters at the American Academy of Arts and Letters in New York, Columbia University, Cornell, Harvard, Pennsylvania State, Princeton, the Universities of Illinois and Southern California, the New York Public Library, the historical societies of Wisconsin and Minnesota, and the Library of Congress.

WORKS OF FICTION

Novels: HIKE AND THE AEROPLANE (1912), OUR MR. WRENN (1914), THE TRAIL OF THE HAWK (1915), THE JOB (1917), THE INNOCENTS (1917), FREE AIR (1919), *MAIN STREET (1920), *BABBITT (1922), *ARROWSMITH (1925), MANTRAP (1926), *ELMER GANTRY (1927), THE MAN WHO KNEW COOLIDGE (1928), *DODSWORTH (1929), ANN VICKERS (1933), WORK OF ART (1934), IT CAN'T HAPPEN HERE (1935), PRODIGAL PARENTS (1938), BETHEL MERRIDAY (1940), GIDEON PLANISH (1943), CASS TIMBERLANE (1945), KINGSBLOOD ROYAL (1947), THE GOD-SEEKER (1949), WORLD SO WIDE (1951).

Stories: SELECTED SHORT STORIES (1935), SEVEN SELECTED SHORT STORIES (1943).

EDITIONS AND REPRINTS

MAIN STREET, BABBITT, ELMER GANTRY, and DODSWORTH were issued as the Nobel Prize Edition of L's works by Harcourt, Brace in 1931, and the last three also have appeared in Modern Library editions. A text edition of ARROW-SMITH with critical apparatus was edited by Barbara Spayd in 1933; revised in 1945.

The publication of Schorer's book in 1961 resulted in a spate of paperback reprints of his novels, but now in print are only Signet editions of ELMER GANTRY, DODSWORTH, and IT CAN'T HAPPEN HERE, plus, of course, MAIN STREET, BABBITT, and ARROWSMITH, which never have been out of print. Schorer also edited in paperback I'M A STRANGER HERE MYSELF AND OTHER STORIES (1962), which is no longer in print. There are in addition paperback reprints in the Popular Library of L's later novels, WORK OF ART, BETHEL MERRIDAY, KINGSBLOOD ROYAL, and THE GOD-SEEKER.

The only hardcover editions available are the Harbrace Classics editions of AR-ROWSMITH, BABBITT, and MAIN STREET, which also are available as a one-volume trilogy entitled L AT ZENITH with introduction by Schorer, and THE

* Of Special Importance

MAN WHO KNEW COOLIDGE (Freeport, N.Y., 1971).

A collection of L's non-fiction pieces was edited by Harry Maule and Melville Cane as THE MAN FROM MAIN STREET: A SL READER (New York, 1953), which contains among other things L's Nobel Prize speech.

BIOGRAPHY

Schorer's 867-page life of L is likely to remain the definitive biography. It is the "official" life, was commissioned by L's executors, and was nearly a decade in the writing. See "My Life and Nine-Year Captivity with SL," NYTBR, 20 August 1961, pp. 7, 26. Despite its having been authorized, it is an objective first-rate work by an able scholar. It is the indispensable work on the life and career of L, and one hardly needs to go beyond it. There are, however, a few other biographical sources that might be noted. The stories of his two marriages have been told, one by his first wife in Grace Hegger Lewis, WITH LOVE FROM GRACIE: SL 1912-1925 (New York, 1955), and the other by Vincent Sheean in DOROTHY AND RED (Boston, 1963), a book based on the Dorothy Thompson papers (see above). Thompson wrote her own memoir of her husband in "SL: A Postscript," AtlM 187 (June 1951): 73-74, and "The Boy and Man from Sauk Center," AtlM 206 (November 1960): 39-48.

There are important glimpses of L in memoirs of friends: Paul De Kruif's THE SWEEPING WIND (New York, 1962) recounts his helping L with ARROWSMITH; Frazier Hunt's ONE AMERICAN (New York, 1938) describes L at the peak of his career; George Jean Nathan's THE INTIMATE NOTEBOOKS (New York, 1932) details L's interest in the theater. Other accounts worth listing are Sheldon Grebstein, "SL's Minnesota Boyhood," MH 34 (1954): 85-89, and "The Education of a Rebel: SL at Yale," NEQ 28 (1955): 372-82; Ramon Guthrie, "The 'Labor Novel' that SL Never Wrote," NYHTB, 10 February 1952, pp. 1, 6; Perry Miller, "The Uncorruptible SL," AtlM 187 (April 1951): 30-34, the last an account of L's final days in Italy. August Derleth's THREE LITERARY MEN (New York, 1963) contains a memoir of L.

There is one book-length collection of letters: Harrison Smith, ed., FROM MAIN STREET TO STOCKHOLM: LETTERS OF SL, 1919-1930 (New York, 1952). These are letters between L and his publisher Alfred Harcourt. Other letters appear in King Hendricks and Irving Shepard, eds., LETTERS FROM JACK LONDON (New York, 1965), and James Napier, "Letters of SL to Joseph Hergesheimer, 1915-1922," AL 38 (1966): 236-46.

CRITICISM

Because the life of L, the social critic and satirist, is so closely tied to his novels, Schorer's SL: AN AMERICAN LIFE is an important critical study as well as a biography. But for students wanting a brief approach to L, Schorer's research and critical views are boiled down in his SL (UMPAW, 1963), a pamphlet that concludes: "He was not a great writer, but without his writing one cannot imagine modern American literature." This is a judgment that may well stand, and L seems to have taken his place as an essential but minor twentieth-century author. That he is essential is suggested by the fact that a SL NEWS-LETTER began publication in 1969 at St. Cloud (Minn.) State College; that he is minor is attested to by the availability of only a few of his novels and the modest level of scholarly attention he receives.

Besides Schorer's pamphlet there are two other brief treatments, both by James Lundquist: GUIDE TO SL (Columbus, 1970) and SL (New York, 1973). A good medium-length book is Grebstein's volume in the Twayne series, which concentrates on L's novels of the 1920's but also manages a comprehensive analysis of L's entire career and assesses the social relevance of his novels. Grebstein, who ranks L as a critical realist on the level of Dickens, sees his subject as more important than Schorer, who tends to damn with faint praise.

There is also a full-length, post-Schorer study in David Dooley's THE ART OF SL (Lincoln, Nebr., 1967). Dooley takes a rather carping view of L, whom he sees as the promulgator of a basically "alien view of America." Although he discusses the 1930 Nobel Prize speech at length and the critical reaction to it, this book does not add substantially to the previous work of Schorer and Grebstein.

An essential gathering of essays for the study of L is Mark Schorer, ed., SL: A COLLECTION OF CRITICAL ESSAYS (Englewood Cliffs, N.J., 1962), which is, as the editor says, "the best critical writing about SL." It's a good collection of 24 pieces, which begins with Schorer's judicious summary of L's critical fortunes. Represented here are early essays by H.L. Mencken, Rebecca West, Sherwood Anderson, Robert Morss Lovett, and Joseph Wood Krutch, all of which review L's novels of the 1920's. There also are summarizing statements by Constance Rourke, Maxwell Geismar, Vernon Parrington, Walter Lippmann, Lewis Mumford, and Alfred Kazin; R.P. Blackmur, Malcolm Cowley, and Edmund Wilson contributed additional essays to the collection. The range is broad--from West's delighted discovery of BABBITT to Walter Lippmann's denunciation of L's barbaric behavior and "compulsion to malice." Mumford's piece expresses some of the widespread dissatisfaction over L's winning the Nobel Prize.

There also are collections of essays devoted to L's best-known novels: Linda Wolfe and Mary Smith, eds., A CRITICAL COMMENTARY: "MAIN STREET" (New York, 1964); Robert Griffith, ed., TWENTIETH-CENTURY INTERPRETATIONS OF "ARROWSMITH": A COLLECTION OF CRITICAL ESSAYS (Englewood Cliffs, N.J., 1968); Martin Light, ed., MERRILL STUDIES IN "BABBITT" (Columbus, 1971).

Because L is very important in the history of the American novel, all the historians of the novel or historians of American literature in general have devoted a considerable amount of space to his work. A few of these are as follows:

Robert Spiller in THE CYCLE OF AMERICAN LITERATURE (New York, 1955), Ludwig Lewisohn in EXPRESSION IN AMERICA (New York, 1932), Van Wyck Brooks in THE CONFIDENT YEARS (New York, 1955), Carl Van Doren in THE AMERICAN NOVEL, 1789-1939 (New York, 1940), Edward Wagenknecht in CAVALCADE OF THE AMERICAN NOVEL (New York, 1952), and H.S. Canby in LHUS.

As suggested earlier, L, along with other lesser American novelists like London, Sinclair, and Buck, has enjoyed great popularity abroad, especially in the German-speaking world. Of the 24 dissertations written on L down through 1971, 11 of them were written in German, seven in Germany and four in Austria. Four doctoral studies of L appeared in German before there was even one in English.

Section 29

JACK LONDON (1876-1916)

Jack London (hereafter JL or L) was born in San Francisco. An illegitimate child raised by his mother and stepfather, he spent his childhood and early adolescence along the Oakland waterfront, a setting he would later use in his writings. In the forty years of his life he produced an enormous number of stories and novels as well as several plays, socialist tracts, and other volumes of nonfiction. In all of his writing he drew heavily on his experiences, particularly as a sailor, a Klondike gold miner, and a foreign correspondent. Rich in excitement and local color, his works have continued to be popular in America and abroad, most notably in Poland, Sweden, Russia, and Germany.

BIBLIOGRAPHY AND MANUSCRIPTS

Half a century after his death the first comprehensive bibliography finally appeared: Hensley Woodbridge, John London, and George Tweney, JL: A BIBLIOGRAPHY (Georgetown, Calif., 1966), a 422-page compilation of both primary and secondary materials. Since its appearance it has been updated and supplemented by Woodbridge in "JL: A Bibliography--A Supplement," ABC 17, iii (1966): 32-35; Earle Labor in "JL: An Addendum," ALR 2 (1968): 91-93; an anonymous contribution, "JL: A Bibliography, A Supplement," JLN 2 (1969): 5-25; John Nichol in "JL: A Bibliography, Addenda I," JLN 2 (1969): 84-87, Robert Woodward in "JL: A Bibliography, Addenda II," JLN 2 (1969): 88-90. Another recent but brief compilation is Dale Walker, THE FICTION OF JL: A CHRONOLOGICAL BIBLIOGRAPHY (El Paso, Tex., 1972), 40 pages. There is an unannotated listing of criticism in James Haydock, "JL: A Bibliography of Criticism," BB 23 (1960): 42-46. Earle Labor's forthcoming JL (TUSAS, 1974) will have a selected annotated bibliography of criticism. Vol. 5 of Jacob Blanck, BIBLIOGRAPHY OF AMERICAN LITERATURE (New Haven, 1955-69), lists L's writings, and the JLN, which began publication in 1967, may be expected to update L bibliography from time to time.

There are special collections of MSS, letters, and other documents at the University of Southern California, the Huntington Library, the San Francisco Public Library, the University of California at Los Angeles and Berkeley, and Stanford. There are also significant holdings at Indiana University, Princeton, Harvard, the New York Public Library, the University of Virginia, and the Wisconsin State Historical Society.

WORKS OF FICTION

Novels: A DAUGHTER OF THE SNOWS (1902), THE CRUISE OF THE DAZZLER (1902), *THE CALL OF THE WILD (1903), *THE SEA-WOLF (1904), THE GAME (1905), *WHITE FANG (1906), BEFORE ADAM (1906), THE IRON HEEL (1907), *MARTIN EDEN (1909), BURNING DAYLIGHT (1910), ADVENTURE (1911), SMOKE BELLEW (1912), THE ABYSMAL BRUTE (1913), THE VALLEY OF THE MOON (1913), THE MUTINY OF THE ELSINORE (1914), THE SCARLET PLAGUE (1915), THE STAR ROVER (1915), THE LITTLE LADY OF THE BIG HOUSE (1916), THE TURTLES OF TASMAN (1916), JERRY OF THE ISLANDS (1917), MICHAEL, BROTHER OF JERRY (1917), HEARTS OF THREE (1920. THE ASSASSINATION BUREAU, LTD. was completed from notes after L's death by Robert Fish and first published in 1963.

Short Stories: THE SON OF THE WOLF; TALES OF THE FAR NORTH (1900), THE GOD OF HIS FATHERS AND OTHER STORIES (1901), CHILDREN OF THE FROST (1902), THE FAITH OF MEN AND OTHER STORIES (1904), TALES OF THE FISH PATROL (1905), MOON-FACE AND OTHER STORIES (1906), LOVE OF LIFE AND OTHER STORIES (1906), LOST FACE (1910), WHEN GOD LAUGHS AND OTHER STORIES (1911), SOUTH SEA TALES (1911), THE HOUSE OF PRIDE AND OTHER TALES OF HAWAII (1912), A SON OF THE SON (1912), THE NIGHT-BORN (1913), THE STRENGTH OF THE STRONG (1914), THE RED ONE (1918), ON THE MAKALOA MAT (1919), DUTCH COURAGE AND OTHER STORIES (1922).

EDITIONS AND REPRINTS

The continued popularity of L is shown by the large number of his works still in print. Story collections in print are THE GOD OF HIS FATHERS AND OTHER STORIES, THE FAITH OF MEN AND OTHER STORIES, MOON-FACE AND OTHER STORIES, LOVE OF LIVE AND OTHER STORIES, STORIES OF HAWAII, and SOUTH SEA TALES. Available novels are THE CALL OF THE WILD (15 editions), WHITE FANG (nine editions), THE SEA-WOLF, THE IRON HEEL, MARTIN EDEN (four editions), BURNING DAYLIGHT, THE STAR ROVER, and THE GAME. There also are many selections of stories in print: in paperback-- SHORT STORIES OF JL (Funk and Wagnalls), SHORT STORIES (Airmont), THE BEST SHORT STORIES OF JL (Fawcett); in hard covers--JL'S TALES OF AD- VENTURE and BEST SHORT STORIES OF JL (Doubleday) and JL STORIES (Platt). There also are collections of longer works, among which are two editions of THE CALL OF THE WILD AND OTHER STORIES and GREAT SHORT WORKS OF JL (THE CALL OF THE WILD, WHITE FANG, and six stories) with an introduction by Earle Labor. James Sisson has edited JL'S ARTICLES AND SHORT STORIES IN THE (OAKLAND) HIGH SCHOOL "AEGIS" (Cedar Springs, Mich., 1971). An eight-volume Russian edition of L's works came out in 1956 and a 14-volume one in 1961. Collected editions are incomplete, but there are the Fitzroy Edition (London, 1963-   ), with each volume edited and introduced by I.O. Evans, and the multi-volume BODLEY HEAD JL (London, 1963-   ),

* Of Special Importance

edited by A.C. Marshall.

BIOGRAPHY

There are two popular, non-scholarly biographies: Irving Stone, SAILOR ON HORSEBACK: THE BIOGRAPHY OF JL (New York, 1938; reissued in 1947 and 1964 with the added sub-title, "A Biographical Novel") and Richard O'Connor, JL: A BIOGRAPHY (Boston, 1964). An unpublished biographical dissertation is Abraham Rothberg's "The House that Jack Built: A Study of JL, the Man, His Times, and His Works," DA 12 (1952): 428. Two rather subjective biographies have been written by L's wife and daughter: Charmian London, THE BOOK OF JL (New York, 1921), and Joan London, JL AND HIS TIMES: AN UNCONVENTIONAL BIOGRAPHY (New York, 1939). The latter was reprinted with an informative new introduction (Seattle, 1968).

L did not write an autobiography, but his various non-fiction volumes are all important for studying his life. THE KEMPTON-WACE LETTERS (written with Anna Strunksy) deal with intellectual issues; THE PEOPLE OF THE ABYSS describes London slum conditions; THE WAR OF THE CLASSES is a socialist tract; THE CRUISE OF THE SNARK recounts travels on L's boat; JOHN BARLEYCORN is an autobiographical memoir written to further the temperance movement. THE ROAD (repr. 1970 with intro. by King Hendricks) describes L's youthful experiences as a hobo. Also MARTIN EDEN is a Bildungsroman that follows closely closely L's own struggles as a young writer.

In addition Charmian London wrote two books about her life with L: THE LOG OF THE SNARK (New York, 1915) and OUR HAWAII (New York, 1917; rev. 1922). Memoirs of L appear in Martin Johnson's THROUGH THE SOUTH SEAS WITH JL (New York, 1913); Georgia Bamford's THE MYSTERY OF JL: SOME OF HIS FRIENDS, ALSO A FEW LETTERS--A REMINISCENCE (Oakland, 1931); Joseph Noel, FOOTLOOSE IN ARCADIA: A PERSONAL RECORD OF JL, GEORGE STERLING, AMBROSE BIERCE (New York, 1940); the JL number of OVERLAND MONTHLY: 90 (1932). Finally, King Hendricks and Irving Shepard have edited a letter collection, LETTERS FROM JL (New York, 1965), and a volume of fugitive material, JL REPORTS: WAR CORRESPONDENCE, SPORTS ARTICLES AND MISCELLANEOUS WRITING (Garden City, N.Y., 1970).

CRITICISM

There has been a great deal written about L, but much of it is popular rather than scholarly. Despite the lack of enthusiasm for L in academia he is still much alive, as the "Editions and Reprints" section above shows. He is especially popular abroad, as a quick glance at THE INDEX TRANSLATIONUM will indicate. Since 1966 there has been a quickening of interest in L, both on the popular and on the scholarly levels. This is reflected in the inauguration of the JLN, which provides tidbits for aficionados as well as more solid fare. The best place to begin serious study of L is with the work of three scholars: C.C. Walcutt, JL (UMPAW, 1966); Earle Labor, JL (TUSAS, scheduled for 1974); Franklin Walker, JL AND THE KLONDIKE: THE GENESIS OF AN AMERICAN WRITER (San Marino, Calif., 1966). Walcutt's pamphlet, though brief, is the work of an authority on literary naturalism. Labor's book suffers from the tight space limitations of the Twayne series, but it is by a knowledgeable London scholar and the most recent book. Walker's book is a careful, thoroughly documented study by a long-time expert on California literary history.

There have been several book-length studies devoted to more specialized aspects of L: Frederick Feied's NO PIE IN THE SKY: THE HOBO AS AMERICAN CULTURAL HERO IN THE WORKS OF JL, JOHN DOS PASSOS, AND JACK KEROUAC (New York, 1964) approaches L from one angle, while V.M. Bykov's JL (Moscow, 1964; rev. 1968) explains L's extreme popularity in Russia. Also there is an older study: Edward Payne's curious little book, THE SOUL OF JL (London, 1926).

L's stories have been treated several times: King Hendricks' pamphlet, JL: MASTER CRAFTSMAN OF THE SHORT STORY (Logan, Utah, 1966); Clara Margolin, JL'S SHORT STORIES: IRHE FORM UND IHRE GEHALT (Heidelberg, 1927); James McClintock, "JL's Short Stories," DA 29 (1968): 1902A-03A, which is one of the 17 dissertations that had been written on L through 1971; Blanche Williams in OUR SHORT STORY WRITERS (New York, 1920).

As one would expect, L has been studied often in relation to his era and as a social critic. One such book-length examination is Philip Foner's JL: AMERICAN REBEL (New York, 1947, 1964), which is a collection of L's social writings as well as a study of the man and his times. Also L's antagonistic views on literary criticism have been discussed: M.A. Isani, "JL on Norris' THE OCTOPUS," ALR 6 (1973): 66-69; David Sloane, "JL on Reviewing: An Addendum," ALR 6 (1973): 70-72; King Hendricks' pamphlet CREATOR AND CRITIC: A CONTROVERSY BETWEEN JL AND PHILO M. BUCK, JR. (Logan, Utah, 1961).

There is space here to cite only a few of the many articles and chapters in books on L. Some of the important ones include: F.L. Pattee's chapter, "The Prophet of the Last Frontier," in his SIDELIGHTS ON AMERICAN LITERATURE (New York, 1922); James McClintock's "JL's Use of Carl Jung's PSYCHOLOGY OF THE UNCONSCIOUS," AL 42 (1970): 336-47; C.C. Walcutt's chapter on L in AMERICAN LITERARY NATURALISM: A DIVIDED STREAM (Minneapolis, 1956); Gordon Mills' "The Symbolic Wilderness: James Fenimore Cooper and JL," NCF 13 (1959): 329-40; Jay Gurian's "The Romantic Necessity in Literary Naturalism; JL," AL 38 (1966): 112-20; Franklin Walker's "Ideas and Action in JL's Fiction" in Clarence Gohdes, ed., ESSAYS ON AMERICAN LITERATURE IN HONOR OF JAY B. HUBBELL (Durham, N.C., 1967); Earle Labor's "JL's Symbolic Wilderness: Four Versions," NCF 17 (1962): 149-61.

Besides this highly selective list it should be noted that ABC 17, iii (1966) devoted an entire issue to L.

Section 30
J(OHN) P(HILLIPS) MARQUAND (1893-1960)

J.P. Marquand (hereafter JPM, JM, or M) was born in Delaware, the son of a civil engineer, but he lived most of his adult life in New England, the scene of his most important fiction. Although his family was socially prominent, it was impecunious, and M went through Harvard on a scholarship. He began his career as a newspaperman in Boston, fought in France during World War I, and published his first novel in 1922. From that time until 1937 he wrote popular fiction and prospered. Then he turned to serious fictional studies of New England society and contemporary American culture. He was always a skilled literary craftsman whose work probably has been undervalued by the academic critics.

BIBLIOGRAPHY AND MANUSCRIPTS

There is no definitive bibliography of M, but several compilations by William White provide fairly extensive lists of primary and secondary materials: "JPM: A Preliminary Checklist," BB 19 (1949): 268-71; "Marquandiana," BB 20 (1950): 8-12; "JPM since 1950," BB 21 (1956): 230-34; "More Marquandiana, 1956-1968," SERIF 6 (1968): 33-36. White also provides bibliographical information for collectors in "On Collecting JPM," ABC 1 (May 1951): 5. In addition, there are selected bibliographies in John Gross's JPM (TUSAS, 1963), annotated; C. Hugh Holman's pamphlet JPM (UMPAW, 1965); Stephen Birmingham's THE LATE JPM: A BIOGRAPHY (Philadelphia, 1972). There are significant MS holdings at Yale, Harvard, the University of Chicago, and the New York Public Library.

WORKS OF FICTION

Novels: THE UNSPEAKABLE GENTLEMAN (1922), THE BLACK CARGO (1925), WARNING HILL (1930), MING YELLOW (1935), NO HERO (1935), THANK YOU, MR. MOTO (1936), THINK FAST, MR. MOTO (1937), *THE LATE GEORGE APLEY (1937), MR. MOTO IS SO SORRY (1938), *WICKFORD POINT (1939), DON'T ASK QUESTIONS (1941), *H.M. PULHAM, ESQ. (1941), LAST LAUGH, MR. MOTO (1942), *SO LITTLE TIME (1943), IT'S LOADED,

* Of Special Importance

MR. BAUER (1943), REPENT IN HASTE (1945), *B.F.'S DAUGHTER (1946), *POINT OF NO RETURN (1949), *MELVILLE GOODWIN, USA (1951), *SIN-CERELY, WILLIS WAYDE (1955), STOPOVER: TOKYO (1957), *WOMEN AND THOMAS HARROW (1958).

Stories: FOUR OF A KIND (1923), HAVEN'S END (1933), THIRTY YEARS (1954), LIFE AT HAPPY KNOLL (1957).

EDITIONS AND REPRINTS

There has been no collected edition of M's works, but many titles are in print. THE LATE GEORGE APLEY was issued by the Modern Library in 1940 with an introduction by the author, and in 1956 an omnibus edition of APLEY, WICK-FORD POINT, and H.M. PULHAM, ESQ. was published as NORTH OF GRAND CENTRAL, also with introductions both by M and Kenneth Roberts. In addition the following titles, among M's ten most important novels, are in print in paperback editions: THE LATE GEORGE APLEY, WICKFORD POINT, H.M. PULHAM, ESQ., SO LITTLE TIME, B.F.'S DAUGHTER, POINT OF NO RETURN, WOMEN AND THOMAS HARROW. The Mr. Moto books also are available in paper.

BIOGRAPHY

Biographically speaking, M has been fairly well served. The first book was Philip Hamburger's JPM, ESQUIRE: A PORTRAIT IN THE FORM OF A NOVEL (New York, 1952), originally published in NY. It is an interesting study of M's life and attitudes, and like most NY profiles it is good literary journalism, though undocumented for scholarly purposes. A recent work, Birmingham's biography (see above), has the advantage of having been written after M's death and has the perspective of time, but it is hastily done and will not satisfy serious readers. Much material in this book comes from Carol Brandt, of the firm of Brandt and Brandt, literary agents. Another shorter sketch is Roger Butterfield's "JPM," LIFE 17 (31 July 1949): 64–66, which preceded Hamburger's book and provided one of the earliest gatherings of biographical data. To these works should be added Josephine Driver's "The Young JM," AtlM 216 (August 1965): 69–72, written by a high school classmate; Kenneth Roberts' essay (mentioned above); and Eric Larrabee's "Two Gentlemen from Newburyport," AH 12 (April 1961): 46–49 (the other gentleman being Timothy Dexter, an eighteenth-century Newburyporter about whom M wrote a biography). There were many interviews with M during his career, a couple of which will have to suffice: Harvey Breit, "An Interview with JPM," NYTBR, 24 April 1949, p. 35; Robert Van Gelder, "M Unburdens Himself," NYTBR, 7 April 1940, pp. 20–21, reprinted in WRITERS AND WRITING (New York, 1946). M also has written about himself in THIRTY YEARS (1954), which in addition to short stories contains commentary, sketches, travel accounts, and lectures; also "Apley, Wickford Point, and Pulham: My Early Struggles," AtlM 198 (September 1956): 71–76. Finally, one should look up the numerous obituary notices that appeared after M's death in 1960.

* Of Special Importance

CRITICISM

There are two separately published critical studies of M: the previously cited works of Gross and Holman. The latter is an excellent brief overview of M and his work in 45 pages and is the obvious place to begin any study of its subject. Holman analyzes succinctly the major works and puts M into the context of contemporary American literature. Gross's book is longer, more detailed, and has time to go into M's critical reputation, but it lacks the mature analysis and expert selection of detail in Holman's pamphlet.

It was not until M began writing serious social novels with THE LATE GEORGE APLEY (1937), which won the Pulitzer Prize, that the critics began writing about him. Some of the useful early discussions: Harlan Hatcher, "JPM," CE 1 (1939): 107-18; Percy Boynton, "The Novels of Puritan Decay," NEQ 13 (1940): 626-27, reprinted in AMERICA IN CONTEMPORARY FICTION (Chicago, 1940); Hershel Brickell, "Miss Glasgow and Mr. M," VQR 17 (1941): 405-17. During the 1950's M began receiving minor but significant attention. Granville Hicks in "M of Newburyport," HM 200 (April 1950): 101-08, found M a very competent sociologist in his fictional studies of Massachusetts society. Leo Gurko in "The High-Level Formula of JPM," ASch 21 (1952): 443-53, discussed M's recurrent use of formula in his fiction as a limitation but placed him high in the literary hierarchy. Charles Brady's "JPM: Martini-Age Victorian" in Harold Gardiner, ed., FIFTY YEARS OF THE AMERICAN NOVEL: A CHRISTIAN APPRAISAL (New York, 1952), dealt generally and favorably with the body of M's work, analyzing themes and character. Later in the 1950's less favorable estimates appeared in Maxwell Geismar's AMERICAN MODERNS: FROM REBELLION TO CONFORMITY (New York, 1958) and in Edward Gordon's "What's Happened to Humor?" EJ 47 (1958): 127-33. Geismar, while admitting M's technical skill, thought he missed being an important novelist, while Gordon measured M against Mark Twain to the former's obvious disadvantage. Another brief but well-informed essay of the same year is Alfred Kazin's "JPM and the American Failure," AtlM 202 (1958): 152-54, and a longer, excellent article, assessing M's major works, is Franz Oppenheimer's "Lament for Unbought Grace: The Novels of JPM," AR 18 (1958): 47-61.

Most of the writers on M have chosen to examine him in toto, but there are a few scrutinies from special angles. Two of these are George Goodwin's "The Last Hurrah: George Apley and Frank Skeffington," MR 1 (1960): 461-71, which is a political look, and A.D. Van Nostrand's "Fiction's Flagging Man of Commerce," EJ 48 (1959): 1-11, which is a probe of the businessman in literature.

In the decade of the 1960's M has taken his place among the significant lesser novelists of this century, and studies of the contemporary novel usually discuss M's accomplishment. Worthwhile works of this sort include Chester Eisinger's FICTION OF THE FORTIES (Chicago, 1963) and Michael Millgate's AMERICAN SOCIAL FICTION: JAMES TO COZZENS (New York, 1964).

Section 31

HENRY MILLER (1891-)

Henry Miller (hereafter HM or M) is a difficult writer to categorize. As one of his critics puts it: "HM is not only a writer, he is a phenomenon." Like Rousseau and Byron in their day "he should probably be viewed as a public figure." Another writes that he is neither the greatest living author, as some of his admirers believe, nor the foulest writer of nonsense, as his detractors would have it. He is a "minor but intriguing writer whose best works are the rhetorical gestures of a rebel-buffoon." His life has led from the streets of Brooklyn to Paris, where he was one of our more colorful expatriates in the 1930's, and back to the United States. Since World War II he has lived in California, first as a sort of cult-leader at Big Sur and in recent years quietly and silently in Los Angeles.

BIBLIOGRAPHY AND MANUSCRIPTS

There is a real need for an up-to-date and complete bibliography of both primary and secondary works. This lacuna is surprising in view of the enormous public attention M has commanded in the past two decades. The best listings available are Thomas Moore, BIBLIOGRAPHY OF HM (Minneapolis, 1961), which is largely primary material; E.L. Riley, HM: AN INFORMAL BIBLIOG-RAPHY, 1924-1960 (Hays, Kans., 1961), which contains both primary and secondary listings; Maxine Renkin, "Bibliography of HM, 1945-1961," TCL 7 (1962): 180-90, which adds secondary items to the previous compilations. Renkin's list was published separately by Alan Swallow (Denver, 1962). For earlier listings of criticism and reviews before 1945, one should consult Bern Porter's HM: A CHRONOLOGY AND BIBLIOGRAPHY (Baltimore, 1945). A more up-to-date but selective checklist of criticism appears as an appendix to Edward Mitchell, ed., HM: THREE DECADES OF CRITICISM (New York, 1971).

Because of the tangled publication history of M's works (many things published as ephemeral pamphlets, entire works or excerpts pirated, books brought out by obscure private publishers, original publication nearly always in Europe, etc.), it is worth noting the location of two extensive collections of M's printed works: The HM Collection at the University of California at Los Angeles; the J. Rives Childs Collection at Randolph-Macon College (for a description of the latter see RALS 1 [1971]: 121-25, and the appendix to the M-Childs letters cited below).

Significant holdings of MSS also are at the University of California at Los Angeles, Harvard, Princeton, the New York Public Library, the University of Virginia, and Randolph-Macon College.

WORKS OF FICTION

M's works defy easy classification. Everything he wrote is more or less auto-biographical, and nothing he wrote can comfortably be called fiction. He wrote narrative and expository prose, and critics usually treat his narratives as fiction. The following list includes only major works (not universally agreed upon) categorized as narrative and exposition.

Narrative: *TROPIC OF CANCER (1934), *BLACK SPRING (1936), *TROPIC OF CAPRICORN (1939), *THE COLOSSUS OF MAROUSSI (1941), THE AIR-CONDITIONED NIGHTMARE (1945), THE ROSY CRUCIFIXION: SEXUS (1949), PLEXUS (1953), NEXUS (1960).

Exposition: ALLER RETOUR NEW YORK (1935), MAX AND THE WHITE PHA-GOCYTES (1938), HAMLET (1943), BIG SUR AND THE ORANGES OF HIERO-NYMUS BOSCH (1957).

EDITIONS AND REPRINTS

Since 1961 when THE TROPIC OF CANCER was first overtly published in the United States M's works have been widely reprinted and freely sold. His works now are generally all in print in paperback and/or hardcover editions. In addition there are a number of editions of his writings by other hands: Kenneth Rexroth introduced a slight anthology, NIGHTS OF LOVE AND LAUGHTER (New York, 1955); Lawrence Powell introduced THE INTIMATE HM (New York, 1959); Lawrence Durrell edited THE HM READER (New York, 1959; Freeport, N.Y., 1972); Thomas Moore edited HM ON WRITING (New York, 1964).

BIOGRAPHY

There is no full-length, objective biography, though there is plenty of biographical material available from H's own work, reminiscences of friends, letters and interviews. Foremost there is Alfred Perles' MY FRIEND HM: AN INTI-MATE BIOGRAPHY (London, 1955), written by one of M's close associates during his Paris years in the 1930's. Perles and Lawrence Durrell, another old friend, collaborated to produce ART AND OUTRAGE (London, 1959), which is a correspondence between the two about M. A gathering by many friends of

* Of Special Importance

recollections, comments, and tributes was edited by Bern Porter as THE HAPPY
ROCK: A BOOK ABOUT HM (Berkeley, 1945).

Many of M's letters have been published, though only a tiny part of the 25,000
he estimated he had written down to 1939. George Wickes edited LAWRENCE
DURRELL AND HM: A PRIVATE CORRESPONDENCE (New York, 1963); Gun-
ther Stuhlmann edited HM: LETTERS TO ANAIS NIN (New York, 1965), another old friend from M's Paris days. Also there is Richard Wood, ed., COL-
LECTOR'S QUEST: THE CORRESPONDENCE OF HM AND J. RIVES CHILDS,
1947-1965 (Charlottesville, Va., 1965); and William Gordon, ed., WRITER AND
CRITIC: A CORRESPONDENCE WITH HM (Baton Rouge, La., 1968), the latter
an exchange that took place while Gordon was preparing his book (see below)
for publication. Four of M's books also are actually letters: ALLER RETOUR
NEW YORK is a long letter to Perles; HAMLET is an exchange of letters with
Michel Fraenkel; SEMBLANCE OF A DEVOTED PAST (Berkeley, 1944) is letters
to Emil Schnellock; THE PLIGHT OF THE CREATIVE ARTIST IN THE UNITED
STATES OF AMERICA (Berkeley, 1944) is a group of open letters.

As noted earlier, most of M's writing is autobiographical, and nearly all of the
more than several million words he has written contributes to his biography. The
trick, of course, is in separating the fact from the fiction. M also has given
many interviews, two of which are George Wickes' "The Art of Fiction--HM,"
PARIS REVIEW, no. 28 (1962): 129-59; and FACE TO FACE WITH HM: CON-
VERSATIONS WITH GEORGES BELMONT (London, 1970; Chicago, 1971). The
latter is a translation of a French radio and television interview conducted by
an old friend. Also of some use for biographical purposes is M's MY LIFE AND
TIMES (Chicago, 1971), a coffee table book which is about half pictures and
half text. The text was worked up by Bradley Smith from taped conversations.

CRITICISM

One needs to tread warily through the rather extensive jungle of M criticism.
M's position as a phenomenon and public figure, the eminence grise in the obscenity trials, has generated a great deal of writing about him. For many years
his books were printed in France and smuggled into the United States by travel-
ers, but he was not really known and he was not taken very seriously by literary journalists and academic critics. During the 1950's, however, when he was
living at Big Sur and becoming well known, he began to interest scholars and
to attract more and more attention. Whereas the criticism a generation ago was
likely to be either shrill attack or uncritical adulation, gradually it became
more and more dispassionate. At the conclusion of the court cases which settled the obscenity matter and allowed M's books to circulate freely, his work
was widely printed and sold. As the public mores changed, it became possible
to read M in a more neutral atmosphere.

There are two excellent collections which enable one to follow the debate over
M's work through the decades: George Wickes, ed., HM AND THE CRITICS
(Carbondale, Ill., 1963), 23 selections ranging from George Orwell's early essay

in praise of M to material on the litigation over M's TROPIC OF CANCER. There are also interesting essays by Frederick Hoffman, Edmund Wilson, Philip Rahv, and Kenneth Rexroth. Nearly a decade later Edward Mitchell edited HM: THREE DECADES OF CRITICISM (New York, 1971), 14 essays with only slight duplication from Wickes' collection, the last six covering the decade of the 1960's. Included here are such pieces as Karl Shapiro's well-known essay, "The Greatest Living Author," and Frank Kermode's acutely dispassionate analysis of what kind of a writer M is.

The best place for the beginner to approach M is through Wickes' lucid pamphlet HM (UMPAW, 1966), which provides a clear introduction to the subject; and after Wickes one may read Kingsley Widmer's HM (TUSAS, 1963). Widmer is not a M cultist and finds a great deal of slag with the pure metal of M's best work. But he's a perceptive critic and his analysis of the "rebel-buffoon" is acute.

There have been a goodly number of books on M in the past dozen years. Preceding Widmer's was Annette Baxter's HM: EXPATRIATE (Pittsburgh, 1961), which began as a Brown University dissertation in American studies. It is a good study of M's expatriate stance and his attacks on America as a major theme in his work, but it is not literary analysis. On the other hand, Jane Nelson's FORM AND IMAGE IN THE FICTION OF HM (Detroit, 1970) is a dense--some may find it impenetrable--Jungian reading of M's works in which M's dream passages are analyzed and archetypal patterns studied. Another academic study, one which couples M and Beckett, is Ihab Hassan's THE LITERATURE OF SILENCE: HM AND SAMUEL BECKETT (New York, 1967). Hassan argues the thesis that "literature turning against itself, aspires to silence" and at the same time writes a good, concise account of M's life and work. William Gordon's THE MIND AND ART OF HM (Baton Rouge, La., 1968), which treats M as a major author, is a very serious, humorless discussion which misses M's ironic playfulness. A rather off-beat book on M is Sidney Omarr's HM: HIS WORLD OF URANIA (London, 1968), a study of the astrological references in M's works.

Because M has gotten inextricably mixed with sociology, one can scarcely consider him apart from his times. Two good studies of the censorship battle appeared after the litigation ended: Charles Rembar's THE END OF OBSCENITY: THE TRIALS OF LADY CHATTERLY, "TROPIC OF CANCER," AND "FANNY HILL" (New York, 1968), Rembar being a Grove Press lawyer who was in the thick of the battle; E.R. Hutchinson's "TROPIC OF CANCER" ON TRIAL: A CASE HISTORY OF CENSORSHIP (New York, 1968).

The public attention that M received in the 1950's and 1960's resulted in 11 dissertations in addition to a great number of critical essays and books. But M is no longer a figure of much controversy, and now that his books have lost the power to shock, his writing must stand on its own merits. Michael Hoffman in "Yesterday's Rebel," WHR 24 (1970): 271-74, summarizes this situation well: academic critics have made M into one of the standard twentieth-century authors, but as his works have lost much of their aura of controversy, they also have lost much of their interest.

Section 32

KATHERINE ANNE PORTER (1890-)

Katherine Anne Porter (hereafter KAP or P) was born in Indian Creek, Texas, but she has lived in Europe, Mexico, and various northern American cities for most of her adult life. She was educated in private schools but ran away at 16 to get married (she was divorced at 19) and during her early years supported herself through journalism. Since publishing her first collection of stories in 1930, she has been a professional writer, and in recent years she has been a lecturer or visiting professor at numerous universities. She writes slowly, revises extensively, and her considerable reputation is based on a fairly small body of work. Although she is generally regarded as a Southern writer, only part of her work uses Southern material, and she also writes about Mexico, the urban East, and Europe.

BIBLIOGRAPHY AND MANUSCRIPTS

The best bibliography for the study of P is Louise Waldrip and Shirley Bauer, A BIBLIOGRAPHY OF THE WORKS OF KAP AND A BIBLIOGRAPHY OF THE CRITICISM OF THE WORKS OF KAP (Metuchen, N.J., 1969). This compilation is up-to-date, annotated, and well organized and supersedes such earlier lists as William Sylvester, "A Selected and Critical Bibliography of the Uncollected Works of KAP," BB 19 (1947): 46, and Edward Schwartz, KAP: A CRITICAL BIBLIOGRAPHY (New York, 1953) reprinted from BNYPL 57 (1953): 211-47. Also useful are the bibliographies by George Core in Louis Rubin, ed., BIBLIOGRAPHICAL GUIDE TO THE STUDY OF SOUTHERN LITERATURE (Baton Rouge, La., 1969), in Lodwick Hartley and George Core, eds., KAP: A CRITICAL SYMPOSIUM (Athens, Ga., 1969), and in George Hendrick's KAP (TUSAS, 1965).

Yale and Princeton have significant collections of P MSS, and there are some letters at the American Academy of Arts and Letters in New York, the Tennessee State Library in Nashville, and in the Horace Liveright Papers at the University of Pennsylvania. P has given her papers to the University of Maryland. There is some material at the University of Texas.

WORKS OF FICTION

Novels: PALE HORSE, PALE RIDER: THREE SHORT NOVELS (1939), SHIP OF FOOLS (1962).

Stories: FLOWERING JUDAS (1930), FLOWERING JUDAS AND OTHER STORIES (1935), THE LEANING TOWER AND OTHER STORIES (1944), COLLECTED STORIES (1964).

EDITIONS AND REPRINTS

FLOWERING JUDAS AND OTHER STORIES (1935) contained the stories in the original FLOWERING JUDAS plus "Hacienda," which had been published separately in 1934, and three others. Then PALE HORSE, PALE RIDER (1939) incorporated with the title novelette "Noon Wine," also published separately in 1937, and "Old Mortality." THE OLD ORDER: STORIES OF THE SOUTH (1955) was a selection of previously published stories about the South. COLLECTED STORIES (1964) contained four tales previously uncollected. P's publisher, Harcourt, Brace, keeps all of her work in print, and the Modern Library edition of FLOWERING JUDAS AND OTHER STORIES (1940) contains a brief introduction by the author. There is a Signet paperback edition of PALE HORSE, PALE RIDER with afterword by Mark Schorer.

BIOGRAPHY

P's biography has yet to be written, and there still are many gaps in what is known about her early life. Two unpublished M.A. theses contain pioneering biographical work: Donald Stalling, "KAP: Life and the Literary Mirror" (Texas Christian University, 1951); K.A. Sexton, "KAP's Years in Denver" (University of Colorado, 1961). George Hendrick's volume in the Twayne series contains a short biographical chapter plus chronology, and there is a good deal of autobiographical material in P's THE COLLECTED ESSAYS AND OCCASIONAL WRITINGS (1970), especially in the sections entitled "Personal and Particular," "Biographical," and "Mexican." Less than half of this material appeared earlier in THE DAYS BEFORE (1952, 1971).

From time to time P's letters have appeared in print: "On First Meeting T.S. Eliot," SHENANDOAH 12, ii (1961): 25-26, and Donald Sutherland, "Old Woman River: A Correspondence with KAP," SR 74 (1966): 754-67; both reprinted in COLLECTED ESSAYS. Also there is "Some Observations on the Genesis of SHIP OF FOOLS: A Letter from KAP," PMLA 84 (1969): 136-37. See in addition three letters to the book editor of the San Antonio EXPRESS NEWS on January 9, March 13, and April 3, 1966. Also useful are the letters to P in Brom Weber, ed., THE LETTERS OF HART CRANE (New York, 1952; Berkeley, 1965).

Additional biographical information may be gleaned from the numerous interviews

P has given, some of which are: Robert Van Gelder, "KAP at Work" in his WRITERS AND WRITING (New York, 1946); Elizabeth Janeway, "For KAP SHIP OF FOOLS Was a Lively Twenty-two Year Voyage," NYTBR, 1 April 1962, pp. 4-5; Barbara Thompson, "KAP: An Interview," PARIS REVIEW, no. 29 (1963): 87-114; reprinted in KAP: A CRITICAL SYMPOSIUM (see above); James Ruoff, "KAP Comes to Kansas," MQ 4 (1963): 396-97; Hank Lopez, "A Country and Some People I Love," HM 231 (September, 1965): 58-68.

Bits of P's journals have been published in "Notes on Writing" in James Laughlin, ed., NEW DIRECTIONS IN PROSE AND POETRY (Norwalk, Conn., 1940; repr. COLLECTED ESSAYS). Also important is the reminiscence of her friend Glenway Wescott, "KAP Personally," in his IMAGES OF TRUTH: REMEMBRANCES AND CRITICISM (New York, 1962; repr. KAP: A CRITICAL SYMPOSIUM).

CRITICISM

A convenient place to begin the study of P is with Ray West's pamphlet, KAP (UMPAW, 1963), a competent 46-page study, or with John Mooney's pamphlet, THE FICTION AND CRITICISM OF KAP (Pittsburgh, 1957; rev. ed., 1962), which was the pioneering monograph on its subject. For those who want a longer discussion Hendrick's book is useful and reliable. Hendrick devotes much of his attention to a careful reading of the stories, approves with reservations of SHIP OF FOOLS, and surveys the voluminous criticism surrounding that novel.

The most ambitious study of P's work is W.L. Nance, KAP AND THE ART OF REJECTION (Chapel Hill, N.C., 1964), which began as one of the ten dissertations written on P so far. This is a detailed reading of the stories and SHIP OF FOOLS and develops the thesis that P's work is united by the theme of rejection of life and love. Nance often links P's life to her fiction because he finds much autobiography in it, and his final view of P is rather unfavorable. Nance's thesis is vigorously contested by Caroline Gordon in "KAP and the ICM," HM 229 (November 1964): 156-58. A more recent book-length study is M.M. Liberman's KAP'S FICTION (Detroit, 1971), which incorporates his earlier defenses of SHIP OF FOOLS (CRITICISM 8, 10 [1966, 1968]: 377-88, 65-71) with additional chapters on the stories, but the book does not provide the overview of P's fiction that one would like. Another separate publication, also a pamphlet, is Winfred Emmons' KAP: THE REGIONAL STORIES (Austin, Tex., 1967), part of a series on Southwestern writers. Since P is only partly a Southwestern writer, the scope of this study is severely limited and allows no chance for a broad view of P's fiction.

Perhaps the most useful recent book on P is KAP: A CRITICAL SYMPOSIUM, which contains 17 essays by various hands. It begins with the pieces by Thompson and Wescott (see above) and includes excellent essays by Robert Penn Warren, Eudora Welty, Cleanth Brooks, and John Aldridge. There also are essays by Ray West and Robert Heilman and Liberman's defense of SHIP OF FOOLS (see above). The essays by Welty and Brooks, along with another piece by Warren, originally appeared in YR 55 (1966) as birthday tributes to P. Warren's YR article, "Uncorrupted Consciousness: The Stories of KAP," pp. 280-90, and should be added to his essay reprinted in A CRITICAL SYMPOSIUM and his introduction to Schwartz' bibliography (see above). All of the essays in CRITICAL SYMPOSIUM are not favorable. Against Warren's view in "Irony with a Center" that many of P's stories are unsurpassed in modern literature, Aldridge believes that P hardly deserves the high praise she has received.

This debate over P's work reached a crescendo in 1962 when she published SHIP OF FOOLS, which had been in progress for twenty years and which became a best seller. As it is her only full-length novel and had been awaited for such a long time, it was widely reviewed and commented upon. The MLA annual bibliography for 1963 and 1964, Hendrick's bibliography, and AAL, 1950-67 list many of the more academic critiques. Stanley Hyman in "Archetypal Woman," NeL 45 (April 1962): 23-24, was disgusted by the book, and Theodore Solotaroff in "SHIP OF FOOLS and the Critic," COMMENTARY 34 (1962): 277-86, thought the book boring, repetitive, and a technical failure. There were many defenders, of course, among whom was Louis Auchincloss, who reviewed the book and then wrote about it again in PIONEERS AND CARETAKERS: A STUDY OF NINE AMERICAN WOMEN NOVELISTS (Minneapolis, 1965), Mark Schorer in NYTBR (1 April 1962), and Heilman and Liberman in the essays previously cited.

There have been a good many excellent articles on P's fiction in the past 20 years, but there is space to mention only a few of particular interest. P has been treated as a Southern writer by Louis Rubin in the book he edited with Robert Jacobs, SOUTHERN RENASCENCE: THE LITERATURE OF THE MODERN SOUTH (Baltimore, 1953), and Frederick Hoffman in THE ART OF SOUTHERN FICTION: A STUDY OF SOME MODERN WRITERS (Carbondale, Ill., 1967). Two articles treat P's interest in Mexico: W.L. Nance, "KAP and Mexico," SWR 55 (1970): 143-53, and Colin Partridge, "My Familiar Country: An Image of Mexico in the Work of KAP," SSF 7 (1970): 597-614. Finally, one might mention as significant Edward Schwartz' discussion of the Miranda stories in "The Fictions of Memory," SWR 45 (1960): 204-15, Marjorie Ryan's partial study of P's debt to Joyce in "DUBLINERS and the Stories of KAP," AL 31 (1960): 464-73, and P's "Noon Wine: The Sources," YR 46 (1956): 22-39; reprinted in COLLECTED ESSAYS with other self-critical statements in a section called "On Writing."

Section 33

WILLIAM SYDNEY PORTER (O. HENRY) (1862-1910)

William Sydney Porter (hereafter WSP or P), better known by his pen name O. Henry (hereafter OH), is probably the most popular writer of short stories that American literature has produced. Although he died more than six decades ago, his stories continue to be read, and his short but colorful career still attracts interest. Born in North Carolina and given little formal education, P gravitated to Texas to seek his fortune. He was a bank teller and then journalist, and when he was accused of embezzling money from the bank, he fled to Honduras. Later he returned to face trial in Texas and was convicted. During his term in prison he began writing stories and after his release went to New York and immediately rocketed to fame as a writer. In six years (1904-1910) he acquired a reputation as a wizard of the short story form. He had a good sense of humor, manipulated ironic coincidence with great skill, and put his trademark on the surprise ending.

BIBLIOGRAPHY AND MANUSCRIPTS

The best bibliography available, though incomplete, is P.S. Clarkson, A BIBLIOGRAPHY OF WSP (Caldwell, Ida., 1938), which lists works by and about P. Briefer listings may be found in the following: the appendix to P's WAIFS AND STRAYS (1917); W.P. Trent, et al, CAMBRIDGE HISTORY OF AMERICAN LITERATURE (New York, 1917-20); G.L. Paine, ed., SOUTHERN PROSE WRITERS: REPRESENTATIVE SELECTIONS (New York, 1947); LHUS; Johnson; E.H. Long, "OH (WSP) (1862-1910)," ALR 1 (1967): 93-99.

There are special collections of MS material at the Greensboro, N.C., Public Library, Duke University, the University of North Carolina at Chapel Hill, and Baylor University. Other significant holdings are at Harvard, Princeton, the New York Public Library, and Mills College.

SHORT STORIES

CABBAGES AND KINGS (1904), *THE FOUR MILLION (1906), THE TRIMMED LAMP (1907), HEART OF THE WEST (1907), THE VOICE OF THE CITY (1908),

* Of Special Importance

THE GENTLE GRAFTER (1908), ROADS OF DESTINY (1909), OPTIONS (1909), STRICTLY BUSINESS (1910), WHIRLIGIGS (1910), SIXES AND SEVENS (1911), ROLLING STONES (1912), WAIFS AND STRAYS (1917).

EDITIONS AND REPRINTS

The standard edition of P now is THE COMPLETE WORKS OF OH, 2 vols. (New York, 1953). Because of P's extreme popularity there have been many complete editions and selections of his work since his death. The first was THE COMPLETE WORKS OF OH, 12 vols. (1912), which was followed by the MANUSCRIPT EDITION, 14 vols. (1912), THE AUTHORIZED EDITION, 14 vols. (1913), THE MEMORIAL EDITION, 14 vols. (1917), THE BIOGRAPHICAL EDITION, 18 vols. (1929). There have been various one-volume editions: Bennett Cerf and V.H. Cartmell, eds., BEST STORIES OF OH (1945); OH'S COPS AND ROBBERS: OH'S BEST DETECTIVE AND CRIME STORIES, selected with intro. Ellery Queen (1948); OH STORIES: THE AMERICAN SCENE AS DEPICTED BY THE MASTER OF SHORT STORIES, intro. Harry Golden (1962); OH'S NEW YORK, selected with intro. Donald Adams (1962), TALES OF OH (1969).

To these editions should be added O. HENRYANA: SEVEN ODDS AND ENDS, POETRY AND SHORT STORIES (1920), POSTSCRIPTS, ed. with intro. Florence Stratton (1923), OH ENCORE: STORIES AND ILLUSTRATIONS USUALLY UNDER THE NAME, THE POST MAN (Dallas, Tex., 1936; New York, 1939), anonymous material from the HOUSTON POST attributed to P by the editor.

BIOGRAPHY

As one might expect of a colorful, popular author, P has not lacked biographers. The best life is Gerald Langford, ALIAS OH: A BIOGRAPHY OF WSP (New York, 1957). Also reliable and scholarly though superseded is E.H. Long, OH: THE MAN AND HIS WORK (Philadelphia, 1949). Of historic interest is the first and authorized biography, C.A. Smith, OH BIOGRAPHY (New York, 1916). In addition there are various reminiscences: Seth Moyle, MY FRIEND: OH (New York, 1914); Al Jennings, THROUGH THE SHADOWS WITH OH (New York, 1921), which deals with P's Latin American and prison experiences; Frances Maltby, THE DIMITY SWEETHEART (Richmond, Va., 1930), about P's courtship; R.H. Davis and Arthur Maurice, THE CALIPH OF BAGDAD (New York, 1931); W.W. Williams, THE QUIET LODGER OF IRVING PLACE (New York, 1936). The latest biography is Richard O'Connor, OH: THE LEGENDARY LIFE OF WSP (New York, 1970), a pleasant narrative biography which is less reliable than Langford's work.

Additional biographical material may be found in P's LETTERS TO LITHOPOLIS FROM OH TO MABEL WAGNALLS (New York, 1922); Clarence Gohdes, "Some Letters by OH," SAQ 38 (1939): 31-39; E.P. Lyle, Jr., and Edward Dieckmann, Jr., "Portrait of OH: the Man on the Second Floor," AM 84 (1957): 89-92; Cathleen Pike, OH IN NORTH CAROLINA, ed. R.C. Moore (Chapel

Hill, N.C., 1957), a 29-page pamphlet; Malcolm McLean, OH in Honduras,"
ALR 3 (1968): 39-46; the records of P's trial, published as WSP . . . VS.
UNITED STATES (Austin, Tex., 1940).

CRITICISM

Although P still gets into the anthologies, his reputation in the academy today
is not very high. Yet he still interests some scholars, and there are plenty of
serious considerations of his work. One should begin the critical study of P
with Eugene Current-Garcia, OH (WSP) (TUSAS, 1965) or with E.H. Long, OH:
AMERICAN REGIONALIST (Austin, Tex., 1969). Both are brief, compact
studies by knowledgeable American scholars. Also useful and informative is
Joseph Gallegly, FROM ALAMO PLAZA TO JACK HARRIS'S SALOON: OH
AND THE SOUTHWEST HE KNEW (The Hague, 1970).

The first serious evaluation of P's stories was H.J. Forman, "OH's Short Stories,"
NAR, 187 (1908): 781-83, but soon after his death there were Hyder Rollins,
"OH," SR 22 (1914): 213-32; Stephen Leacock, "The Amazing Genius of OH,"
in his ESSAYS AND LITERARY STUDIES (New York, 1916); Carl Van Doren,
"OH," TR 2 (1917): 248-59. All of these essays were admiring, but there
were dissenters: F.L. Pattee, "The Journalization of American Literature,"
UNPOPULAR REVIEW 7 (1917): 374-94, and in his THE DEVELOPMENT OF
THE AMERICAN SHORT STORY (New York, 1923); also see N.B. Fagin in
SHORT STORY WRITING: AN ART OR A TRADE? (New York, 1923).

P is another writer who interests Europeans. Although only one American has
written a dissertation on P, two Germans, one Austrian and one Frenchman have
so treated him (See DAL), and in Russia he has been continuously popular: see
Deming Brown, SOVIET ATTITUDES TOWARD AMERICAN WRITING (Princeton,
1962). A good example of favorable Russian comment is Roman Samarin, "OH:
'A Really Remarkable Writer,'" SovR 3 (1962): 55-58. Other articles on P
appeared in Germany and Japan in the 1960's.

Some useful specialized studies: F.M. Kercheville, "OH and Don Alfonso,"
NMQ 1 (1931): 367-88, on P's knowledge of Spanish; P.S. Clarkson, "A De-
composition of Cabbages and Kings," AL 7 (1935): 195-202, a scholarly analysis of how the stories were originally cut and spliced; L.W. Courtney, "OH's
Case Reconsidered," AL 14 (1943): 261-71, proof that P received a fair trial
and was unquestionably guilty of embezzlement; W.B. Gates, "OH and Shakespeare," SHAKESPEARE ASSOC. BUL. 19 (1944): 20-25; E.C. Echols, "OH's
Shaker of Attic Salt" and "OH and the Classics," CJ 43, 44 (1948): 488-89,
209-10; E.H. Long, "OH as a Regional Artist," in Clarence Gohdes, ed.,
ESSAYS ON AMERICAN LITERATURE IN HONOR OF JAY B. HUBBELL (Durham, N.C., 1967). A more recent general study of P is D.F. Peel, "A
Critical Study of the Short Stories of OH," N.W. MO. STATE COLLEGE
STUDIES 25 (1961): 3-24. Finally, two interesting evaluations by other writers
are Upton Sinclair, BILL PORTER: A DRAMA OF OH IN PRISON (Pasadena,
Calif., 1925) and William Saroyan, "O What a Man Was OH," KR 29 (1967):
671-75.

Section 34

ELIZABETH MADOX ROBERTS (1881-1941)

Elizabeth Madox Roberts (hereafter EMR or R) was born in rural Kentucky, the scene of her fiction. Although she lived at various times in Colorado, New York, and California, she spent most of her creative life in her native state. She taught public school for a decade after leaving high school and did not go to college until she was 36. After graduating from the University of Chicago in 1921, she began writing fiction, and her first novel, THE TIME OF MAN (1926), was a great critical success as well as a Book-of-the-Month Club selection. Her novels and stories derive their strength from a meticulous use of the speech and folkways of Kentucky and a poetic imagination.

BIBLIOGRAPHY AND MANUSCRIPTS

There is no complete bibliography available, and one must make do with the meager listing in AAL, Gerstenberger, and Johnson plus the selected bibliographies accompanying F.P.W. McDowell, EMR (TUSAS, 1963), and Earl Rovit, HERALD TO CHAOS: THE NOVELS OF EMR (Lexington, Ky., 1960). The MS sources, however, are abundant. R's papers were given to the Library of Congress after her death: see Allen Tate, "The EMR Papers," QJLC 1 (1943): 29-31. The University of Chicago and the New York Public Library have extensive holdings, the Filson Club of Louisville has a special collection, and the Viking Press has a large number of letters.

WORKS OF FICTION

Novels: *THE TIME OF MAN (1926), MY HEART AND MY FLESH (1927), JINGLING IN THE WIND (1928), *THE GREAT MEADOW (1930), A BURIED TREASURE (1931), HE SENT FORTH A RAVEN (1935), BLACK IS MY TRUE-LOVE'S HAIR (1938).

Stories: THE HAUNTED MIRROR (1932), NOT BY STRANGE GODS (1941).

* Of Special Importance

ELIZABETH MADOX ROBERTS

THE TIME OF MAN has been reprinted frequently: in the Modern Library with an introduction by Donald Adams (1935); twice by Viking (1945) and with an introduction by Robert Penn Warren (1963). Three paperback editions are in print: The New American Library, The Popular Library and Viking. The Popular Library also has reissued HE SENT FORTH A RAVEN, BLACK IS MY TRUE-LOVE'S HAIR, MY HEART AND MY FLESH, JINGLING IN THE WIND, and A BURIED TREASURE. The New American Library in addition reprinted THE GREAT MEADOW with an afterword by Willard Thorp (1961).

BIOGRAPHY

The most extensive biographical study is an unpublished dissertation: Woodridge Speares, "EMR: A Biographical and Critical Study," DA 20 (1960): 3753-54. Most accessible, however, is the initial biographical chapter in H.M. Campbell and R.E. Foster, EMR: AMERICAN NOVELIST (Norman, Okla., 1956). There also is a biography in McDowell's Twayne volume. R did not write an auto-biography but she wrote an article about her Kentucky ancestors: "Over the Trace to 'the Great Meadow,'" WINGS 4 (March, 1930): 6-9; and there is material in an interview with Donald Davidson (Louisville COURIER-JOURNAL, 24 February 1929). See also Rena Niles, "Kentucky Profiles: She Writes the Way She Weaves," Louisville COURIER-JOURNAL (8 January 1939), in which R talks about her work, methods of composition, and style, and Glenway Wescott, "A Personal Note about Miss R," in EMR (New York, 1930), a 27-page pamphlet.

CRITICISM

When R's first novel appeared in 1926, she immediately became a major novelist, and her next two books confirmed her reputation. Her novels in the 1930's, however, were less successful, and after her death in 1941 she fell into critical neglect, from which she now is being rescued. McDowell's Twayne volume is a brief, competent place to begin the study of R's work. More elaborate and the best work of criticism is Earl Rovit, HERALD TO CHAOS (see above), a full-length treatment that concerns itself with aesthetic and thematic matters and makes use of the R papers at the Library of Congress. Rovit's work began as a dissertation (Boston University, 1957), which was followed by several good articles later subsumed into his book.

Another book-length study, Campbell and Foster (see above), preceded Rovit's work, but it is less useful. Its tone is adulatory, its evaluations uncritical, the book lacks an index and bibliography. Two articles by Campbell (SHENAN-DOAH 5 [Summer 1954]: 42-59, and SWR 39 [1954]: 337-46) are incorporated in this study.

Among the early essays on R worth reporting are these: Donald Davidson,

"Analysis of EMR's A BURIED TREASURE," CREATIVE READING 6 (1931): 1235-49; Mark Van Doren, "EMR," EJ 21 (1932): 521-28; Donald Adams in THE SHAPE OF BOOKS TO COME (New York, 1934) and "EMR," VQR 12 (1936): 80-90; F.L. Janney, "EMR," SR 45 (1937): 388-410; Shields McIlwaine in THE SOUTHERN POOR-WHITE FROM LUBBERLAND TO TOBACCO ROAD (Norman, Okla., 1939), which links R to Caldwell, Faulkner, and Glasgow; A.M. Buchan, "EMR," SWR (1940): 463-81. In the same pamphlet to which Wescott contributed a memoir (see above), there are critical comments by R.M. Lovett, Edward Garnett, Mary Ross, Allan Nevins, Carl Van Doren, and Louis Untermeyer. Viking published a similar pamphlet in 1938.

Although only one essay on R appeared in a composite study in the 1940's, there were two in the 1950's and three in the 1960's, as renewed interest in her work accelerated. See Mark Van Doren, "EMR: Her Mind and Style," in his THE PRIVATE READER (New York, 1942); Edward Wagenknecht, "Novelists of the Twenties: The Inner Vision: EMR" in his CAVALCADE OF THE AMERICAN NOVEL (New York, 1952); Blair Rouse, "Time and Place in Southern Fiction," in Louis Rubin and R.D. Jacobs, eds., SOUTHERN RENASCENCE: THE LITERATURE OF THE MODERN SOUTH (Baltimore, 1953); Willard Thorp in AMERICAN WRITING IN THE TWENTIETH CENTURY (Cambridge, Mass., 1960); Louis Auchincloss in PIONEERS AND CARETAKERS: A STUDY OF NINE AMERICAN WOMEN NOVELISTS (Minneapolis, 1965); Herman Spivey, "The Mind and Creative Habits of EMR" in R.A. Bryan et al., eds., ALL THESE TO TEACH: ESSAYS IN HONOR OF C.A. ROBERTSON (Gainesville, Fla., 1965).

Robert Penn Warren commented on R's work in "Life Is From Within," SatR 46 (2 March 1963): 20-21, 38, about the same time he was introducing a new edition of THE TIME OF MAN; and two fairly recent articles are J.J. Murphy, "EMR and the Civilizing Consciousness," KHSR 64 (1967): 110-20; J.R. Smith, "New Troy in the Bluegrass; Vergilian Metaphor and THE GREAT MEADOW," MissQ 22 (1969): 39-46.

Section 35

WILLIAM SAROYAN (1908-)

William Saroyan (hereafter WS or S) was born in Fresno, California, of Armenian immigrant parents, and some of his most memorable fiction draws on his experience in growing up in the San Joaquin Valley. Although he first established his reputation as a short story writer, he also has written many novels and plays, some of which have been staged very successfully, and in the last decade has produced a series of autobiographical volumes. A sort of literary Horatio Alger, he writes fluently and optimistically of the American experience.

BIBLIOGRAPHY AND MANUSCRIPTS

Since S still is writing industriously, there is no up-to-date bibliography, but 30 years of his career are covered by David Kherdian, A BIBLIOGRAPHY OF WS: 1934-1964 (San Francisco, 1965), a compilation listing both primary and secondary materials. In addition, there is a selected bibliography in H.R. Floan, WS (TUSAS, 1966), and he is included in LHUS. There are MSS at Mills College, the University of Chicago, Harvard, the New York Public Library, and California State University at Fresno. Also there is significant material in the George Jean Nathan Collection at Cornell.

WORKS OF FICTION

Novels: *THE HUMAN COMEDY (1943), THE ADVENTURES OF WESLEY JACKSON (1946), ROCK WAGRAM (1951), TRACY'S TIGER (1951), THE LAUGHING MATTER (1953), MAMA, I LOVE YOU (1956), PAPA, YOU'RE CRAZY (1957), BOYS AND GIRLS TOGETHER (1963), ONE DAY IN THE AFTERNOON OF THE WORLD (1964).

Short Stories: *THE DARING YOUNG MAN ON THE FLYING TRAPEZE AND OTHER STORIES (1934), INHALE AND EXHALE (1936), THREE TIMES THREE (1936), THE TROUBLE WITH TIGERS (1937), LITTLE CHILDREN (1937), LOVE, HERE IS MY HAT (1938), A NATIVE AMERICAN (1938), PEACE, IT'S WONDERFUL (1939), *MY NAME IS ARAM (1940), DEAR BABY (1944), THE ASSYR-

*Of Special Importance

169

IAN AND OTHER STORIES (1950), THE WHOLE VOYALD AND OTHER STORIES (1956), MY KIND OF CRAZY, WONDERFUL PEOPLE (1966).

EDITIONS AND REPRINTS

Harcourt, Brace issued THE SAROYAN SPECIAL (1948), a selection of "best stories," while a decade later Braziller brought out THE WS READER with an introduction by the author. Still later appeared AFTER THIRTY YEARS: THE DARING YOUNG MAN ON THE FLYING TRAPEZE (1964), which included 38 essays plus the text of the first edition of THE DARING YOUNG MAN. In 1968 a Dell paperback was issued, MAN WITH THE HEART IN THE HIGHLANDS AND OTHER STORIES. All but the first of these are now in print.

BIOGRAPHY

There is biographical material in Floan's TUSAS volume, but the best source for S's life is his own series of autobiographical volumes: TWIN ADVENTURES (1950), THE BICYCLE RIDER IN BEVERLY HILLS (1952), HERE COMES, THERE GOES, YOU KNOW WHO (1961), NOT DYING (1963), SHORT DRIVE, SWEET CHARIOT (1966), LETTERS FROM 74 RUE TAITBOUT [Paris, where S now lives] (1969), DAYS OF LIFE AND DEATH AND ESCAPE TO THE MOON (1970), PLACES WHERE I'VE DONE TIME (1972). S also reminisced in "The Time of My Life," TArts 39 (January 1955): 22-24, 95, and in "Twenty Years of Writing," AtlM 195 (May 1955): 65-68.

CRITICISM

The only published book-length study of S is Floan's brief volume in the Twayne series. There have, however, been two dissertations: David Morris, "A Critical Analysis of WS" (Denver, 1960) and Walter Petricek, "WS als Dramatiker" (Vienna, 1949), but both of these studies are concerned with S as dramatist. The Austrian dissertation was among the first of a considerable number of foreign articles, which began with an Italian piece in 1946. Articles have appeared in French, Italian, Japanese, Polish, Spanish, British, and German journals, and S's foreign reputation is greater than that of many more important writers.

Although many of the articles on S deal with him as dramatist, a topic beyond the scope of this bibliographic essay, there was, at least until recent years, a small but steady interest in his fiction. It began when Clifton Fadiman discovered him, NY 12 (February 1936): 67-69; Edmund Wilson discussed him, NR 103 (18 November 1940): 697-98; and H.S. Canby wrote in SRL 23 (28 December 1940): 5 that MY NAME IS ARAM "is a genuine, significant contribution to American literature." Harlan Hatcher in EJ 28 (1939): 169-77 thought there was some truth to the charge that S was half genius and half phony, but on balance praised his work. Alfred Kazin in NR 108 (1 March 1943): 289-91 thought the novel version of THE HUMAN COMEDY contained effective scenes but was deficient as a novel. Unfavorable commentators were Philip Rahv, "WS: A Minority Report," AM 57 (1943): 371-77, and Joseph Remenyi, "WS: A Portrait," CE 6 (1944): 92-100.

Later Frederic Carpenter, "The Time of WS's Life," PS 1 (1947): 88-98, found that S reaffirmed the old American faith of Emerson and Whitman; Nona Balakian, "So Many Ss," NR 123 (7 August 1950): 19-20, found allegory in S's writing; and Elizabeth Bowen, "In Spite of Words," NR 128 (9 March 1953): 18-19, believed S had performed a service for the short story form.

Again S was written off by William Fisher, "What Ever Happened to WS?" CE 16 (1955): 336-40 but treated respectfully by H.R. Floan, "S and Cervantes' Knight," THOUGHT 33 (1958): 81-92, and Levon Sarkisian, "S's 'Rock Wagram': A Psycho-Social Character Study," ARMENIAN REV. 11 (1959): 61-68. As a currently unfashionable writer, S only occasionally is treated in composite studies, but there are chapters in Charles Angoff, THE TONE OF THE TWENTIES AND OTHER ESSAYS (New York, 1966), and E.B. Burgum, THE NOVEL AND THE WORLD'S DILEMMA (New York, 1947). During the past dozen years few critics have given S more than a passing nod, one such being Edward Krickel, "Cozzens and S: A Look at Two Reputations," GaR 24 (1970): 281-96.

Section 36
UPTON SINCLAIR (1878-1968)

Upton Sinclair (hereafter US or S), who became one of the leading muckrakers of the early twentieth century, was born in a socially prominent but poor Baltimore family. He began writing popular fiction at the age of 15 to put himself through New York's City College, and by the time he graduated at the age of 19 he was able to support himself by grinding out stories for pulp magazines. He wrote several novels without much success before publishing THE JUNGLE (1906), his famous fictionalized expose of the meat-packing industry in Chicago. He was a prominent socialist in real life and literary gad-fly in his fiction, which continued in an undiminished flow throughout his long life. He ran unsuccessfully for governor of California in 1934 and devoted much of his life to fighting injustice and social ills.

BIBLIOGRAPHY AND MANUSCRIPTS

For a minor writer S has been well served bibliographically. The work of Ronald Gottesman is crucial: "US: A Bibliographical Catalogue, 1894-1932" (available from University Microfilms) is a 1964 Indiana University dissertation which tries to identify "in full descriptive bibliographical form, first printings of S's works and to establish the complete canon for the period 1894-1932"; US: AN ANNOTATED CHECKLIST (Kent, Ohio, 1973) organizes all of S's work in checklist form, describes translations and foreign editions, and provides an extensive listing of secondary materials. Another bibliography, though superseded by Gottesman's work, is Joseph Gaer's US: BIBLIOGRAPHY AND BIOGRAPHICAL DATA (n.p., 1935; New York, 1971), which also contains a checklist of criticism. Also useful is the appendix to S's AUTOBIOGRAPHY (New York, 1962), which lists works planned, begun, or completed but never published. S has had a great vogue abroad, and any study of his work must include his foreign reputation. Helpful in this respect is BOOKS OF US IN TRANSLATION AND FOREIGN EDITIONS: A BIBLIOGRAPHY OF 772 TITLES IN 47 LANGUAGES AND 39 COUNTRIES (Pasadena, Calif., 1938), a list prepared by S. S reported in 1949 that the list by then probably was over 1000 titles. Also, O SHEPHERD SPEAK! (1949), the tenth volume of the Lanny Budd novels, lists in its appendix the foreign editions of that series.

The Lilly Library at Indiana University owns the vast S Archives, an eight-ton collection of MSS, letters and correspondence, documents, notes, first editions. The key to this collection is Ronald Gottesman and Charles Silet's THE LITERARY MANUSCRIPTS OF US (Columbus, Ohio, 1972). Earlier the Lilly Library issued A CATALOGUE OF BOOKS, MANUSCRIPTS, AND OTHER MATERIALS FROM THE US ARCHIVES (Bloomington, Ind., 1963), with an introduction by Gottesman. In addition to these vast holdings other libraries have letter collections: Stanford, The Huntington, Duke, Virginia, Yale, Pennsylvania, Occidental College, to mention the largest. Other significant holdings may be found at the University of California at Berkeley, the University of North Carolina, the Wisconsin State Historical Society, and the Library of Congress.

WORKS OF FICTION

Novels (A selected list): SPRINGTIME AND HARVEST (1901), MANASSAS (1904), *THE JUNGLE (1906), THE METROPOLIS (1908), THE MONEYCHANGERS (1908), SAMUEL THE SEEKER (1910), SYLVIA (1913), KING COAL (1917), JIMMY HIGGINS (1919), OIL! (1927), BOSTON (1928), MOUNTAIN CITY (1930), ROMAN HOLIDAY (1931), THE WET PARADE (1931), CO-OP (1936), WORLD'S END (1940), BETWEEN TWO WORLDS (1941), DRAGON'S TEETH (1942), WIDE IS THE GATE (1943), PRESIDENTIAL AGENT (1944), DRAGON HARVEST (1945), A WORLD TO WIN (1946), PRESIDENTIAL MISSION (1947), ONE CLEAR CALL (1948), O SHEPHERD SPEAK! (1949), THE RETURN OF LANNY BUDD (1953).

EDITIONS AND REPRINTS

A number of S's novels written before 1930 have been reprinted: SPRINGTIME AND HARVEST (n.d.), MANASSAS (1968), THE MONEYCHANGERS (1968), SYLVIA (1970), JIMMY HIGGINS (1970), OIL! (1966); BOSTON (1970), which was condensed and issued as AUGUST 22ND (1965). In addition, S's most famous novel, THE JUNGLE, has had numerous reprintings: Viking Press with intro. by US (1946); Harper Modern Classics with intro. by US and John Fischer (1951); New American Library with afterword by Robert Downs (1961); Limited Editions Club and Heritage Press with new pref. by US (1965). There are currently three editions in print, two paperback. There never has been any effort to collect S's work, but AN US ANTHOLOGY, compiled by I.O. Evans with pref. by US, was issued in 1934.

BIOGRAPHY

An up-to-date critical biography of S is a desideratum. The only book on S is Floyd Dell's US: A STUDY IN SOCIAL PROTEST (Long Beach, Calif., 1927; New York, 1927). It is an adequate study of S's life and work done to its date of writing. For S's later career the sources are fragmentary. An unpublished dissertation by Martin Zanger, "US's Reform Activities in California,

* Of Special Importance

1915-1950," DA 32 (1972): 5725A is available; also a number of brief sketches or reminiscences: Robert Cantwell, "US," NR 90 (1937): 69-71; Ed Ainsworth, "Remembering Uppie," SatR 50 (30 September 1967): 32-33, the memories of a former political opponent; Judson Grenier, "US: A Remembrance," CHSQ 48 (1969): 165-69.

The best available source of S's life is his AUTOBIOGRAPHY (1962), but he also wrote earlier autobiographical works: AMERICAN OUTPOST: A BOOK OF REMINISCENCES (1932, 1969); and two novels, THE JOURNAL OF ARTHUR STIRLING (1903) and LOVE'S PILGRIMAGE (1911). S also published a collection of letters written to him: MY LIFETIME IN LETTERS (Columbia, Mo., 1960), and there is an unpublished dissertation devoted to S's correspondence: D.A. Remley, "The Correspondence of Henry Louis Mencken and US: 'An Illustration of How Not to Agree,'" DA 28 (1967): 3682A.

CRITICISM

S never has had much standing among literary critics, and what criticism there is deals with him as a muckraker or reformer and assesses the social content in his work. Early views, pro and con, may be found in Carl Van Doren's CONTEMPORARY AMERICAN NOVELISTS (New York, 1922) and Van Wyck Brooks' EMERSON AND OTHERS (1927). Other discussions in the 1930's include Harry Hartwick, THE FOREGROUND OF AMERICAN FICTION (New York, 1934), Harlan Hatcher, CREATING THE MODERN AMERICAN NOVEL (New York, 1935), and Robert Cantwell's essay in Malcolm Cowley, ed., AFTER THE GENTEEL TRADITION (New York, 1937; Carbondale, Ill., 1964). Later treatments worth looking into are in Alfred Kazin's ON NATIVE GROUNDS (New York, 1942) and Joseph Blotner's THE MODERN AMERICAN POLITICAL NOVEL, 1900-1960 (Austin, Tex., 1966). A particularly good summary of S's accomplishments is in Walter Rideout's THE RADICAL NOVEL IN THE UNITED STATES, 1900-1954 (Cambridge, Mass., 1956). As the outstanding socialist novelist of the first two decades of this century, Rideout says, S "almost was radical American literature."

Of the few periodical articles on S over the years several may be recommended: R.M. Lovett, "US," EJ 17 (1928): 706-14; Granville Hicks, "The Survival of US," CE 4 (1943): 213-20; G.J. Becker, "US: Quixote in a Flivver," CE 21 (1959): 133-40; S.G. Putt's "World Without End: US and Lanny Budd" in his SCHOLARS OF THE HEART: ESSAYS IN CRITICISM (London, 1962). The last two are rare essays that deal with S as writer and not as propagandist. There also is an unpublished dissertation (Chicago, 1948) by E.N. Lockhart on "Technique in the Novels of US."

Anyone interested in S as social reformer and politician should consult DAL for listings of unpublished dissertations on S as crusader, S on education, and S and his campaign for governor of California. A more recent dissertation is R.B. Fisher, "The Last Muckraker: The Social Orientation of the Thought of US," DA 33 (1972): 250A. S is generally treated in standard works on the muckraking movement, the most recent of which is R.J. Cook, MUCKRAKERS: CRUSADING JOURNALISTS WHO CHANGED AMERICA (New York, 1972).

Section 37

GERTRUDE STEIN (1874-1946)

A quarter of a century after her death the career of Gertrude Stein (hereafter GS or S) seems greater in its sum than in its parts. As a writer, she cannot claim major stature, but had she never written a line, she would still enjoy a modest place in the history of twentieth-century culture. As collector of art and friend of painters, as teacher and critic of greater writers like Sherwood Anderson and Hemingway, as the demiurge of avant-gardism, she has left her mark on the world of literature and art. Born in Pennsylvania, educated in California and at Radcliffe, she studied psychology under William James, almost finished a medical degree at Johns Hopkins; then she went abroad in 1902 and in the following year settled permanently in France. During her life she was a very controversial and enigmatic figure, popularly known as the writer of incomprehensible, experimental prose and poetry, but since her death her solid importance has clearly emerged from the literary gossip and obfuscations.

BIBLIOGRAPHY AND MANUSCRIPTS

Before her death S designated Yale University as the repository of her MSS, and one should begin the bibliographical study of S with the compilation of R.B. Haas and Donald Gallup, A CATALOGUE OF THE PUBLISHED AND UNPUBLISHED WRITINGS OF GS . . . (New Haven, 1941), a 64-page pamphlet describing Yale's holdings of S material. After S's death Gallup also described the S Collection in YULG 22 (October 1947): 22-32. The most extensive bibliography of primary materials, though not complete, as it was done before S's death, is Julian Sawyer, GS: A BIBLIOGRAPHY (New York, 1941). Sawyer added to this work with "GS: A Bibliography, 1941-1948," BB 19 (1948): 152-56, 183-87; he also has published "GS: A Checklist Comprising Critical and Miscellaneous Writings about Her Work, Life, and Personality from 1913-1942," BB 17 (1943): 211-12; 18 (1943): 11-13; 19 (1948): 128-31. Although there are selected bibliographies in some of the critical studies that have appeared since S's death, one especially useful being Richard Bridgman's (see below), which also contains a key to the Yale Catalogue, there now is a need for a complete and up-to-date listing of both primary and secondary work. Such a compilation would reflect the increasing critical interest and the posthumous publication program of previously unpublished MSS. As already noted, Yale University has most of the S MSS, but there is significant MS material at Har-

177

vard, the University of Chicago, the New York Public Library, and the Wisconsin State Historical Society.

WORKS OF FICTION

*THREE LIVES (1909), *THE MAKING OF AMERICANS (1925), *LUCY CHURCH AMIABLY (1930), IDA, A NOVEL (1941), BREWSIE AND WILLIE (1946), *FOUR IN AMERICA (1947), BLOOD ON THE DINING-ROOM FLOOR (1948), *TWO: GS AND HER BROTHER (1951), *MRS. REYNOLDS AND FIVE EARLIER NOVELETTES (1952), AS FINE AS MELANCTHA (1954), A NOVEL OF THANK YOU (1958), FERNHURST, Q.E.D., AND OTHER EARLY WRITINGS (1971).

EDITIONS AND REPRINTS

The Yale Edition of the Unpublished Writings of GS (under the general editorship of Carl Van Vechten, her literary executor, with an advisory committee of Donald Gallup, Donald Sutherland, and Thornton Wilder), consists of eight uniform volumes issued between 1951 and 1958. These volumes were reprinted by Books for Libraries Press in 1969.

The reprinting of S's published works has gone on simultaneously with the publication of her unpublished MSS. THE SELECTED WRITINGS OF GS, ed. with intro. and notes by Van Vechten, appeared in 1946 and was put into the Modern Library in 1962. THE GS FIRST READER AND THREE PLAYS came out in 1948. GS: WRITINGS AND LECTURES, 1911-1945, ed. Patricia Meyerowitz, was issued in London in 1967 and became a Penguin paperback in 1971. To these should be added SELECTED OPERAS AND PLAYS OF GS, ed. J.M. Brinnin (Pittsburgh, 1970), and MATISSE, PICASSO, AND GS, WITH TWO SHORTER STORIES (Millerton, N.Y., 1972).

A number of individual titles also have been reissued. LECTURES IN AMERICA was a Beacon paperback in 1957, PICASSO in 1959; THE MAKING OF AMERICANS was reprinted from the full 1925 Paris text (New York, 1966), while Harcourt, Brace put its 1934 abridged edition into a Harvest paperback in 1962; Haskell House reissued GEOGRAPHY AND PLAYS (1967) and TENDER BUTTONS (1970); Pitman published WHAT ARE MASTERPIECES? (1970); Cooper Square Publishers brought out IDA and EVERYBODY'S AUTOBIOGRAPHY (1971); Avon Books reissued THE WORLD IS ROUND, a juvenile (1972), and PARIS FRANCE is a Liveright paperback (1970). Even S's undergraduate essays on MOTOR AUTOMATISM were reprinted as a pamphlet by the Phoenix Book Shop (1969) from the PSYCHOLOGICAL REVIEW of 1896 and 1898. THREE LIVES and THE AUTOBIOGRAPHY OF ALICE B. TOKLAS are available as Vintage paperbacks.

BIOGRAPHY

Because S was the topic of much literary gossip during the first two decades of

* Of Special Importance

her career and a sort of football between admirers and detractors, reliable biographical material had to wait until after her death. In the mid-1930's, however, a great deal began to be written about her, especially after her successful lecture tour of the United States in 1934-35; but it was not very objective.
Early works are admiring like Bravig Imbs, CONFESSIONS OF ANOTHER YOUNG
MAN (New York, 1936), or angry attacks like Eugene Jolas et al., TESTIMONY
AGAINST GS (TRANSITION, Pamphlet no. 1, February 1935), in which a group
of her Paris associates denounced her. The best way to begin the study of S's
life is to start with THE AUTOBIOGRAPHY OF ALICE B. TOKLAS (1933), which
was written by S but purports to be (and in part was) by her friend and companion. It is, however, unreliable as biography. A memoir actually written
by Toklas did appear in 1963 as WHAT IS REMEMBERED, and a biographer should
not ignore THE ALICE B. TOKLAS COOKBOOK (New York, 1954). Nor should
he ignore S's late autobiographical works, WARS I HAVE SEEN (1944) and
EVERYBODY'S AUTOBIOGRAPHY (1937). Two additional early recollections,
written by friends, are Hutchins Hapgood, A VICTORIAN IN THE MODERN
WORLD (New York, 1939), and Mable Dodge Luhan, EUROPEAN EXPERIENCES
(New York, 1935).

After S's death additional memoirs appeared such as W.G. Rogers, WHEN THIS
YOU SEE REMEMBER ME (New York, 1948), favorable, and Ernest Hemingway
in A MOVEABLE FEAST (New York, 1964), unfavorable. In the 1950's two
works, largely biographical, were issued: J.M. Brinnin, THE THIRD ROSE: GS
AND HER WORLD (New York, 1959), and Elizabeth Sprigge, GS: HER LIFE
AND WORK (New York, 1957). Most of the writers on S in the last two decades have been interested in analyzing her work and only incidentally in her
life. But an engaging short introduction to S combining biography and criticism
is George Wickes, AMERICANS IN PARIS (New York, 1969). One also should
look at the MS material in the Yale Edition entitled TWO: GS AND HER
BROTHER (New Haven, 1951), the brother being Leo Stein with whom S lived
during her early years in Paris; Donald Gallup, ed., THE FLOWERS OF FRIEND-
SHIP: LETTERS WRITTEN TO GS (New York, 1953); and Edmund Fuller's edition of Leo Stein's JOURNEY INTO THE SELF (New York, 1950). Bridgman's
book (see below) has a useful chronology. There is additional biographical material in Barbara Pollack, THE COLLECTORS: DR. CLARIBEL AND MISS ETTA
CONE (Indianapolis, 1962), a book about two Baltimore ladies who were friends
of the Steins, and R.B. Haas, GS: A PRIMER FOR THE GRADUAL UNDER-
STANDING OF GS (Los Angeles, 1971), which reprints "A Transatlantic Interview, 1946" and "There Once Was a Family Called Stein" by S's niece.

CRITICISM

Frederick Hoffman, GS (UMPAW, 1961), is a sound, brief, and convenient
place to begin the study of S, but for those who want more than 45 pages, the
best full-length critical study is now Richard Bridgman, GS IN PIECES (New
York, 1970), a work of impeccable scholarship. The first major study, however,
Donald Sutherland, GS: A BIOGRAPHY OF HER WORK (New Haven, 1951),
still is excellent and reliable. In addition, an excellent medium-length study
will soon be available in the Twayne series by Michael Hoffman, who also

wrote a useful monograph, THE DEVELOPMENT OF ABSTRACTIONISM IN THE WRITINGS OF GS (Philadelphia, 1965). The latter work, which began as one of the six dissertations (see DAL) that have been written on S since her death, deals with S's first decade of writing down to and including THE MAKING OF AMERICANS.

Besides these books, there have been five other full-length critical studies of S since her death. The first, Rosamond Miller, GS: FORM AND INTELLIGIBILITY (New York, 1949), contains a 95-page introduction to S "written for the average reader," then reprints S's essays written at Radcliffe for a composition course taken under William Vaughn Moody. B.L. Reid, ART BY SUBTRACTION: A DISSENTING OPINION OF GS (Norman, Okla., 1958), revives the old polemics and reminds one of the earlier cudgeling S took from critics like Oscar Cargill (INTELLECTUAL AMERICA, 1941), who treated her rudely in a chapter called "The Decadents," or her brother Leo, who wrote a friend after THE AUTO-BIOGRAPHY OF ALICE B. TOKLAS came out that "I simply cannot take Gertrude seriously as a literary phenomenon." To Reid S is "a vulgar genius talking to herself" and "already effectively dead as a writer." But the critical attention she has received and the number of reprint editions appearing during the past 15 years suggest that the epitaph may be premature.

Or so it would seem from such works as Allegra Stewart, GS AND THE PRE-SENT (Cambridge, Mass., 1967), which William Wasserstrom called "the most persuasive case yet offered in support of Miss S's genius" and a thoroughly convincing one; also Norman Weinstein, GS AND THE LITERATURE OF THE MODERN CONSCIOUSNESS (New York, 1970), which is as broadly sympathetic as Reid's is antagonistic, and Bridgman's study (cited above), which Michael Hoffman believes "will be the foundation for all future studies of S."

S has been treated often in composite studies, many of which are good. Besides Wickes (see above) others that may be recommended include Frederick Hoffman, "GS: The Method and the Subject," in his THE MODERN NOVEL IN AMERI-CA, 1900-1950 (Chicago, 1951), and Edwin Burgum, "The Genius of Miss GS," in THE NOVEL AND THE WORLD'S DILEMMA (New York, 1947). One also should not miss Edmund Wilson's early essay on S in AXEL'S CASTLE (New York, 1931), and of less usefulness are chapters on S in two other works: Francis Russell, THREE STUDIES IN TWENTIETH CENTURY OBSCURITY (Aldington, Kent, 1954), unfavorable, and Laura Riding, CONTEMPORARIES AND SNOBS (New York, 1928), favorable. Katherine Anne Porter also has a piece on S in THE DAYS BEFORE (New York, 1952).

Lewis Leary (AAL, 1900-50, 1950-67) lists more than 70 items on S, but many are unimportant or have been written by the authors of studies cited above and subsumed into their works. A few articles, not all in Leary, are worth noting: Kenneth Burke, "Engineering with Words," DIAL 74 (1923): 408-12; Harvey Eagleson, "GS: Method in Madness," SR 44 (1936): 164-77; Donald Gallup, "The Making of THE MAKING OF AMERICANS," NCol 3 (1950): 54-74; W.H. Gass, "GS: Her Escape from Protective Language," ACCENT 18 (1958): 233-44; George Haines, "GS and Composition," SR 57 (1949): 411-24; Marianne Moore, "The Spare American Emotion," DIAL 80 (1926): 153-56. A provocative recent article is Strother Purdy, "GS at Marienbad," PMLA 85 (1970): 1096-1105, and finally one should not miss Thornton Wilder's introduction to FOUR IN AMERICA (New Haven, 1947), Van Vechten's introduction to the SELECTED WRITINGS, and Sherwood Anderson's essay on S, which is reprinted with GEOGRAPHY AND PLAYS (1967).

Section 38

JOHN STEINBECK (1902-1968)

John Steinbeck (hereafter JS or S), who was the seventh American writer to win the Nobel Prize for Literature (1962), is best known for his novels and stories laid in his native California. Born in Salinas, he grew up in the "Long Valley" of his fiction, attended Stanford University without taking a degree, worked on farms and did other odd jobs before publishing his first novel in 1929. His interest in the plight of the migrant farm laborer led him to write IN DUBIOUS BATTLE, OF MICE AND MEN, and his most famous work, THE GRAPES OF WRATH, a story of Oklahoma farmers driven west by the drought in the 1930's. After World War II Steinbeck left California, and his last novel has an Eastern setting.

BIBLIOGRAPHY AND MANUSCRIPTS

There is no complete descriptive bibliography of S's works or any up-to-date listing of works about him. The following are the best or latest available: Tetsumaro Hayashi, JS: A CONCISE BIBLIOGRAPHY (1930-1965) (Metuchen, N.J., 1967), for both primary and secondary works, and Maurice Beebe and Jackson Bryer, "Criticism of JS: A Selected Checklist," MFS 11 (1965): 90-103, for criticism. Although Hayashi lists many reviews, unpublished theses and dissertations and 157 pages of material altogether, there still is need for a comprehensive listing of foreign editions of S's works and works about him published abroad. A start was made with JS: AN EXHIBITION OF AMERICAN AND FOREIGN EDITIONS (Austin, Tex., 1963), which describes a display at the University of Texas. A S NEWSLETTER (now the S QUARTERLY) began in 1968 and will serve as a clearing house for bibliographical information. The best place to begin any bibliographical study of S is Warren French's fine essay in SMAA, which judiciously summarizes the state of S scholarship in a compact, 18-page review. Also Peter Lisca's book (see below) contains a good summary of the scholarship down to his writing, and he has updated his survey of S criticism to 1971 in Tetsumaro Hayashi, ed., S'S LITERARY DIMENSION: A GUIDE TO COMPARATIVE STUDIES (Metuchen, N.J., 1973). In the same volume Hayashi has added a section of updated bibliography.

Most of S's papers still are in private hands, and not too many of his letters have found their way into libraries. There are good letter collections, however, at the University of Virginia, Harvard, and the University of California at Berkeley. Hayashi discusses letter collections in his bibliography (see above). As for MSS, Virginia has a signed draft of THE GRAPES OF WRATH, and the Library of Congress has a typescript with MS corrections. The Pierpont Morgan Library has the MSS of S's last three books.

WORKS OF FICTION

Novels: CUP OF GOLD (1929), TO A GOD UNKNOWN (1933), *TORTILLA FLAT (1935), *IN DUBIOUS BATTLE (1936), *OF MICE AND MEN (1937), *THE GRAPES OF WRATH (1939), THE MOON IS DOWN (1942), *CANNERY ROW (1944), THE WAYWARD BUS (1947), THE PEARL (1948), BURNING BRIGHT (1950), EAST OF EDEN (1952), SWEET THURSDAY (1954), THE SHORT REIGN OF PIPPIN IV (1957), THE WINTER OF OUR DISCONTENT (1961).

Stories: THE PASTURES OF HEAVEN (1932), THE LONG VALLEY (1938).

EDITIONS AND REPRINTS

There is no collected edition of S's works, though his books have been enormously popular, widely reprinted, and often translated. All of his fiction is available in paperback editions, some books in more than one, and THE GRAPES OF WRATH in three. Four novels were put into Modern Library editions by 1941: TORTILLA FLAT, IN DUBIOUS BATTLE, OF MICE AND MEN, and THE GRAPES OF WRATH; and THE PORTABLE S has gone through two editions and also is in paperback. There is a much-reprinted edition of THE SHORT NOVELS OF JS (1953), which contains TORTILLA FLAT, OF MICE AND MEN, THE RED PONY, THE MOON IS DOWN, CANNERY ROW, and THE PEARL. THE RED PONY has been published separately, in paper and in hard covers, in THE LONG VALLEY, and in THE PORTABLE S. A S OMNIBUS (1950), published in London, has similar contents to THE PORTABLE S, both containing mostly stories and excerpts from longer works. Several of S's works have been published in elegant editions, particularly THE GRAPES OF WRATH in a two-volume edition with lithographs by Thomas Hart Benton (1940).

BIOGRAPHY

Although there have been some good critical books on S, he has yet to find his biographer. In the absence of autobiography and published letter collections, information about S's life is rather sparse. Richard O'Connor's JS (New York, 1970) is a popular, undocumented life written by a skillful professional author, but it is aimed at a young audience instead of students and scholars. The best brief account of S's life is Peter Lisca's "JS: A Literary Biography," in E.W. Tedlock, Jr., and C.V. Wicker, eds., S AND HIS CRITICS: A RECORD OF TWENTY-FIVE YEARS (Albuquerque, N.M., 1957). Lisca was given access to

* Of Special Importance

the files of both S's agent and his publisher and was aided by S, who checked the accuracy of the facts and supplied additional information. Other biographical data may be found in Lewis Gannett's preface to THE VIKING PORTABLE S (New York, 1946) and J.H. Jackson's "JS: A Portrait," SRL 16 (25 September 1937): 11-12, 18. Jackson, who was a San Francisco book-reviewer, was the recipient of 35 letters from S now at Berkeley. A brief essay published as a pamphlet deals with S's youth: Robert Bennett's THE WRATH OF JS (Los Angeles, 1939). There is also material in Frank Scully's ROGUE'S GALLERY (Hollywood, Calif., 1943), and an interesting memoir in Webster Street, "JS: A Reminiscence," in S: THE MAN AND HIS WORK (see below). Hayashi's bibliography lists 16 pages of biographical items, but many are news stories or encyclopedia entries.

Even if S did not write an autobiography, he did talk about himself occasionally, especially in "About Ed Ricketts," which prefaces THE LOG FROM THE SEA OF CORTEZ (New York, 1951). This book recounts the collecting expedition in marine biology that S took part in after writing THE GRAPES OF WRATH. Also see S's piece, "The Making of a New Yorker," NYTM (1 February 1953): 26; S's Nobel Prize acceptance speech, which was widely reprinted (see Hayashi, pp. 26-27). A few letters also have been printed in scattered places, but one series is noteworthy: "Letters to Alicia" the wife of the editor and publisher of NEWSDAY, which appeared in the Long Island paper beginning November 20, 1965. These have not been reprinted, however. In addition, much of S's nonfiction is autobiographical, such as his war reporting during World War II, A RUSSIAN JOURNAL (1948), TRAVELS WITH CHARLEY IN SEARCH OF AMERICA (1962). Finally, his long novel, EAST OF EDEN, is based on family history, and there are biographical data as well as glimpses of the author at work in S's JOURNAL OF A NOVEL: THE "EAST OF EDEN" LETTERS (New York, 1969). These "letters" actually are journal entries cast in the form of letters to "Pat" (Pascal Covici, S's editor), written while the novel was in progress. They were not intended to be published.

CRITICISM

The volume of criticism that S's readers have produced is far less than the Fitzgerald, Faulkner, or Hemingway floods. He did not attract much attention until the mid-1930's, and after THE GRAPES OF WRATH came out, much of the writing was polemical, pro or con. After the flurry of interest in that novel died down, S began to be treated seriously by critics and literary historians, but during the last two decades of his life (the 1950's and 1960's) his work fell off in quality, and his stature today seems less than it did a quarter of a century ago. New interest in his work seems to be kindling, however, as the appearance of the S QUARTERLY and a greater number of items listed annually in the recent serial bibliographies would suggest.

A good place to begin a brief overview of S is James Gray's JS (UMPAW, 1971), one of the last publications in this useful pamphlet series; but for the student who wants a longer summary, there is Warren French's excellent JS

(TUSAS, 1961), which deals with S's writings down to 1960. French's views on S's last novel may be seen in "S's Winter Tale," MFS 11 (1965): 66-74. French links S to the native American transcendentalism of Emerson and Whitman and sees overall unity in his work. An earlier book but still a very good one is Peter Lisca's THE WIDE WORLD OF JS (New Brunswick, N.J., 1958), which began as one of the 20 dissertations that have been written on S. This is pioneering work that gives S's works a sympathetic reading, gives the fiction careful analysis down through PIPPIN. Lisca sees S as declining as a writer after World War II, partly as a result of the death of his friend Ed Ricketts, the "Doc" of CANNERY ROW and SWEET THURSDAY. Lisca carries on his summary seven years later in "S's Image of Man and His Decline as a Writer," MFS 11 (1965): 3-10, in which he sees him as trying unsuccessfully in his last years to reconstruct his image of man and to regain his earlier significance. Somewhat the same general view of S's decline after the 1940's is seen in James Woodress' "JS: Hostage of Fortune," SAQ 63 (1964): 385-97, a summary of S's life and work to the time of the Nobel Prize (repr. in Donohue's CASE-BOOK, see below).

Because S published no fiction after 1961, books written after that date but before his death were able to survey all his fictional output. F.W. Watt's JS (London and New York, 1962) and Joseph Fontenrose's JS: AN INTRODUCTION AND AN INTERPRETATION do that. The former, however, is a brief work that does not go beyond earlier books; the latter, on the other hand, breaks some new ground in discussing the myths underlying S's fiction. This book is full of interesting insights. The most recent work is L.J. Marks's THEMATIC DESIGN IN THE NOVELS OF JS (The Hague, 1969), only the second of the American dissertations so far to become books. Marks organizes S's work into three thematic patterns: (1) which views man as a religious animal; (2) which views man as a group animal; (3) which views man as searching for values "without knowledge of the cause of his existence." The last is the "non-teleological" thinking that stems from THE LOG FROM THE SEA OF CORTEZ and runs as a strong motif in much S criticism. In addition to the five general books already discussed, there is another, actually the first published: Harry Moore's THE NOVELS OF JS (Chicago, 1939; repr. Port Washington, N.Y., 1968). This book, of course, deals with S only down through THE GRAPES OF WRATH. Moore liked S's early lyrical novels but did not care for S when he shifted to sociological fiction. The reprint of this book contains an "Epilogue: Some Notes on JS's Later Works."

There have been six volumes of reprinted criticism thus far, and students of S now can lay their hands on a considerable body of material without having to search through original book or periodical sources. The earliest was Tedlock and Wicker (see above), which collected 26 essays including five pieces by S himself. These are arranged topically under the headings "Man and Career," "S on Criticism," "Artist and Thinker," "THE GRAPES OF WRATH," "The Later Work," and they are summarized in the introduction. A recent gathering is R.M. Davis, ed., S: A COLLECTION OF CRITICAL ESSAYS (Englewood Cliffs, N.J., 1972), which contains 11 essays, all written after World War II as S's reputation began to decline, plus a page from Gide's journal (1940) about IN DUBIOUS BATTLE. Five are reprinted from books by Lisca, French, and Fon-

tenrose and the special issue of MFS. Also included is a chapter on THE
GRAPES OF WRATH from George Bluestone's NOVELS INTO FILM (Baltimore,
1957). Hayashi's S'S LITERARY DIMENSION (see above) reprints 11 essays on
such topics as S and Dickens, S and Faulkner, S and Hemingway, etc.

Three volumes dealing with S's most famous novel have appeared. Warren
French, ed., A COMPANION TO "THE GRAPES OF WRATH" (New York,
1963), is a well-chosen and edited collection of contemporary material about
migrant farm workers and essays about the novel's reception and reputation.
Particularly interesting is the reprinting of newspaper articles that S wrote about
the migrant laborers for the San Francisco NEWS in 1936 and later published in
a rare pamphlet, THEIR BLOOD IS STRONG (San Francisco, 1968). French
also has a good chapter on THE GRAPES in his THE SOCIAL NOVEL AT THE
END OF AN ERA (Carbondale, Ill., 1966). Another collection on THE GRAPES
is Agnes Donohue's A CASEBOOK ON "THE GRAPES OF WRATH" (New York,
1968), which reprints more than three dozen essays under two general headings,
"THE GRAPES OF WRATH as a Social Document" and "THE GRAPES OF WRATH
as Literature." This is a rich gathering of essays from periodicals and chapters
from books. There is F.I. Carpenter's "The Philosophical Joads" (also in Tedlock and Wicker); a section from Leo Gurko's THE ANGRY DECADE (New York,
1947); an excerpt from Maxwell Geismar's WRITERS IN CRISIS (Boston, 1942);
an important essay by Chester Eisinger on Jeffersonian Agrarianism in the novel;
something from Charles Walcutt's AMERICAN LITERARY NATURALISM (Minneapolis, 1956); Edmund Wilson's rather unfavorable views of S from his CLASSICS
AND COMMERCIALS (New York, 1950); Arthur Mizener's objection to the
Nobel Prize (from the NYTBR); "Our Man in Helsinki," a piece from NY describing S's feelings on winning the prize; and S's prize acceptance speech. The
final volume of this group is Peter Lisca's "THE GRAPES OF WRATH": TEXT
AND CRITICISM (New York, 1972).

There are two other volumes of original criticism available: the special MFS
issue in Spring, 1965, which published ten articles, and Richard Astro and Tetsumaro Hayashi, eds., S: THE MAN AND HIS WORK (Corvallis, Oregon,
1971), a collection of ten papers presented at a S conference. Although the
latter have an air of special pleading, they provide some new perspective for
S criticism. They are summarized in Astro's introductory essay.

Although most American critics were startled and some were annoyed when S
won the Nobel Prize, the international honor reflects the fact that S has a
world-wide audience. Of the 20 dissertations on S listed in DAL nine were
done in Europe: seven in Germany, one in France, and one in Austria. Three
of these were written before the first was undertaken in America. Two of the
German dissertations have appeared as books: H.R. Rauter, BILD UND SYMBOL
IM WERKE JSS (Cologne, 1960), and Walter Rahn, DIE FUNKTIONEN DER
KALIFORNISCHEN LANDSCHAFT IM EPISCHEN FRUHWERK JSS (Munich, 1962).
Another German study, this one of German translations of S, has come out in
English: Helmut Liedloff, S IN GERMAN TRANSLATION: A STUDY OF
TRANSLATIONAL PRACTICES (Carbondale, Ill., 1965). The serial bibliogra-
phies have listed many foreign articles on S in the past decade, and to give
some samples of S's international reputation: the MLA bibliography lists one

article and one book in Japanese in 1967; articles in Danish, Romanian, French in 1968; articles in Greek, Italian, Romanian, French, Portuguese (Brazil), and seven in Japanese in 1969; and in 1970 Swedish was added to this list.

Section 39

JESSE STUART (1907-)

Stuart (hereafter JS or S) is a regional writer of Kentucky who has steadily grown in popularity and critical attention since he began his career as a poet in 1930. While he has continued to write poetry, he had by 1973 also published nine novels, eight collections of stories, several volumes of autobiography, and six juvenile books. S's work is traditional in form and content, but it derives strength from his complete immersion in his native state where he continues to live and write.

BIBLIOGRAPHY AND MANUSCRIPTS

The most recent book-length bibliography is Hensley Woodbridge, JS AND JANE S: A BIBLIOGRAPHY (Murray, Ky., 1969), which updates the same author's JS: A BIBLIOGRAPHY (Harrogate, Tenn., 1960) and lists works by and about S. Since publication of the former, bibliographical supplements have begun appearing in the JLN: 2 (1969): 118-20; 3 (1970): 65-69, 132-34. Further bibliographical data may be found in SIXTY AMERICAN POETS, 1896-1944 (Washington, D.C., 1945; rev. ed., 1954) and Blair's biography (see below).

S MSS have been acquired chiefly by the Murray (Ky.) State College Library, but S's publisher McGraw-Hill also has extensive correspondence. Smaller collections are located at the University of Chicago, University of Kentucky, and the Wisconsin Historical Society at Madison. A JS NEWSLETTER has been appearing as a supplement to the JLN.

WORKS OF FICTION

Novels: TREES OF HEAVEN (1940), TAPS FOR PRIVATE TUSSIE (1943), MONGREL METTLE (1944), FORETASTE OF GLORY (1946), THE THREAD THAT RUNS SO TRUE (1949), HIE TO THE HUNTERS (1950), THE GOOD SPIRIT OF LAUREL RIDGE (1953), DAUGHTER OF THE LEGEND (1965), MR. GALLION'S SCHOOL (1967), THE LAND BEYOND THE RIVER (1973).

Stories: HEAD O' W-HOLLOW (1936), MEN OF THE MOUNTAINS (1941),

TALES FROM THE PLUM GROVE HILLS (1946), CLEARING IN THE SKY AND OTHER STORIES (1950), MY LAND HAS A VOICE (1966), COME GENTLE SPRING (1969), COME BACK TO THE FARM (1971), DAWN OF A REMEM-BERED SPRING (1972).

EDITIONS AND REPRINTS

There are only two collections of S's works: A JS HARVEST (1965), a Dell paperback with 18 stories; A JS READER: STORIES AND POEMS SELECTED AND INTRODUCED BY JS (1963). The same volume with a foreword by Max Bogart has been issued as a Signet paperback. Most of S's works are still available (see BOOKS IN PRINT).

BIOGRAPHY

S has been reasonably well served biographically for a writer still living. Four dissertations, three of which deal with S biographically, were written between 1960 and 1970. One of these, the most comprehensive general work, has been published: Everetta Blair, JS: A SURVEY OF HIS LIFE AND WORKS (Colum-bia, S.C., 1967). Two others are J.R. LeMaster, "JS: Kentucky's Chronicler-Poet," DAI 31 (1970): 2925A, and F.H. Leavell, "The Literary Career of JS," DA 26 (1966): 6045. S himself has provided a good bit of material for his biographers in BEYOND DARK HILLS (1938, 1972), covering his first 25 years; THE THREAD THAT RUNS SO TRUE, an autobiographical novel; THE YEAR OF MY REBIRTH (1956), about his recovery from a heart attack; and GOD'S ODD-LING (1960), the story of his father. Also see "Autobiographical Reminiscence," UKCR 27 (1960): 57-64; "My Land Has a Voice," ArQ 21 (1965): 197-211; "Come Take This Tour with Me," KHSR 64 (1966): 1-13; and TO TEACH, TO LOVE (1970), which records S's opinions and experiences as a teacher. Also see John Bird, "My Friend JS," SEP 232 (25 July 1959): 32-33, 79, 81-83, and Blair, "JS: Schoolmaster," GaR 15 (1961): 311-23.

CRITICISM

There are two general studies of S's work which appeared as if in answer to Frank Leavell, "Desiderata in JS Studies," ABC, 16, vi (1966): 13-14, which called for more serious consideration. Lee Pennington, THE DARK HILLS OF JS (Cincinnati, 1967), is an intensive analysis of a single theme dominant in eight of S's novels and argues that S is more than a regional writer, and Ruel Foster's JS (TUSAS, 1968) is one of the compact general studies in the Twayne series. Foster also contributed a chapter on S as a short story writer in W.E. Walker and Robert Welker, eds., REALITY AND MYTH: ESSAYS IN AMERI-CAN LITERATURE IN HONOR OF RICHMOND CROOM BEATTY (Nashville, 1964.

As one might expect of a regionalist, much of the critical attention devoted to

S has centered on his skillful exploitation of Kentucky. This is seen in another useful article by Foster, "JS's W-Hollow: Microcosm of the Appalachians," KanQ 2 (1970): 66-72, and Dayton Kohler, "JS and James Still, Mountain Regionalists," CE 3 (1942): 523-33, but more specifically in the consideration of S as folklorist. Mary Washington Clarke's Pennsylvania dissertation (the first on S) eventuated in a detailed study, JS'S KENTUCKY (New York, 1968). She previously had contributed articles on S's folklore in SFQ 28 (1964): 157-98; 29 (1965): 142-63, and in KFR 9 (1963): 75-86. Also one should consult S on S's folklore in "New Wine in Old Bottles," KFR 13 (1967): 20-24.

Section 40

BOOTH TARKINGTON (1869-1946)

Tarkington (hereafter BT or T) was a popular and successful novelist whose career spanned almost five decades. Although he had more talent than most of his contemporaries, his work never quite achieved major significance, and he had to content himself with a large rather than a discriminating audience. Despite his popular appeal, however, his work has importance for the student of American literature, who finds in his novels an accurate picture of urban mid-America in the transitional years of its growth from rural innocence to urban sophistication. T was a versatile writer also and wrote 28 plays (often with a collaborator), some of which achieved a considerable success on the stage.

BIBLIOGRAPHY AND MANUSCRIPTS

The pioneer volume listing T's works is Barton Currie, BT: A BIBLIOGRAPHY (New York, 1932). After his death the Indiana Historical Society sponsored a complete listing in Dorothy Russo and Thelma Sullivan, A BIBLIOGRAPHY OF BT, 1869-1946 (Indianapolis, 1949). This work is exhaustive, reliable, and lists works about T as well as by him. Additional listings are found in Fred Millett, CONTEMPORARY AMERICAN AUTHORS (New York, 1940); PULC 16 (1955): 89-94; and in the notes to Woodress' biography (see below).

The T Papers, given to Princeton after T's death, contain a large number of MSS of literary works, some unpublished, many holograph letters to and from T, and much printed material. The collection is described in James Woodress, "The T Papers," PULC 16 (1955): 45-53. Both the public and state libraries in Indianapolis have extensive clipping files, and there are smaller letter collections at Purdue and Harvard Universities.

WORKS OF FICTION

Novels: *THE GENTLEMAN FROM INDIANA (1899), *MONSIEUR BEAUCAIRE (1900), THE TWO VANREVELS (1902), CHERRY (1903), THE BEAUTIFUL LADY (1905), THE CONQUEST OF CANAAN (1905), HIS OWN PEOPLE (1907), THE

* Of Special Importance

GUEST OF QUESNAY (1908), BEASLEY'S CHRISTMAS PARTY (1909), THE FLIRT (1913), *PENROD (1914), *THE TURMOIL (1915), *PENROD AND SAM (1916), *SEVENTEEN (1916), *THE MAGNIFICENT AMBERSONS (1918), RAMSEY MIL-HOLLAND (1919), *ALICE ADAMS (1921), HARLEQUIN AND COLUMBINE (1921), GENTLE JULIA (1922), *THE MIDLANDER (1924), WOMEN (1925), THE PLUTOCRAT (1927), CLAIRE AMBLER (1928), YOUNG MRS. GREELEY (1929), PENROD JASHBER (1929), MIRTHFUL HAVEN (1930), MARY'S NECK (1932), WANTON MALLY (1932), PRESENTING LILY MARS (1933), LITTLE ORVIE (1934), THE LORENZO BUNCH (1936), RUMBIN GALLERIES (1937), THE HERI-TAGE OF HATCHER IDA (1941), THE FIGHTING LITTLES (1941), KATE FEN-NIGATE (1943), IMAGE OF JOSEPHINE (1945), THE SHOW PIECE (1947), THREE SELECTED SHORT NOVELS: WALTERSON, UNCERTAIN MOLLY COL-LICUT, RENNIE PEDDIGOE (1947).

Stories: IN THE ARENA: STORIES OF POLITICAL LIFE (1905), THE FASCI-NATING STRANGER AND OTHER STORIES (1923), MR. WHITE, THE RED BARN, HELL, AND BRIDEWATER (1935).

EDITIONS AND REPRINTS

THE WORKS OF BT (The Autograph Edition), 27 volumes, limited to 565 copies, appeared between 1918 and 1932, and the Seawood Edition, also 27 volumes, limited to 1075 copies, was issued between 1922 and 1932. Several less compre-hensive editions were brought out between 1915 and 1933, but there is no col-lected edition containing work published during the last 13 years of T's life. A trilogy containing THE MAGNIFICENT AMBERSONS, THE TURMOIL, and NA-TIONAL AVENUE (originally called THE MIDLANDER) was published in one volume as GROWTH (1927). PENROD: HIS COMPLETE STORY appeared in 1931 with a "Dedicatory Word by the Author" and included all three of the Penrod books. The last collection of T's work was John Beecroft, ed., THE GENTLEMAN FROM INDIANAPOLIS (New York, 1957), which contains three novels, seven stories, and excerpts from three novels.

While most of T's lesser works have long been out of print, the most significant titles always have been available. ALICE ADAMS, his best and most important novel, and THE MAGNIFICENT AMBERSONS, both of which won Pulitzer prizes, belong in this category, along with the Penrod books, those boy stories which long have appealed to young and old alike, T's memorable tale of Midwest adolescence, SEVENTEEN, and MONSIEUR BEAUCAIRE, the perennial costume romance that furnished movies both for Valentino and Bob Hope.

In addition to these, as of 1973 reprint editions also were available of the fol-lowing: THE CONQUEST OF CANAAN, THE GENTLEMAN FROM INDIANA, WOMEN, LOOKING FORWARD AND OTHERS, SOME OLD PORTRAITS.

BIOGRAPHY

The only full-length critical biography is James Woodress, BT: GENTLEMAN FROM INDIANA (Philadelphia, 1955; New York, 1969). It is based on the T

* Of Special Importance

Papers at Princeton and other MS holdings and strikes a balance between narrative biography and criticism. Other useful materials for a life of T may be found in three letter collections: YOUR AMIABLE UNCLE: LETTERS TO HIS NEPHEWS [in 1903-04] (Indianapolis, 1949); Alan Downer, ed., ON PLAYS, PLAYWRIGHTS, AND PLAYGOERS: SELECTIONS FROM THE LETTERS OF BT TO GEORGE C. TYLER AND JOHN PETER TOOHEY, 1913-1925 (Princeton, 1959); and "T's New York Literary Debut: Letters Written to His Family in 1899," PULC 16 (1955): 54-79. To these should be added two autobiographical works: AS I SEEM TO ME, SEP 214 (5 July-23 August 1941), and THE WORLD DOES MOVE (Garden City, N.Y., 1928), the former covering youth and literary apprenticeship and the latter containing middle-aged reminiscences and opinions.

CRITICISM

Academic critics never have paid much attention to T, regarding him as an articulator of his time and place, not as a literary pioneer. As a result he received a great deal of attention in his own day from literary journalists, and since his death his reputation has steadily faded. Besides the one book-length critical biography mentioned above, there have been two dissertations: Albert Van Nostrand, "The Novels and Plays of BT" (Harvard, 1951), and Keith Fennimore, "A Case Study of BT as a Novelist," DA 16 (1956): 1140.

Among the critical articles of the past 20 years, the following are serious, worthwhile discussions of T's fiction: C.R. Coxe, "The Pre-Publication Printings of T's PENROD," SB 5 (1952-53): 153-57, the only textual study of a T work to date; W.T. Scott, "T and the 1920's," ASch 26 (1957): 181-94, a sharp but fair balance sheet of T's strengths and weaknesses (both considerable) with excellent discussion of ALICE ADAMS as one of the most significant novels of the 1920's; J.D. Seelye, "That Marvelous Boy--Penrod Once Again," VQR 37 (1961): 591-604, a shrewd analysis of Penrod as an embodiment of Midwest, middle-class values; W.E. Wilson "The Titan and the Gentleman," AR 23 (1963): 25-34, a superficial discussion of T and Dreiser as Hoosier contrasts; and three articles by James Woodress: "BT's Attack on American Materialism," GaR 8 (1954): 440-46, which finds social criticism in T's work of the World War I era; "BT's Political Career," AL 26 (1954): 209-22, which studies the biographical background for the political stories in IN THE ARENA; "Popular Taste in 1899: BT's First Novel," in Max Schulz, ed., ESSAYS IN AMERICAN AND ENGLISH LITERATURE PRESENTED TO BRUCE ROBERT MCELDERRY, JR. (Athens, Ohio, 1967), an analysis of why T's novel was a best seller.

Section 41

B. TRAVEN (TRAVEN TORSVAN) (1890-1969)

B. Traven (hereafter BT or T) was born in Chicago, the son of working-class Scandinavian immigrant parents. He had no formal schooling and went to sea at the age of 12, but after a number of years as a sailor, about 1914, he settled in Mexico where he lived the rest of his life. Most of his fiction is laid in Mexico and reflects a strong sympathy for workers, particularly the exploited Mexican Indians. For decades he was the mystery man of American literature, and as a result much that has been written about him is wildly inaccurate. He demanded anonymity from his publishers and insisted that his life was in his work.

BIBLIOGRAPHY AND MANUSCRIPTS

The most recent listing was published in Germany: Rolf Recknagel, "BT: BETRAGE ZUR BIOGRAFIE" (Reclams Universal Bibliotek, vol. 269, Leipzig, 1966). More accessible is an earlier compilation: E.R. Hagemann, "Checklist of the Work of BT . . ." PBSA 53 (1959): 40-67, which includes primary and secondary materials. At the date of this writing T's MSS have not yet turned up in institutional holdings.

WORKS OF FICTION

The publication history of T's works is a morass. All of his fiction was first published in Europe, and the first of his novels to be published in America appeared only in 1934. Nine of his 12 novels, plus the novella MACARIO, now have been published in the United States and another, THE WHITE ROSE, in London, but TROZA and ASLAN NORVAL have appeared only in German.

Novels (The following list gives the English titles of the novels with the original date of publication): THE DEATH SHIP (1926), THE COTTON PICKERS (1926) [called DER WOBBLY in German], *THE TREASURE OF THE SIERRA MADRE (1927), THE BRIDGE IN THE JUNGLE (1929), THE WHITE ROSE (1929), THE CARRETA (1930), GOVERNMENT (1931), MARCH TO THE MONTERIA

* Of Special Importance

(1933), THE REBELLION OF THE HANGED (1936), TROZA (1936), THE GEN-
ERAL FROM THE JUNGLE (1939), MACARIO (1949), ASLAN NORVAL (1961).

Stories: BUSH (1928).

EDITIONS AND REPRINTS

T has been one of the most popular writers of the twentieth century, but he is
only now being recognized in the United States. His works have been translated into 21 languages and down to 1959 there had been some 237 editions of
his books. Eight of his novels and the novella MACARIO are in print, including four novels recently published in English for the first time. There are Signet and Modern Library editions of THE TREASURE OF THE SIERRA MADRE, and
there have been two story collections: STORIES BY THE MAN NOBODY KNOWS:
NINE TALES (Evanston, Ill., 1961); THE NIGHT VISITOR AND OTHER STORIES,
intro. Charles Miller (New York, 1966); also available in paperback.

BIOGRAPHY

There is no biography of T in English and little is known about him. However,
much of his fiction is narrated in the first person and seems clearly based on
his own experience. When he insisted that his publishers not advertise his books
or even give out his address, he wrote them: "In every work of a writer the
man behind it reveals his personality." The only reliable biographical sketch
is Charles Miller, "BT, American Author," TQ 6 (1963): 162-68, but even
there T's birthdate is incorrect. The NEW YORK TIMES obituary (27 March
1969) also is useful. The first crack in T's anonymity came from a Mexican
journalist who investigated immigration records. See Luis Spota, "MANANA
Descubre la Identidad de BT," MANANA 258 (7 August 1948): 10-26. Beware
of Judy Stone, "The Mystery of BT," RAMPARTS 6, ii, iii (1967): 31-49, 55-
75, who believes T was really named Ret Marut, was the illegitimate son of
Wilhelm II, and published an anti-war newspaper in Munich during World War
I. Also beware of Rolf Recknagel (see above), who wrote an entire book to
prove that the mysterious revolutionary Marut, who disappeared in the 1920's,
and T were the same person.

CRITICISM

That T finally is being recognized in his native country is shown by the recent
reprinting of his works and a growing body of criticism about him. There have
been two dissertations: C.R. Humphrey, "BT: An Examination of the Controversy over His Identity with an Analysis of His Major Work and His Place in
Literature," DA 27 (1967): 3049-50A; J.H. Irsfeld, "The American as a Symbol of the Conflict between Industry and Nature in the First Five Novels of
BT," DAI 30 (1970): 3011A. These studies were preceded by John Fraser,
"The Novels of BT," GSE 2 (1958): 7-15, and a special section in TQ in

1963. This reprinted some of T's work that had not previously appeared in the United States and assessed his importance. See Charles Miller, "BT in the Americas," TQ 6 (1963): 208-11, and Neville Braybrooke, "The Hero without a Name: Some Notes on BT's THE DEATH SHIP," TQ 6 (1963): 140-44.

Miller has made two more contributions to this criticism in "Our Great Neglected Wobbly," MQR 6 (1967): 57-61, and "BT: Pure Proletarian Writer" in David Madden, ed., PROLETARIAN WRITERS OF THE THIRTIES (Carbondale, III., 1968); and there is another article by Fraser: "Splendor in the Darkness: BT's THE DEATH SHIP," DR 44 (1964): 35-43. A useful analysis of a story is J.M. Warner, "Tragic Vision in BT's 'The Night Visitor'," SSF 7 (1970): 377-84.

Section 42

CARL VAN VECHTEN (1880-1964)

Carl Van Vechten (hereafter CVV, VV, or V) made his way from his native Iowa to New York by way of the University of Chicago. He spent a number of years as a music critic for the NEW YORK TIMES, later contributed essays as a free lance critic to literary and musical publications, and at the age of 40 began writing novels. His novels follow no pattern but reflect the topical interests of the 1920's. Despite the lack of any consistent attitude towards life or philosophy, he was, in the view of one critic (Oscar Cargill, INTELLECTUAL AMERICA), "the best creative artist among the American Intelligentsia."

BIBLIOGRAPHY AND MANUSCRIPTS

The most recent listing is Paul Padgette, CVV: 1880-1964 (San Francisco, 1965), the catalogue for a memorial exhibit at the San Francisco Public Library. Earlier compilations include K.W. Jonas, CVV: A BIBLIOGRAPHY (New York, 1955), which was updated by the same writer in "Additions to the Bibliography of CVV," PBSA 55 (1961): 42-45. See also J.D. Gordon, "CVV: Notes for an Exhibition in Honor of His 75th Birthday," BNYPL 59 (1955): 331-66. The earliest listing was Scott Cunningham, A BIBLIOGRAPHY OF THE WRITINGS OF CVV (Philadelphia, 1924).

Both Yale and the New York Public Library have special collections, the former having 41 MSS, 600 letters and 10,000 pieces of correspondence. In addition, Princeton, Harvard, and the University of Chicago have extensive holdings.

WORKS OF FICTION

Novels: PETER WHIFFLE: HIS LIFE AND WORKS (1922), THE BLIND BOW-BOY (1923), THE TATTOOED COUNTESS (1924), FIRECRACKERS: A REALISTIC NOVEL (1925), *NIGGER HEAVEN (1926), SPIDER BOY (1928), PARTIES: SCENES FROM CONTEMPORARY NEW YORK LIFE (1930).

* Of Special Importance

EDITIONS AND REPRINTS

All of V's novels were sufficiently popular to have had contemporary reprintings in inexpensive editions. PETER WHIFFLE was an early title in the Modern Library, BLIND BOW-BOY a Borzoi pocket book; THE TATTOOED COUNTESS was reissued by A.L. Burt, NIGGER HEAVEN, FIRECRACKERS, and SPIDER BOY by Grosset. PARTIES was reprinted by Books for Libraries Press (Freeport, N.Y., 1971), and NIGGER HEAVEN is a Harper-Row paperback.

BIOGRAPHY

There are two books that treat V and his era. The more recent is Bruce Kellner, CVV AND THE IRREVERENT DECADE (Norman, Okla., 1968), which is rich in personal detail but has few critical judgements. Also it is illustrated lavishly with the famous photographs that V took after giving up writing for photography. The other work is Edward Lueders, CVV AND THE TWENTIES (Albuquerque, N.M., 1955), a better balance of criticism and biography and an outgrowth of an earlier (1952) dissertation. V is also his own biographer, having written "Notes for an Autobiography," COLOPHON 1 (September 1930): part 3; SACRED AND PROFANE MEMORIES (New York, 1932; Freeport, N.Y., 1971); FRAGMENTS FROM AN UNWRITTEN AUTOBIOGRAPHY (New Haven, 1955), papers originally in YULG; "Rogue Elephant in Porcelain," YULG 38 (1963): 41-50, reminiscence of Wallace Stevens. In addition others have recorded their memories of V: Emily Clark, INNOCENCE ABROAD (New York, 1931); Lincoln Kirstein, "CVV (1880-1964), YULG 39 (1964): 158-62; A.A. Knopf, "Reminiscences of Hergesheimer, VV, and Mencken," YULG 25 (1950): 145-64; Langston Hughes, THE BIG SEA (New York, 1945); Eleanor Wylie, "CVV" in THE BORZOI 1925 (New York, 1925); Gertrude Stein, "Van or 20 Years After," REVIEWER 4 (1924): 176-77. The V-Stein relationship was summarized by Donald Gallup, "CVV's Gertrude Stein," YULG 27 (1952): 77-86.

CRITICISM

V remains an important figure in his era but of minor intrinsic significance. Lueders has written a second book, CVV (TUSAS, 1965), which is a competent treatment within the Procrustean Twayne format. Most of the recent interest in V centers on his Harlem novel, NIGGER HEAVEN. There is a complete dissertation: L.D. Coleman, "The Contribution of CVV to the Negro Renaissance, 1920-1930," DAI 30 (1970): 3453A. For earlier review-essays by black writers, see (favorable) James Weldon Johnson, "Romance and Tragedy in Harlem," OPPORTUNITY 4 (1926): 316-17, 330, and (unfavorable) W.E.B. DuBois in THE CRISIS (December 1926). Three articles in PHYLON (a journal devoted to black writing) deal with V: H.M. Gloster, "The VV Vogue," 6 (1945): 310-14; G.S. Schuyler, "The VV Revolution," 11 (1950): 362-68; Eugene Arden, "The Early Harlem Novel," 20 (1959): 25-31. Though V was white, he is included in H.M. Gloster, NEGRO VOICES IN AMERICAN FICTION (Chapel Hill, N.C., 1948), a reprinting of the article cited above. Another study of NIGGER HEAVEN is C.R. Larson, "Three Harlem Novels of the Jazz Age,"

Crit 11, iii (1969): 66-78.

V was the subject of critical attention almost as soon as he began writing novels. Gertrude Stein devoted a brief chapter to him in GEOGRAPHY AND
PLAYS (Boston, 1922); J.W. Beach treated him in "The Peacock's Tail," AS 1
(1925): 65-73, repr. THE OUTLOOK FOR AMERICAN PROSE (Chicago, 1926);
the most recent article is James Ringo, "A Three-Quarter-Length Portrait of
CVV," CABELLIAN 1, ii (1969): 68-71. V also has often been included in
books on the novel or in general studies. Some of them are Edmund Wilson,
THE SHORES OF LIGHT (New York, 1952); Charles Baldwin, THE MEN WHO
MAKE OUR NOVELS (New York, 1924); Harlan Hatcher, CREATING THE
MODERN AMERICAN NOVEL (New York, 1935); Oscar Cargill, INTELLECTUAL
AMERICA (New York, 1941); Alfred Kazin, ON NATIVE GROUNDS (New
York, 1942).

Section 43

NATHANAEL WEST (1903-1940)

Nathanael West (hereafter NW or W) was born Nathan Wallenstein Weinstein in New York City, the son of a building contractor. He attended New York public schools and Brown University, from which he graduated in 1924. After two years in Paris he returned to New York to begin writing, but his bitter, satiric fiction attracted little attention. He later moved to Hollywood as a script writer and there gathered the material that went into his devastating, surrealistic picture of the movie community in THE DAY OF THE LOCUST. He was still virtually unknown when he died, but in the past ten or 15 years he has been discovered, praised, and explicated extensively, and now he seems to belong in the Pantheon of modern American masters.

BIBLIOGRAPHY AND MANUSCRIPTS

A definitive bibliography of both primary and secondary sources is badly needed. A start was made by William White in "NW: A Bibliography," SB 11 (1958): 207-25, which describes first editions and lists reviews. White also includes criticism and "Movies by NW," but the latter item needs to be supplemented by lists in Jay Martin's NW: THE ART OF HIS LIFE (New York, 1970). Later White brought his bibliography up to date in "NW: A Bibliography Addenda," SERIF 2 (March 1965): 5-18, and there are in addition listings in several recent books: Randall Reid, THE FICTION OF NW: NO REDEEMER, NO PROMISED LAND (Chicago, 1967); Jay Martin, ed., NW: A COLLECTION OF CRITICAL ESSAYS; Thomas Jackson, ed., TWENTIETH-CENTURY INTERPRETATIONS OF "MISS LONELYHEARTS" (both Englewood Cliffs, N.J., 1971); David Madden, ed., NW: THE CHEATERS AND THE CHEATED (Deland, Fla., 1973). The last three bibliographies are annotated.

Because West was unknown and unsung when he died relatively young, no one was interested in collecting his MSS, and there is therefore very little W material in institutional collections. W's literary remains, however, passed into the hands of his executor and brother-in-law, S.J. Perelman, who has in recent years made them available to scholars. Princeton reports significant MS holdings, however, and there are small letter collections at Yale and the State University of New York at Buffalo.

WORKS OF FICTION

Novels: THE DREAM LIFE OF BALSO SNELL (1931), *MISS LONELYHEARTS (1933), A COOL MILLION (1934), *THE DAY OF THE LOCUST (1939).

EDITIONS AND REPRINTS

Original editions of W's works are virtually unobtainable, but W's recent surge to critical acclaim has resulted in many reprints. THE COMPLETE WORKS (1957) contains all the novels in a 421-page volume, and in the 1960's paper-back editions appeared of MISS LONELYHEARTS, A COOL MILLION, and THE DAY OF THE LOCUST. The first carried an introduction by S.E. Hyman and the last by Budd Schulberg, who had been a friend of W's. The novels also have been brought out in combinations in paperback editions, and in this form A COOL MILLION and THE DAY OF THE LOCUST both are available with BALSO SNELL within the same covers.

BIOGRAPHY

The first comprehensive and adequate life of W is Jay Martin's work (see above). Martin had access to the papers in Perelman's possession and conducted numerous interviews with friends and associates. There is an enormous amount of material here that future writers on W will find invaluable. Martin's work supersedes the earliest book on W by James Light, NW: AN INTERPRETATIVE STUDY (Evanston, Ill., 1961, 1971), which was written without access to W's papers. A brief biographical account also is included in Hyman's pamphlet NW (UMPAW, 1962).

Although W did not write about himself, there are various reminiscences of interest by literary friends: S.J. Perelman, "NW: A Portrait," CONTEMPO 2 (25 July 1933): 3; William Carlos Williams, AUTOBIOGRAPHY (New York, 1951); Erskine Caldwell, CALL IT EXPERIENCE (New York, 1951); Josephine Herbst, "NW," KR 23 (1961): 611-27; Budd Schulberg, THE FOUR SEASONS OF SUCCESS (New York, 1972); John Sanford, "NW," THE SCREEN WRITER 2 (December 1946): 10-13; Ruth McKenney, LOVE STORY (New York, 1950). W was married to the heroine of McKenney's play about her younger sister, MY SISTER EILEEN. In addition to these articles and chapters James Light's "Genius on Campus: NW at Brown," CONTACT 3 (1959): 98-111, is important.

CRITICISM

Almost the only critical attention that W received during his lifetime was in book reviews, although some of these were very enthusiastic. Malcolm Cowley in EXILE'S RETURN (New York, 1934) discussed MISS LONELYHEARTS as a bril-

* Of Special Importance

liant book with few readers. After W died in 1940, he continued to be neglected and did not get into Fred Millett's CONTEMPORARY AMERICAN AUTHORS (1940); nor did he make the OXFORD COMPANION TO AMERICAN LITERATURE until the third edition (1956), and he still has not broken into the latest bibliographical supplement to LHUS (1972).

Light's essays on W began to appear with the publication of "MISS LONELY-HEARTS: The Imagery of Nightmare," AQ 8 (1956): 316-27, and culminated in his book (1961), which was the first full-length study and still is an important critical work. Light's book, which began as the first dissertation on W, is useful for its extensive treatment of the inter-relationship between W's life and themes. Light regards surrealism as a major influence on W. Hyman's Minnesota pamphlet is perhaps the best brief critical overview and has been reprinted in W.V. O'Connor, ed., SEVEN MODERN AMERICAN NOVELISTS (Minneapolis, 1964).

Two more of the ten dissertations that were written on W through 1970 have been turned into books: Victor Comerchero, NW: THE IRONIC PROPHET (Syracuse, 1964); Randall Reid (see above). Comerchero gives W a Freudian and mythic reading and concludes that W is a visionary whose best novels, "are his visionary nightmares." Reid's study develops the thesis that W was a parodist. W never developed a systematic view of American culture but attacked the ills and grotesqueries of American society by parodying them. Another more recent book-length work is Irving Malin's NW'S NOVELS (Carbondale, Ill., 1972), a medium-length volume in the Cross-Current series.

There now is available on W about as much material as one is likely to need in the three collections (see above) of reprinted criticism. Martin's edition, CRITICAL ESSAYS, includes pieces by W.H. Auden, Norman Podhoretz, and Edmund Wilson, as well as biographical material by Perelman and Herbst. In addition there are two prose essays by W: "Some Notes on Violence" and "Some Notes on Miss L." Podhoretz' essay, "NW: A Particular Kind of Joking," NY 33 (18 May 1957): 156-65, sees W as "first and last a writer of comedy" and in so far as he deals with serious matters as greater than either Fitzgerald or Hemingway. Auden's piece, "W's Disease," reprinted from THE DYER'S HAND AND OTHER ESSAYS (New York, 1960), argues that W's view is that "creation is essentially evil and that goodness is contrary to its laws." The collection edited by Jackson, devoted entirely to MISS LONELYHEARTS, selects from more than thirty articles which have by now been written on this novel. Among these two should be singled out: Robert Andreach, "Between the Dead Pan and the Unborn Christ," MFS 12 (1966): 251-60, and Edmond Volpe, "The Waste Land of NW," RENASCENCE 13 (1961): 69-77. The latter sees W's novel as the answer of the 1930's to Eliot's poem. Madden's gathering begins with "A Confluence of Voices," in which various writers and critics discuss W, and follows with 14 essays both general and on specific works.

Other significant general essays that should be noted: Daniel Aaron's "Late Thoughts on NW," MR 6 (1965): 307-16, looks at W as a writer of the 1930's; Kingsley Widmer's "The Sweet Savage Prophecies of NW" in Warren French, ed., THE THIRTIES (Deland, Fla., 1967), is a coherent discussion of W's unique genius; Bruce Olson's "NW: The Use of Cynicism" in Charles Hoyt, ed., MINOR AMERICAN NOVELISTS (Carbondale, Ill., 1970), concludes that W is the author of one and one-half novels: MISS LONELYHEARTS and the "unfulfilled novel about Hollywood," THE DAY OF THE LOCUST.

Section 44

EDITH WHARTON (1862-1937)

Edith Wharton (hereafter EW or W) was born into an old and socially prominent
New York family. She made her debut at the age of 17 and married a Boston
banker at the age of 23. But totally unlike the rest of her family, she was
interested in books and tried writing a novel at 11. As a young society matron,
she began writing seriously and published a collection of short stories in 1899.
From then on she wrote steadily and produced an entire shelf of novels, some
of them distinguished contributions to American literature. After 1907 she lived
in France, was active in relief work during World War I, and was a friend of
Henry James, with whose writing hers often is compared. She probably was
the most distinguished American novelist born in the 1850's and 1860's.

BIBLIOGRAPHY AND MANUSCRIPTS

A definitive bibliography of W, who is almost one of our major authors, is
badly needed. The most recent compilation is in LHUS, Bibliography Supplement II (New York, 1972), but this is highly selective. More complete and
fairly recent is Vito Brenni's EW: A BIBLIOGRAPHY (Morgantown, W.Va.,
1966), which contains 708 entries of primary and secondary material including
some reviews, theses, and dissertations.

Earlier listings which still have some validity for primary sources are these: the
appendix to Blake Nevius' EW: A STUDY OF HER FICTION (Berkeley, 1953);
L.M. Melish's A BIBLIOGRAPHY OF THE COLLECTED WRITINGS OF EW (New
York, 1927); Lavinia Davis' A BIBLIOGRAPHY OF THE WRITINGS OF EW (Port-
land, Maine, 1933); the appendix to E.K. Brown's EW: ETUDE CRITIQUE
(Paris, 1935). For secondary material one needs to use the standard serial bibliographies and checklists (see "Part One") plus the appendices to Grace Kellogg's THE TWO LIVES OF EW: THE WOMAN AND HER WORK (New York,
1965); Geoffrey Walton's EW: A CRITICAL INTERPRETATION (Rutherford, N.J.,
1970); also the books by Nevius and Brown (see above). Also valuable though
less accessible is Patricia Plante's unpublished dissertation: "The Critical Reception of EW's Fiction in America and England with an Annotated Enumerative
Bibliography of W Criticism from 1900-1961," DA 23 (1962): 1706.

W's papers were given to Yale in 1938 with the stipulation that they were not to be made available until 1968. Now that the restriction has expired R.W.B. Lewis is at work on an authorized biography making use of this material. This collection contains 170 MSS and over five thousand items in all, including journals and letters. There also are collections of W's letters to W.C. Brownell at Amherst College; her correspondence with Scribner's remains in the publisher's archives. There are other significant letter collections at Smith College, the University of California at Berkeley, Harvard, Princeton, Columbia, the University of Chicago, the Wisconsin Historical Society, and the American Academy of Arts and Letters.

WORKS OF FICTION

Novels: THE TOUCHSTONE (1900), A GIFT FROM THE GRAVE (1900), THE VALLEY OF DECISION (1902), SANCTUARY (1903), *THE HOUSE OF MIRTH (1905), THE FRUIT OF THE TREE (1907), MADAME DE TREYMES (1907), *ETHAN FROME (1911), THE REEF (1912), *THE CUSTOM OF THE COUNTRY (1913), SUMMER (1917), THE MARNE (1918), *THE AGE OF INNOCENCE (1920), THE GLIMPSES OF THE MOON (1922), A SON AT THE FRONT (1923), OLD NEW YORK: NEW YEAR'S DAY; THE SPARK; THE OLD MAID; FALSE DAWN (1924), THE MOTHER'S RECOMPENSE (1925), TWILIGHT SLEEP (1927), THE CHILDREN (1928), HUDSON RIVER BRACKETED (1929), THE GODS ARRIVE (1932), THE BUCCANEERS (1938).

Stories: THE GREATER INCLINATION (1899), CRUCIAL INSTANCES (1901), THE DESCENT OF MAN (1904), THE HERMIT AND THE WILD WOMAN (1908), TALES OF MEN AND GHOSTS (1910), *XINGU (1916), HERE AND BEYOND (1926), CERTAIN PEOPLE (1930), HUMAN NATURE (1933), THE WORLD OVER (1936), GHOSTS (1937).

EDITIONS AND REPRINTS

There is no collected edition of W's works and many have long been out of print. Some of the best novels have been reprinted and the following are useful text editions with introductions and critical apparatus: THE CUSTOM OF THE COUNTRY with introduction by Nevius (1956) and ETHAN FROME: THE STORY WITH SOURCES AND COMMENTARY, also ed. by Nevius (1968); THE HOUSE OF MIRTH with introduction by Irving Howe (1962) and with introduction by R.W.B. Lewis (1963). The latter reproduces sample MS pages in the appendix. Lewis also has edited THE AGE OF INNOCENCE (1968) and THE COLLECTED SHORT STORIES OF EW, 2 vols. (1968), while Louis Auchincloss brought out THE EW READER (1965) and A.H. Quinn AN EW TREASURY (1950). Earlier Wayne Andrews edited and introduced THE BEST SHORT STORIES OF EW (1958). In addition there are paperback reprints of THE REEF and SUMMER, and eight other titles in hardback reprints. Nineteen titles, however, never have been reprinted or, if reprinted, have been allowed to go out of print.

* Of Special Importance

THE AGE OF INNOCENCE was put in the Modern Library in 1943, and there now are three editions in print. ETHAN FROME exists in five editions, and so does THE HOUSE OF MIRTH. The Scribner paperback ETHAN FROME contains the preface EW wrote for the 1922 edition.

BIOGRAPHY

Until Lewis' biography-in-progress is published, there will be many unanswered questions about W's life. There are two chief sources for biographical information. The first is W's own A BACKWARD GLANCE (1934), one of the good literary autobiographies but a reticent one. W was very circumspect in talking about her personal life, her relationship with her husband, which ended in divorce in 1913, and her long love for Walter Berry. But the book is important for W's views on life and art and her family background. The other source book for W's life is Percy Lubbock's PORTRAIT OF EW (New York, 1947), but Lubbock is no more candid than W herself. Yet his book is important because he was a friend and because he prints letters and reminiscences by friends. See Edmund Wilson's essay, "EW: A Memoir by an English Friend," in his CLASSICS AND COMMERCIALS (New York, 1950). Also see W's travel books on France and Morocco.

Three other books of varying value contain biographical data: Oliva Coolidge's EW: 1862-1937 (New York, 1964) is a competent, straightforward life which does not try to penetrate W's silences or psychoanalyze her; Grace Kellogg's book on the other hand (see above) must be read with caution, as it does speculate and it documents few of its assumptions. The most important book is Millicent Bell's EW AND HENRY JAMES: THE STORY OF THEIR FRIENDSHIP (New York, 1965), a first-rate study of a relationship that extended from 1902 to 1916. It is based on meticulous examination of original sources and is well documented. A more recent addition to W biography is Auchincloss' EW: A WOMAN IN HER TIME (New York, 1971), a handsome book that is half text and half illustrations. As Auchincloss is a novelist, the book is full of well-written anecdotes and character sketches, but it does not add to available biographical knowledge.

Some of W's letters have been published: 27 in Lubbock's edition of THE LETTERS OF HENRY JAMES (New York, 1920); her letters to Fitzgerald in E.H. Lockridge, ed., TWENTIETH CENTURY INTERPRETATIONS OF "THE GREAT GATSBY" (Englewood Cliffs, N.J., 1968); Hilda Fife's "Letters from EW to Vernon Lee," CLQ 3 (1953): 139-44. Other brief contributions to biography include: Peter Buitenhuis, "EW and the First World War," AQ 18 (1966): 493-505; Arthur Mizener, "Scott Fitzgerald and EW," TLS, 7 July 1966, p. 595; J.W. Tuttleton, "The President and the Lady: EW and Theodore Roosevelt," BNYPL 69 (1965): 49-57. Andrews' introduction to THE BEST SHORT STORIES is entitled, "The World of EW: Fragment of a Biography in Progress."

CRITICISM

W's critical reputation had sagged badly by the time she died in 1937. She completed her important work with THE AGE OF INNOCENCE, and in the

1930's she seemed an excessively conservative voice from the past. But interest in her revived in the 1950's and 1960's, and while only six dissertations had been written on her before 1950, 23 more were produced in the next 20 years. Other critical activity and the reprinting of her works have paralleled the academic interest.

There were two books written about W before she died: R.M. Lovett's EW (New York, 1925) and E.K. Brown's EW: ETUDE CRITIQUE (see above). Lovett's book is a sympathetic reading of the works by a distinguished critic who saw the complexities and recognized the artistry. Brown's study began as the first dissertation on W. Written by a first-rate critical intelligence, his book has had a strong influence on later W scholars, but unfortunately it has never been translated. Some of Brown's views, however, are included in his "EW," EA 2 (1938): 16-26 (translated in Howe's collection, see below).

There were two critical works in the 1950's: Blake Nevius' (see above) and Marilyn Lyde's EW: CONVENTION AND MORALITY IN THE WORK OF A NOVELIST (Norman, Okla., 1959). Nevius' work is the best study available, a comprehensive critical appraisal of the entire canon, which argues convincingly that W's great theme was the "trapped sensibility." Lyde's work, which began as a dissertation, is more narrowly focused. The central problem in W's fiction, she believes, is to define "the exact nature of the relation Mrs. W conceived to exist between social convention and morality."

More recent contributions to W exegesis include Auchincloss' pamphlet EW (UMPAW, 1961), which is a very satisfactory brief overview, but it is too brief to do more than suggest the outlines for further study. Walton's study (see above) analyzes the novels under the headings of tragedy in society, comedy in society, social change and morals in society, and satire on society. But perhaps even more useful in studying W's fiction is her own critical work, THE WRITING OF FICTION (1925), which provides a good insight into her perception of the problems and strategies of the writer. This work has been kept in print.

W's work has been discussed innumerable times in historical and critical studies of twentieth-century literature and in individual essays. Only a few may be cited here. Some of the better and more interesting ones: J.W. Beach's THE TWENTIETH-CENTURY NOVEL: STUDIES IN TECHNIQUE (New York, 1932); Josephine Jessup's FAITH OF OUR FEMINISTS (New York, 1950), which studies W, Ellen Glasgow, and Willa Cather; H.W. Morgan's WRITERS IN TRANSITION: SEVEN AMERICANS (New York, 1963); Alfred Kazin's ON NATIVE GROUNDS (New York, 1942), which contrasts W and Dreiser in a single chapter; D.E.S. Maxwell's AMERICAN FICTION: THE INTELLECTUAL BACKGROUND (New York, 1963); Lionel Trilling in Robert MacIver, ed., GREAT MORAL DILEMMAS (New York, 1956); Edmund Wilson's THE WOUND AND THE BOW (Boston, 1941).

A great many articles have been written about W, and fortunately Irving Howe has collected 17 of them in EW: A COLLECTION OF CRITICAL ESSAYS

(Englewood Cliffs, N.J., 1962). The essays by Wilson, Brown, and Kazin (previously cited) appear here along with Percy Lubbock's "The Novels of EW" and Auchincloss' "EW and Her New Yorks." These and the other essays in the collection address themselves to the four major problems in studying W: the range of her achievement, her role as heiress of Henry James, her attempt to deal with social and economic change, and her vision that "society was profoundly inhospitable to human need and desire." The standard bibliographies list many articles on W's best novels, ETHAN FROME, THE HOUSE OF MIRTH, and THE AGE OF INNOCENCE.

Section 45

THORNTON WILDER (1897-   )

Thornton Wilder (hereafter TW or W) was born in Madison, Wisconsin, the son of a newspaper editor and grew up partly in China where his father was consul general in Hong Kong and Shanghai. He attended Oberlin but received his bachelor's degree from Yale and a master's degree from Princeton. He has taught at Lawrenceville School, the University of Chicago, and lectured at Harvard, but since he wrote his best-selling, Pulitzer-prize-winning novel, THE BRIDGE OF SAN LUIS REY (1927), he has been able to devote as much of his time to writing as he has wanted. A large part of his energy has gone into writing plays, and he has won two Pulitzer Prizes for OUR TOWN (1938) and THE SKIN OF OUR TEETH (1942). In the long run he probably will turn out to be a more significant writer than his present critical acclaim would suggest.

BIBLIOGRAPHY AND MANUSCRIPTS

The best bibliography available is Jerome Edelstein's A BIBLIOGRAPHICAL CHECKLIST OF THE WRITINGS OF TW (New Haven, 1959), which limits it-self to first editions of English-language publications, but it lists novels, plays, articles, lectures, and contributions to books. For criticism one should consult Heinz Kosok's "TW: A Bibliography of Criticism," TCL 9 (1963): 93-100. Kosok also has written "TW: Ein Literaturbericht," JA 9 (1964): 196-227, which surveys all the important critical writing on W to the date of publication. To these should be added Jackson Bryer's "TW and the Reviewers," PBSA 58 (1964): 35-49. The time has come for someone to do a complete, definitive, up-to-date bibliography of primary and secondary works.

W has given most of his MSS to Yale, but there are additional MSS at the New York Academy of Arts and Letters. Other significant collections are at the University of Chicago, the New York Public Library, Princeton, Harvard, and Longmans, Green and Co., publishers, New York City. Many of W's letters are in institutional collections, including the New York Academy of Arts and Letters, Yale, Kent State University (see "Letters by TW: A Catalogue," SERIF 3 [June 1966]: 39-40), Syracuse University, Boston University, the University of Illinois, and the Newberry Library.

WORKS OF FICTION

Novels: THE CABALA (1926), *THE BRIDGE OF SAN LUIS REY (1927), THE WOMAN OF ANDROS (1930), HEAVEN'S MY DESTINATION (1934), *THE IDES OF MARCH (1948), THE EIGHTH DAY (1967), THEOPHILUS NORTH (1973).

EDITIONS AND REPRINTS

There has been no collected edition of W's works, but THE CABALA and THE WOMAN OF ANDROS were published together (1968) and earlier those two and THE BRIDGE appeared as A TW TRIO (1956) with an introduction by Malcolm Cowley. THE BRIDGE, THE CABALA, THE EIGHTH DAY, HEAVEN'S MY DESTINATION, and THE IDES OF MARCH all are available in paperback editions. W's plays also have been reprinted in several collections.

BIOGRAPHY

As W wants no biography written during his lifetime, there is no satisfactory account yet of his career; but one may go to standard biographical sources for information. Also there are numerous interviews available: Walther Tritsch, "TW in Berlin," LIVING AGE 341 (1931): 44-47; Flora Lewis, "TW at 65 Looks Ahead--and Back," NYTM 15 April 1962, pp. 28-29; Ross Parmenter, "Novelist into Playwright," SRL 18 (11 June 1938): 10-11; Richard Goldstone, "TW," in Malcolm Cowley, ed., WRITERS AT WORK: THE PARIS REVIEW IN-TERVIEWS (New York, 1958). There also is biographical information in Malcolm Goldstein's THE ART OF TW (Lincoln, Nebr., 1965) and Bernard Grebanier's pamphlet TW (UMPAW, 1964). There are several sketches of W: NY 35 (23 May 1959): 34-35; "An Obliging Man," TIME 61 (12 January 1953): 44-46, 48-49; Hermine Popper, "The Universe of TW," HM 230 (June 1965): 72-78; Richard Goldstone, "The W 'Image,'" FOUR QUARTERS 16 (May 1967): 1-7. W has not written an autobiography, though he occasionally has written about his own work, and his letters remain unpublished.

CRITICISM

W has been neglected by the academic critics, perhaps because he has won three Pulitzer prizes and reached a wide, popular audience. W has not sought publicity, nor has he tried to promote his own work. He pays no attention to the critics, and his work is so varied that it cannot be put into convenient pigeonholes. A good part of the W criticism is devoted to his plays, but since consideration of W as playwright lies outside the scope of this essay, that aspect of W will not be considered here.

Grebanier's pamphlet (see above) is a convenient brief and reliable summary of W's achievement in 44 pages. This may be supplemented by Rex Burbank's TW (TUSAS, 1961), a slender volume which is a competent, straightforward analysis of W's works from the standpoint of style, recurrent myths, religious humanism,

* Of Special Importance

and belief in human dignity. Burbank shows W to be a more significant writer than he generally had been regarded before the 1960's. Goldstein's book (see above) also is a valuable contribution, concentrating as the title suggests on W as artist. It has good essays on individual works. Two other general treatments are worth examining: Helmut Papajewski's TW (New York, 1969), which originally was written in German, concerns itself with W's relation to American philosophy and intellectual history, finding him a "product of rationalist American protestantism"; he concludes that W's main theme is that "the self-perfecting of selfless love is the sole purpose that gives life meaning." A brief but excellent summary of W's work is Alexander Cowie's "The Bridge of TW" in Clarence Gohdes, ed., ESSAYS ON AMERICAN LITERATURE IN HONOR OF JAY B. HUBBELL (Durham, N.C., 1967).

There have been a number of discussions of themes and techniques in W's novels. Cowley's introduction to A TW TRIO (see above) is good, and there are four unpublished dissertations on the novels: Evelyn Dugan, "The Novels of TW: Themes through Characterization," DAI 31 (1971): 6050A; Allen Loyd, "The Shudder of Awe: A Study of the Novels of TW," DA 29 (1968): 1541A; Evelyn Claxton, "The Novels of TW," DAI 32 (1971): 959A; M.E. Williams, "The Novels of TW," DAI 32 (1971): 1536A.

THE BRIDGE provoked a considerable literary controversy. Michael Gold and Granville Hicks, Marxist critics, attacked the novel in "TW: Prophet of the Genteel Christ," NR 64 (22 October 1930): 266-67, and in THE GREAT TRA-DITION (New York, 1935). Later E.K. Brown in "A Christian Humanist: TW," UTQ 4 (1935): 356-70, discussed HEAVEN'S MY DESTINATION as W's answer to the Marxist critics.

Two studies of the influences on W are provocative: H.S. Canby in AMERI-CAN MEMOIR (Boston, 1947) suggests that the strongest influence on W is Gertrude Stein, while Edmund Wilson in THE SHORES OF LIGHT (New York, 1952) believes that W was the first American writer to be influenced by Proust. L.C. Perez compares THE EIGHTH DAY to DON QUIXOTE in "W and Cervantes: In the Spirit of the Tapestry," SYMPOSIUM 25 (1971): 249-59. Finally, there was a special issue of FOUR QUARTERS 16 (1967) devoted to W, containing, besides the articles previously cited by Goldstone, Donald Haberman on "The Americanization of TW," and Joseph Firebaugh on "Farce and the Heavenly Destination."

The same issue also carried an article by Hans Sahl on "TW and the Germans," only one of many European studies, especially German, of W. See F.R. Frey, "Postwar German Reactions to American Literature," JEGP 54 (1955): 173-94. Although THE BRIDGE was widely read in Europe, most of the foreign interest in W has been in his plays.

Section 46

OWEN WISTER (1860-1938)

Owen Wister (hereafter OW or W) came from a prominent Pennsylvania family, graduated from Harvard in 1882, and then went West for his health. His experiences in Wyoming provided him with unexploited literary material and made his reputation, but after writing THE VIRGINIAN, which did more than any other book to establish the stereotypical "Western," he turned to other subjects and non-fiction.

BIBLIOGRAPHY AND MANUSCRIPTS

The most recent listing is Dean Sherman, "OW: An Annotated Bibliography," BB 28 (1971): 7-16. See also "The OW Papers in the Library of Congress . . .," PENNSYLVANIAN 10 (August 1952): 1-3; Theodore Hornberger, "American 1st Editions at Texas University: OW," LCUT 1 (1945): 33-34; and Johnson. Extensive holdings of manuscript material may be found at the Library of Congress, Harvard, the New York Public Library, Princeton, and the University of North Carolina at Chapel Hill. There are in addition large letter collections at the University of Michigan, University of California at Berkeley, University of South Carolina, and the Wisconsin State Historical Society. There are other smaller letter collections in various libraries (see ALM).

WORKS OF FICTION

Novels: *THE VIRGINIAN (1902), PHILOSOPHY 4: A STORY OF HARVARD UNIVERSITY (1903), LADY BALTIMORE (1906).

Stories: RED MEN AND WHITE (1896), LIN MCLEAN (1898), THE JIMMY-JOHN BOSS AND OTHER STORIES (1900), MEMBERS OF THE FAMILY (1911), WHEN WEST WAS WEST (1928).

EDITIONS AND REPRINTS

THE WRITINGS OF OW, Definitive Ed., 11 vols. (New York, 1928). In this

* Of Special Importance

collection THE JIMMYJOHN BOSS is called HANK'S WOMAN. RED MEN AND WHITE and JIMMYJOHN BOSS have been reprinted by Garrett Press (1969), while LIN MCLEAN was reissued by Literature House (1970). The last and six different editions of THE VIRGINIAN are available in paperback. THE VIRGINIAN has been reprinted many times since its original publication. Also in print is THE WEST OF OW: SELECTED SHORT STORIES, intro. by R.L. Hough (Lincoln, Nebr., 1972).

BIOGRAPHY

Although there is no published biography of W, an unpublished dissertation exists: G.T. Watkins, III, "OW and the American West: A Biographical and Critical Study," DA 20 (1959): 1772. Also one may consult W's autobiographical volume, ROOSEVELT: THE STORY OF A FRIENDSHIP, 1880-1919 (New York, 1930). There is an important volume of letters and journals: Fanny Kemble Wister, ed., OW OUT WEST: HIS JOURNALS AND LETTERS (Chicago, 1958). Also significant is B.M. Vorpahl, ed., MY DEAR WISTER: THE FREDERICK REMINGTON-OW LETTERS (Palo Alto, Calif., 1972). Other letters and information published by Fanny Kemble Wister are in "Letters of OW: Author of THE VIRGINIAN," PMHB 83 (1959): 3-28, and "OW's West," AtlM 195 (May, June 1955): 29-35, 52-57. And finally there are G.E. White, THE EASTERN ESTABLISHMENT AND THE WESTERN EXPERIENCE: THE WEST OF FREDERICK REMINGTON, THEODORE ROOSEVELT, AND OW (New Haven, 1968), and Julian Mason, "OW: Boy Librarian," QJLC 26 (1969): 200-12, material on W's secondary school days at St. Paul's Academy.

CRITICISM

As one might expect, most of the critical interest in W focuses on his use of the West, his perceptions, his mythologizing, his contrasts. The only full-length critical study is an unpublished dissertation: N.E. Lambert, "The Western Writings of OW: The Conflict of East and West," DA 27 (1967): 2503A. Lambert has published parts of his work in "OW's 'Hank's Woman': The Writer and His Comment," WAL 4 (1969): 39-50; "OW's Lin McLean: The Failure of the Vernacular Hero," WAL 5 (1970): 219-32; "The Values of the Frontier: OW's Final Assessment," SDR 9 (1971): 78-87. A more general study of W's western fiction is Mody Boatright, "The American Myth Rides the Range: OW's Man on Horseback," SWR 36 (1951): 157-63, and an article dealing with W's anti-democratic bias in his treatment of Western life is Marvin Lewis, "OW: Caste Imprints in Western Letters," ArQ 10 (1954): 147-56. A provocative review-article contrasting Remington's realistic West and W's romantic views by John Seelye appeared in NR 167 (2 September 1972): 28-33.

THE VIRGINIAN alone continues to attract critical interest: N.E. Lambert, "OW's Virginian: The Genesis of a Cultural Hero," WAL 6 (1971): 99-107; N.R. Rush, "Fifty Years of THE VIRGINIAN," PBSA 46 (1952): 117-20; J.T. Bratcher, "OW's THE VIRGINIAN: Two Corrections," WF 21 (1962): 188-90; H.S. Fiske, PROVINCIAL TYPES IN AMERICAN FICTION (New York, 1903).

W's relations with other more famous people also commands the attention of critics: D.D. Walker, "W, Roosevelt, and James: A Note on the Western," AQ 12 (1960): 358-66; Carl Bode, "Henry James and OW," AL 26 (1954): 250-52; John Barsness, "Theodore Roosevelt as Cowboy: The Virginian as Jacksonian Man," AQ 21 (1969): 609-19; B.M. Vorpahl, "Ernest Hemingway and OW," LCUP 36 (1970): 126-37, and "'Very Much Like a Firecracker,': OW on Mark Twain," WAL 6 (1971): 83-98. Also a slight literary relationship is assessed in John Solensten, "Richard Harding Davis, OW, and THE VIRGINIAN: Unpublished Letters and a Commentary," ALR 5 (1972): 122-33.

Section 47

THOMAS WOLFE (1900-1938)

Thomas Wolfe (hereafter TW or W) was born in Asheville, N.C., the "Alta-mont" of his autobiographical novel LOOK HOMEWARD, ANGEL (1929). He graduated from the University of North Carolina in 1920, went on to Harvard to study playwriting and took an M.A. degree. He taught English at New York University until his first novel was published, after which he devoted all his time to writing. He had scarcely begun his career, however, when he died, having published only two novels and a collection of stories and short novels; but he left an enormous amount of manuscript material, from which three more volumes were quarried. Despite his early death Wolfe has taken his place as one of the major fiction-writers of this century. His positive, yea-saying view of America and his evocative lyric prose have attracted a large following.

BIBLIOGRAPHY AND MANUSCRIPTS

Elmer Johnson's TW: A CHECKLIST (Kent, O., 1970) is a useful and reason-ably complete compilation of primary and secondary sources. Of its 278 pages the first third lists W's works; the remainder lists books, articles, chapters from books, theses and dissertations about W. It supersedes an earlier list by John-son and G.R. Preston, TW: A BIBLIOGRAPHY (New York, 1943). A briefer compilation but one by a knowledgeable W scholar is Paschal Reeves' CHECK-LIST OF TW (Columbus, 1970). A selected list of W criticism compiled by Maurice Beebe appears in Leslie Field, ed., TW: THREE DECADES OF CRITI-CISM (New York, 1968). Bruce McElderry's TW (TUSAS, 1964) contains a good selected, annotated bibliography. By far the best place to begin a bib-liographical study of W is Hugh Holman's admirable essay in SMAA, a remark-ably lucid, concise, and well-informed summary.

A vast collection of W's letters, MSS, inscribed works, galley and page proofs, notebooks, school papers, and even checkbooks and bank statements has been gathered at Harvard. See Thomas Little, "The TW Collection of William B. Wisdom," HLB 1 (1947): 280-87. A smaller collection consisting of both prin-ted and MS materials is at the University of North Carolina, and there is a collection mostly of printed materials but some letters at the Pack Memorial Library, Asheville.

WORKS OF FICTION

Novels: *LOOK HOMEWARD, ANGEL (1929), *OF TIME AND THE RIVER (1935), THE WEB AND THE ROCK (1939), YOU CAN'T GO HOME AGAIN (1940).

Stories: FROM DEATH TO MORNING (1935), THE HILLS BEYOND (1941).

EDITIONS AND REPRINTS

As one notes from the dates of W's fiction, three of the above titles were published after W's death. THE WEB AND THE ROCK appeared pretty much as W had intended, but the other two volumes were assembled from W's literary remains. The textual problems in editing W, which are difficult and complicated, are summarized succinctly in Holman's essay in SMAA. Also since W's death the following editions have been issued: Maxwell Geismar edited THE PORTABLE TW (1946); Hugh Holman edited THE SHORT NOVELS OF TW (1961) and THE TW READER; J.S. Barnes selected and arranged lyrical passages in free verse form as A STONE, A LEAF, A DOOR (1945); John Hall Wheelock selected poetical passages about America under the title THE FACE OF A NATION (1939). All of the above editions and reprints except the last are in print, and all of the above works of fiction are available both in hard covers and paper.

BIOGRAPHY

W's fiction is so autobiographical that writers on him have had trouble separating the fictional characters from the real prototypes. To grasp this problem one should read Floyd Watkins' TW'S CHARACTERS: PORTRAITS FROM LIFE (Norman, Okla., 1957). There have been two significant biographies: Elizabeth Nowell's TW: A BIOGRAPHY (Garden City, N.Y., 1960) and Andrew Turnbull's TW (New York, 1968). The first is by the woman who was an editor at Scribner's when W began publishing and who was his agent after 1933. She had access to the primary materials but was too close to the subject for complete objectivity. Turnbull's life is the work of an accomplished biographer and creates a credible, flesh-and-blood TW. This is the biography to read if one does not intend to look at both. A more specialized study but an important biographical source is Richard Kennedy's THE WINDOW OF MEMORY: THE LITERARY CAREER OF TW (Chapel Hill, N.C., 1962). As the title suggests, it deals primarily with W's life as a writer, but it is carefully put together and well documented. A good brief portrait of W may be found in Malcolm Cowley's THINK BACK ON US (Carbondale, Ill., 1967).

There is an abundance of primary material such as lectures, letters, and notebooks which provide sources for studying W's life. The last work published in his lifetime was THE STORY OF A NOVEL, a critical-autobiographical essay

* Of Special Importance

based on lectures he delivered at a writers' conference in Colorado. Also in this category is William Braswell and Leslie Field, eds., TW'S PURDUE SPEECH: "WRITING AND LIVING" (Lafayette, Ind., 1964), a speech delivered shortly before W died. There are several letter collections: Hugh Holman and Sue Ross, THE LETTERS OF TW TO HIS MOTHER (Chapel Hill, N.C., 1968), a revised and corrected edition of the same letters edited earlier by J.S. Terry; Elizabeth Nowell, ed., THE LETTERS OF TW (New York, 1956); Oscar Cargill and T.C. Pollock, eds., THE CORRESPONDENCE OF TW AND HOMER ANDREW WATT (New York, 1954). It is important to supplement these letters with the letters of Maxwell Perkins, W's editor at Scribner's, in EDITOR TO AUTHOR (New York, 1950). W's notebooks also have been published in two volumes: Richard Kennedy and Paschal Reeves, eds., THE NOTEBOOKS OF TW (Chapel Hill, N.C., 1970). W's 1938 journal appeared as A WESTERN JOURNAL: A DAILY LOG OF THE GREAT PARKS TRIP, June 20-July 2, 1938 (Pittsburgh, 1951).

There have been other studies of partial aspects of W's life. Hayden Norwood, THE MARBLE MAN'S WIFE: TW'S MOTHER (New York, 1947); Mabel Wolfe Wheaton and LeGette Blythe, TW AND HIS FAMILY (Garden City, N.Y., 1961), the former being W's sister; Agatha Adams, TW, CAROLINA STUDENT: A BRIEF BIOGRAPHY (Chapel Hill, N.C., 1950); Wisner Kinne, GEORGE PIERCE BAKER AND THE AMERICAN THEATER (Cambridge, Mass., 1954), which deals with W at Harvard; Oscar Cargill, TW AT WASHINGTON SQUARE, which deals with W as a New York University faculty member; Vardis Fisher, TW AS I KNEW HIM AND OTHER ESSAYS (Denver, 1963), who also treats the New York University period. Aline Bernstein, the "Esther Jack" of W's fiction, makes W the title character in a story "Eugene" in her THREE BLUE SUITS (New York, 1933) and recounts her affair with him fictionally in a novel, THE JOUR-NEY DOWN (New York, 1938). W's letters to Mrs. Bernstein, which have not yet been published, are at Harvard. In addition, the impact of Europe on W has been studied by George Reeves in TW ET L'EUROPE (Paris, 1955) and Hugh Holman in "Europe as a Catalyst for TW," Max Schulz et al., eds., ES-SAYS IN AMERICAN AND ENGLISH LITERATURE PRESENTED TO BRUCE ROB-ERT MCELDERRY, JR. (Athens, O., 1967).

CRITICISM

Hugh Holman's pamphlet TW (UMPAW, 1960) is an excellent starting point for a critical study of W. It is a felicitously written brief study by one of the best W scholars. Holman believes W is artistically most successful in his short novels. Two short books that are solidly informed and may be relied upon are Richard Walser's TW: AN INTRODUCTION AND INTERPRETATION (New York, 1961) and Bruce McElderry's TW (TUSAS, 1964). Both are based on a thorough knowledge of the sources and neither contains critical eccentricities. Among the earlier books on W Louis Rubin's TW: THE WEATHER OF HIS YOUTH (Baton Rouge, La., 1955) is an important one, full of discerning criticism, and insistent that W's novels be judged as novels. Rubin believes that LOOK HOME-WARD, ANGEL is W's best novel and the one most likely to endure. The first book-length study, Herbert Muller's TW (Norfolk, Conn., 1947), treated W as a major writer in the American tradition and still is a book worth reading. Pamela Hansford Johnson's TW: A CRITICAL STUDY (London, 1947) contains perceptive analyses of W's novels. It was published in America as HUNGRY GULLIVER (New York, 1948) and again as THE ART OF TW (New York, 1963).

The most recent books on W are less important. Paschal Reeves' TW'S ALBATROSS: RACE AND NATIONALITY IN AMERICA (Athens, Ga., 1969) is a study of W's incidental references to various races, while William Snyder's TW: ULYSSES AND NARCISSUS (Athens, O., 1971) puts W on the psychoanalyst's couch, determines that he should be classified as a psychoneurotic, and finds "evidences of paranoidal behavior of subpsychotic intensity" (see Warren French in ALS 1971, p. 238).

There have been four collections of essays about W: Richard Walser, ed., THE ENIGMA OF TW (Cambridge, Mass., 1953); Hugh Holman, ed., THE WORLD OF TW (New York, 1962); Field's TW: THREE DECADES OF CRITICISM (see above); Louis Rubin, TW: A COLLECTION OF CRITICAL ESSAYS (Englewood Cliffs, N.J., 1973). Taken together these volumes provide a wide spectrum of the most important comment on W since 1929. There is some duplication among these collections, but Walser provides eight biographical and 17 critical essays, Holman includes 30 essays or extracts in a gathering prepared as a "research anthology," and Field has rounded up 23 essays, all critical.

From these gatherings one may follow W's reputation from the beginning when LOOK HOMEWARD, ANGEL burst on the literary horizon until the 1960's when he had taken his place among the major voices of this century. There is H.S. Canby's essay on OF TIME AND THE RIVER which found the book "an artistic failure," Robert Penn Warren's well-known "The Hamlet of TW," Bernard De Voto's nasty review, "Genius Is Not Enough," which was at least in part responsible for W's leaving Scribner's for Harper's. Holman's volume presents, besides the critical excerpts, W's THE STORY OF A NOVEL and Clifton Fadiman's parody, "The Wolfe at the Door." The Field collection is mostly recent criticism, more than half of the selections having been published since 1960. In the more than four decades since W's first novel appeared W has been one of the more controversial figures in American literature.

Some of the shorter general essays that are worth looking at include: J.W. Beach in AMERICAN FICTION, 1920-1940 (New York, 1941); Alfred Kazin in ON NATIVE GROUNDS (New York, 1942); Maxwell Geismar in LHUS; Robert Spiller in THE CYCLE OF AMERICAN LITERATURE; and J.B. Priestly in LITERATURE AND WESTERN MAN. Priestly saw W as the archetypal American. A recent symposium held at the University of Georgia has been edited by Paschal Reeves as TW AND THE GLASS OF TIME (Athens, Ga., 1971) in which Kennedy, Holman, and Walser all present significant extensions of their earlier work on W.

W's foreign reputation deserves a brief comment, for he is one of the more popular American authors abroad. Of the 39 dissertations written on W between

1948 and 1971 no less than nine were written in Germany and Austria. There have been five books on W in German, and one each in Italian, French, Spanish, and Japanese, plus many critical articles.

Section 48
RICHARD WRIGHT (1908-1960)

Richard Wright (hereafter RW or W) has become in the 1970's the most important American black writer of the first half of the century. Born the son of a Mississippi sharecropper who deserted his family, W grew up in rural poverty until he went to Chicago in 1927. There he exchanged the repressed life of a Southern Negro for the marginal existence of a ghetto black and (soon thereafter) the poverty of the Great Depression. But somehow he managed to educate himself and to write. He was much influenced by the sociologists of the University of Chicago of that period and Marxism and joined the Communist Party in 1932; but he repudiated Communism 12 years later and after World War II moved to France for the rest of his life.

BIBLIOGRAPHY AND MANUSCRIPTS

The fullest listing of W's works is in Michel Fabre and Edward Margolies, "RW (1908-1960): A Bibliography," BB 24 (1965): 131-33, 137, which is reprinted in Constance Webb's RW: A BIOGRAPHY (New York, 1968) and in NegroD 18, iii (1969): 86-92. An earlier and now superseded listing is M.D. Sprague, "RW: A Bibliography," BB 22 (1953): 39. The most recent compilation appears in R.C. Brignano, RW: AN INTRODUCTION TO THE MAN AND HIS WORKS (Pittsburgh, 1970), which also contains secondary materials. For additional listings about W one should consult Jackson Bryer, "RW: A Selected Checklist of Criticism," WSCL 1 (1960): 22-33, which is annotated and useful for items down to the year of W's death. The first attempt at a bibliographical essay was Donald Gibson, "RW: A Bibliographical Essay," CLAJ 12 (1969): 360-65; but the best, most extensive, and most up-to-date effort is John Reilly, "RW: An Essay in Bibliography," RALS 1 (1971): 131-80.

Most of W's papers remain in the hands of his widow in Paris. These include MSS of published and unpublished works, notes, and journals. The New York Public Library has the original typescript of NATIVE SON; Yale and Princeton both have MSS and letters, the latter's holding including about 500 letters exchanged between W and Harper and Brothers.

RICHARD WRIGHT

WORKS OF FICTION

Novels: *NATIVE SON (1940), THE OUTSIDER (1953), SAVAGE HOLIDAY (1954), THE LONG DREAM (1958), LAWD TODAY (1963).

Stories: UNCLE TOM'S CHILDREN (1938), EIGHT MEN (1961).

EDITIONS AND REPRINTS

Six of W's seven volumes of fiction are available in paperback editions: UNCLE TOM'S CHILDREN, NATIVE SON, and THE OUTSIDER from Harper and Row; THE LONG DREAM from Ace; SAVAGE HOLIDAY from Award; EIGHT MEN from Pyramid. Also there are "Five Episodes" from an uncompleted novel in Herbert Hill, ed., SOON, ONE MORNING (New York, 1963). Michel Fabre has edited a bi-lingual edition of the story, "The Man Who Lived Underground" (included in EIGHT MEN), with a long preface (Paris, 1971).

BIOGRAPHY

Thirteen years after W's death a first-rate critical biography finally appeared: Michel Fabre's THE UNFINISHED QUEST OF RW (New York, 1973). This is a 652-page work that provides indispensable information for the study of W's life and work. It is a more significant work, but it does not entirely supersede Constance Webb's RW: A BIOGRAPHY (see above), which makes use of the unpublished third of W's autobiography, BLACK BOY, had the cooperation of W's widow, and is based on a friendship with W and talks with him about his life and works. Another biography, accurate though slight and directed at young readers, is John Williams' THE MOST NATIVE OF SONS: A BIOGRA-PHY OF RW (New York, 1970). The author is the same person who wrote THE MAN WHO CRIED I AM (Boston, 1967), a roman à clef with W as the protagonist.

There are also briefer accounts that supplement the book-length studies. The earliest is E.R. Embree's treatment of W in 13 AGAINST THE ODDS (New York, 1944), and one of the most recent is Blyden Jackson, "RW: Black Boy from America's Black Belt and Urban Ghettos," CLAJ 12 (1969): 287-309, an excellent first chapter which will be part of a forthcoming book. Many people who knew W have written about him: Herbert Hill's ANGER AND BEYOND (New York, 1966) devotes a chapter to "Reflections on RW," in which Saunders Redding, Arna Bontemps, and Horace Clayton reminisce. Clayton in his auto-biography, LONG OLD ROAD (New York, 1965), recalls his association with W, as does Albert Halper in his memoirs, GOODBYE, UNION SQUARE (Chicago, 1970).

Another point of view in W's life comes to light in the celebrated quarrel be-

* Of Special Importance

230

tween W and James Baldwin. See Baldwin's NOBODY KNOWS MY NAME (New York, 1961) and Maurice Charney, "James Baldwin's Quarrel with RW," AQ 15 (1965): 65-75. There are a good many accounts of W's life in exile, some of which are: Saunders Redding, "The Alien Land of RW," in Hill's SOON, ONE MORNING (see above); Ben Burns, "They're Not Uncle Tom's Children," REPORTER 14 (8 March 1956): 21-23; W.G. Smith, "Black Boy in France," EBONY 8 (July 1953): 32-36, 39-42; Ollie Harrington, "The Last Days of RW," EBONY 17 (February 1961): 83-94. More recently Fabre interviewed Simone de Beauvoir, who knew W (SBL 1 [1970]: 3-5), and published a letter from Dorothy Padmore concerning W's anti-colonialist activities (SBL [1970]: 5-9).

W has written eloquently about his own life, though he had trouble separating things that happened to him from things he was told about. See BLACK BOY (1945), a book-length account of his life down to age 19, and in addition these essays: "The Ethics of Living Jim Crow," in AMERICAN STUFF: A WPA WRITERS' ANTHOLOGY (New York, 1937); "How Bigger Was Born," SRL 22 (1 June 1940): 17-20, reprinted as a pamphlet (New York, 1940); "I Tried to Be a Communist," AtlM 174 (August-September 1944): 61-70, 48-56; "Early Days in Chicago," in Edwin Seaver, ed., CROSS SECTION (New York, 1945).

W's letters are in the process of being edited by Fabre and Margolies. The first volume was to appear in 1973 but as of mid-1974 had not come out. In addition see Thomas Knipp, ed., RW: LETTERS TO JOE C. BROWN (Kent, Ohio, 1968), 10 letters written to a childhood friend.

CRITICISM

Criticism of W provides a sort of paradigm of political and social developments in the United States in the past 35 years. As the author of a bestselling novel of social protest and as a member of the Communist Party, W was inevitably judged at first as a polemicist rather than as an artist. UNCLE TOM'S CHILDREN, NATIVE SON, and BLACK BOY (1938-45) generated much discussion, most of it sub-literary and ephemeral. This ranged all the way from David Cohn's review of NATIVE SON in AtlM (165 [1940]: 659-61), which argued that Negroes should make the best of their plight and shut up, to Samuel Sillen's series in the NEW MASSES (35 [23 April, 21 May 1940]: 25-26, 23-28), which hailed W's brilliant achievement with Marxist fervor. A handy shortcut to observe the phenomenon of W's best seller is Richard Abcarian, ed., RW'S "NATIVE SON": A CRITICAL HANDBOOK (Belmont, Calif., 1970), which reprints 20 contemporary reviews. W left the Communist Party during World War II and in 1947 moved permanently to France. Gradually his work began to be judged as art rather than artifact, and in the 1960's he began to move into the ranks of major American writers. The first of six dissertations (three of which already have become books) was written in 1964, and by the end of the decade, with the appearance of several new journals devoted to black studies, the growth of academic programs in ethnic studies, and affirmative action employment policies, interest in W boomed. In 1968, 1969, and 1970 there were three special issues of journals devoted to him, five books, two pamphlets, three dissertations, one letter collection, and a spate of articles. The end is not yet in sight.

There is space here to list only a few of the early essays, but there are some that have permanent value. Good essays on both UNCLE TOM'S CHILDREN ("The Art of RW's Short Stories") and NATIVE SON ("The Promise of Democracy in RW's NATIVE SON") by Edwin Burgum were reprinted in his THE NOVEL AND THE WORLD'S DILEMMA (Oxford, 1947). Perhaps the best Marxist analysis of the novel appeared in Harry Slochower's NO VOICE IS WHOLLY LOST (New York, 1945), which discussed thoughtfully themes, characterization, and W's sense of alienation. The appearance of BLACK BOY (1945) also produced some worthwhile criticism, especially Horace Clayton's examination of the social content of the book in "Frightened Children of Frightened Parents," TWICE-A-YEAR (1945): 262-69; and Ralph Ellison's "RW's Blues," AR 5 (1945): 198-211, which probed the psychology underlying the work. The summing-up article of early W criticism was written by his friend and future biographer, Constance Webb, after W left for France: "What Next for RW?" PHYLON 10 (1949): 161-66. Webb recapitulated W's career to that date as a rejection of both Communism and bourgeois society and then posed her question.

In the early 1950's two essays, one by a philosopher and the other by a sociologist, helped broaden the scope of W criticism. Morris Weitz in his PHILOSOPHY OF THE ARTS (Cambridge, Mass., 1950) examined the universality of W's themes in philosophical terms, while David Riesman in "Marginality, Conformity, and Insight," PHYLON 14 (1953): 241-57, discussed W's development of a survival mechanism through his powers of the imagination. Also belonging to the early 1950's are James Baldwin's essays attacking W, which are a part of criticism as well as biography. Two of his pieces, "Everybody's Protest Novel" and "Many Thousands Gone," reprinted in NOTES OF A NATIVE SON (Boston, 1955), charged that W had perpetuated Harriet Beecher Stowe's stereotype of the Negro and had failed in his social purpose.

When W produced his first novel in 13 years, THE OUTSIDER (1953), a new era in criticism began. Some critics saw the novel as a new departure, such as N.A. Ford, "The Ordeal of RW," CE 15 (1953): 87-94, who contrasted the Marxism in NATIVE SON with the existentialism in THE OUTSIDER; but others, such as Steven Marcus, "The American Negro in Search of Identity," COMMENTARY 16 (November 1953): 456-63, thought W had merely repeated his stereotype of the cultureless black victim of society. The existentialism of the novel attracted a considerable amount of attention. Two good articles should be cited: Nathan Scott, "Search for Beliefs: Fiction of RW," UKCR 23 (1956): 131-38; and Kingsley Widmer, "The Existential Darkness: RW's THE OUTSIDER," WSCL 1 (1960): 13-21. The latter deals with the novel as an American existentialist fable. A similar discussion which puts W into a larger context is Richard Lehan, "Existentialism in Recent American Fiction: The Demonic Quest," TSLL 1 (1959): 181-202.

The final phase of W criticism, a phase which is still going on, began after his death in 1960. With the publication of THE LONG DREAM (1958), the posthumous collection of stories in EIGHT MEN and the appearance of W's last novel, LAWD TODAY (1963), it became possible to see W in larger perspective and to sum up. The process began auspiciously in Blyden Jackson, "The Negro's Image of the Universe as Reflected in His Fiction," CLAJ 4 (1960): 22-31. Of varying importance are three recent books: Edward Margolies, THE ART OF RW (Carbondale, Ill., 1969); Dan McCall, THE EXAMPLE OF RW (New York, 1969); R.C. Brignano, RW: AN INTRODUCTION TO THE MAN AND HIS WORKS (see above). Margolies approaches W thematically and feels that he "wove his theme of human fear, alienation, guilt, and dread into the overall texture of his work." This book is the fullest and most accurate summing up so far. McCall's study, as Warren French says (ALS 1969), is "simply a piece of bellicose journalism, designed to arouse a new generation's interest in the voice of a lonely, furious, proud black man from the South, telling us that our culture is crazy.'" Brignano's contribution to W scholarship also attempts to sum up, but it argues a thesis that many readers will not agree with: W was basically a western humanist who believed fundamentally that man by reason alone could abolish injustice.

Two recent pamphlets have appeared: Robert Bone's RW (UMPAW, 1969) and Milton and Patricia Rickels, RW (Austin, Tex., 1970). Bone, who also wrote THE NEGRO NOVEL IN AMERICA (New Haven, 1958; rev. ed., 1965) provides a brief but useful introduction to W, while the Rickels' pamphlet, which is part of a series on Southern writers, is unique in dealing with W's imagery and his roots in black folk culture. Two books also have appeared recently: David Bakish's sketch, RW (New York, 1973), and an ambitious study, Keneth Kinnamon's THE EMERGENCE OF RW: A STUDY IN LITERATURE AND SOCIETY (Urbana, Ill., 1972).

There have been many recent books containing chapters on W and journal articles, but only a few can be cited here. Margolies has a good chapter in his NATIVE SONS: A CRITICAL STUDY OF TWENTIETH CENTURY NEGRO AUTHORS (Philadelphia, 1968), as does Warren French in THE SOCIAL NOVEL AT THE END OF AN ERA (Carbondale, Ill., 1966). French's essay is a well-balanced estimate that focuses mostly on NATIVE SON. Other books that should be consulted are: Davis Littlejohn, BLACK ON WHITE: A CRITICAL SURVEY OF WRITING BY AMERICAN NEGROES (New York, 1966); Nelson Blake, NOVELISTS' AMERICA: FICTION AS HISTORY, 1910-1940 (Syracuse, 1969); Chester Eisinger, FICTION OF THE FORTIES (Chicago, 1963); Harold McCarthy, "RW: The Expatriate as Native Son," AL 44 (1972): 97-117. Finally, one should not overlook the three special journal issues devoted to W, which taken together provide approximately three volumes of additional critical and biographical material: CLAJ 12, iv (1969); NegroD 18, ii (1968); SBL 1, iii (1970).

INDEX

Underlined page numbers refer to sections devoted to an individual author.

INDEX

Perkins, G.   17

Perkins, M.   225

Perles, A.   154, 155

Perosa, S.   17, 106, 108

Peter, E.   48

Peterson, R.   122

Petricek, W.   170

Phillips, W.   18

Picasso, P.   178

Pike, C.   162

Pinsker, S.   21

Piper, H. D.   9, 105, 106

Pitavy, F.   97

Pizer, D.   81, 82, 85, 94

Plante, P.   209

Podhoretz, N.   207

Poli, B.   108

Polk, N.   93

Pollack, B.   179

Pollock, T. C.   225

Popper, H.   216

Porter, B.   153, 155

Porter, Katherine Anne   24, 27, 33, 157-60, 180

Porter, W. S. (O. Henry)   26, 28, 161-63

Portz, J.   64

Potter, J.   77

Pound, E.   74

Powell, L.   154

Powell, L. C.   61

Powers, J. F.   29

Praz, M.   121

Presley, J.   132, 133

Preston, G. R.   223

Price, L. M.   27

Price-Stephens, G.   92, 94

Priestley, J. B.   127, 226

Prigozy, R. M.   108

Prizel, Y.   123

Proust, M.   217

Purdy, S.   181

Putt, S. G.   175

Q

Queen, E.   162

Quinn, A. H.   8, 13, 59, 210

R

Ragan, D.   114

Rahn, W.   187

Rahv, P.   156, 171

Raimbault, R. N.   97

Randall, J.   59

Raper, J. R.   110, 112

253